Rethinking Contract Law and Contract Design

RETHINKING LAW

The *Rethinking Law* series is a forum for innovative scholarly legal writing from across all substantive fields of law. The series aims to enrich the study of law by promoting a cutting-edge approach to legal analysis.

Despite the old maxim that nothing is new under the sun, it is nevertheless true that laws evolve and contexts in which laws operate change. Law faces new and previously unforeseen challenges, responds to shifting motivations and is shaped by competing interests and experiences. Academic scrutiny and challenge is an essential component in the development of law, and the act of re-thinking and re-examining principles and precepts that may have been long-held is imperative.

Rethinking Law showcases authored books that address their field from a new angle, expose the weaknesses of existing frameworks, or 're-frame' the topic in some way. This might be through the introduction of a new legal framework, through the integration of perspectives from other fields or even other disciplines, through challenging existing paradigms, or simply through a level of analysis that elevates or sharpens our understanding of a subject. While each book takes its own approach, all the titles in the series use an analytical lens to open up new thinking.

Titles in the series include:

Rethinking Contract Law and Contract Design
Victor P. Goldberg

Rethinking Cyberlaw
A New Vision for Internet Law
Jacqueline Lipton

Rethinking Contract Law and Contract Design

Victor P. Goldberg

Jerome L. Greene Professor of Transactional Law, Columbia University, USA

RETHINKING LAW

Edward Elgar PUBLISHING

Cheltenham, UK • Northampton, MA, USA

Published by
Edward Elgar Publishing Limited
The Lypiatts
15 Lansdown Road
Cheltenham
Glos GL50 2JA
UK

Edward Elgar Publishing, Inc.
William Pratt House
9 Dewey Court
Northampton
Massachusetts 01060
USA

A catalogue record for this book
is available from the British Library

Library of Congress Control Number: 2014952143

This book is available electronically in the **Elgar**online
Law subject collection
DOI 10.4337/9781783471546

MIX
Paper from responsible sources
FSC® C013056

ISBN 978 1 78347 153 9 (cased)
ISBN 978 1 78347 154 6 (eBook)

Typeset by Columns Design XML Ltd, Reading
Printed and bound in Great Britain by T.J. International Ltd, Padstow

Contents

Acknowledgments

Nearly a decade ago I published a book of essays, *Framing Contract Law*, in which I took an economist's perspective on some issues of contract law. I have collected a number of my essays since then, along with some new material, as a follow-up. Some of the previously published material has received only a light edit, the main change being the elimination of the excessive footnoting imposed by law review editors. Other essays have been substantially revised. I have received comments, advice, and assistance from participants in workshops at a number of law schools and at conferences. I would like to thank a number of individuals, and apologize in advance to those who I have inadvertently failed to acknowledge: Sarah Biser, Barbara Black, Doug Bregman, Marvin Chirelstein, Lord Lawrence Collins, Hanoch Dagan, Eugene Geekie, Judge Robert Gerber, Ronald Gilson, Steve Horowitz, Avery Katz, Jody Kraus, Mark Lawson, Alex Layton, Eugene Meehan, Jennifer Morgan, Barak Richman, Sir Bernard Rix, Ruti Ronnen, Bob Rubin, Donald Schneider, Bob Scott, Mark Shaikin, George Triantis, Florian Wagner von Papp, J.J. White, and George Zhou. I also want to acknowledge the helpful work of my research assistants: Christa Bieker, Brooke Gottlieb, James Larsen, Zach Moore, John Powell, Ni Qian, Haiwei Wang, and Carson Zhou.

The earlier versions of the chapters are as follows; full citations are given in the references under Goldberg, Chapter 2 (2014); Chapter 7 (2008a); Chapter 8 (2014); Chapter 10 (2013b); Chapter 11 (2010); Chapter 12 (2011b); Chapter 13 (2013a); Chapter 15 (2011a).

The author and publisher gratefully acknowledge permission to reprint the following:

2008a. "Cleaning Up *Lake River*," 3.2 *Virginia Law & Business Review* (2008) 427–45.

2010. "Excuse Doctrine: The Eisenberg Uncertainty Principle," 2(1) *Journal of Legal Analysis* 359–72.

2011a. "Traynor (*Drennan*) versus Hand (*Baird*): Much Ado about (Almost) Nothing," 3 *Journal of Legal Analysis* 1–47.

2011b. "After Frustration: Three Cheers for *Chandler v. Webster*," 68 *Washington & Lee Law Review* 1133–69.
2013a. "A Precedent Built on Sand: *Norcon v. Niagara Mohawk*," 2013 *Columbia Business Law Review* 138–78.
2013b. "*The Achilleas*: Forsaking Foreseeability," 66 *Current Legal Problems* 107–30.
2014. "Protecting Reliance," 114 *Columbia Law Review* 1033–81.

Table of cases

UNITED STATES CASES

INTERNATIONAL CASES

1. Introduction

After I had submitted the manuscript, the editor asked whether I would consider including the book in the new "Rethinking Law" series. This struck me as fortuitous on two grounds. First, when I first began thinking about and teaching contract law nearly two decades ago, I came to it with the mindset of many of my colleagues who share a law and economics perspective, namely that contract doctrine is efficient. However, it now seems to me that in many instances contract doctrine is terribly inefficient; doctrine is a hurdle that good lawyers must overcome. Second, I have come to think about contract law differently. My approach now is to focus on how parties design their contractual relations and to glean from that insights into both doctrinal reform and contract interpretation.

Contract law allows parties to set their own rules within constraints. It provides a set of default rules and if the parties do not like them, they can change them. Some of the rules, however, are mandatory, and others are, to varying degrees, sticky. That stickiness is in part due to the costs of tailoring a transaction. A more subtle source of stickiness is the beliefs of judges, scholars, and lawyers about the nature of contracts and contractual duties. The notion that a breach is a wrong and that victims of a breach of contract should be made whole is a powerful one.

My concern, I must emphasize, is with the contracts of sophisticated parties. I am not concerned with consumer contracts or agreements between amateurs – for example, uncle's promise of cash to pay for nephew's car, which was featured in the debate over the adoption of Section 90. There can, of course, be some dispute over whether a particular contract falls in that category. For my purposes, the category is defined by agreements for which both parties could be expected to have access to counsel.

A generation ago, Judge Posner bemoaned the mismatch of the facts as presented in judicial opinions with the actual facts, and argued that this had adverse consequences for the development of doctrine:

> If factual uncertainty is disproportionately characteristic of litigated cases … then, given the difficulty of dispelling such uncertainty by the methods of

> litigation, we can expect the factual recitals in published judicial opinions to be wrong much of the time … .
>
> And especially in cases where there is no published dissent, judicial opinions exemplify "winners' history." The appellate court will usually state the facts as favorably to its conclusions as the record allows, and often more favorably. … The tendency I have described is abetted by the reluctance of academic commentators to expand their study of cases beyond judicial opinions. Rarely will the commentator get hold of the briefs and record to check the accuracy of the factual recitals in the opinion.
>
> … One of the distinctive features of judges as policy makers – and it should be clear by now that judges in our system *are*, to a significant degree, policy-making officials – is that they obtain much of their knowledge of how the world works from materials that are systematically unreliable sources of information. (1990, 210–11)

By and large, the academic commentators of the Contracts wing of the profession have remained reluctant. In my previous book (Goldberg (2006)) I analysed a number of cases in which the court's presentation of the facts was seriously deficient. In this book I will add a few more pieces to the "data base." I do hope others will be encouraged to engage in more such studies, although the response to my earlier book does not inspire much confidence.

Not all the chapters in this book are detailed analyses of specific cases. Others concern broader questions, for example, the role of the "tacit assumption" in claims for consequential damages and the role of restitution when performance is excused because of impracticability. The common theme running throughout the book is the focus on contract design – the economic problems confronting contracting parties and the tools for coping with them.

The first two sections of the book deal with remedies. Part I concerns direct claims. The standard contract law rhetoric emphasizes the notion that victims of a breach should be compensated to make them as well off as they would have been had the contract been performed. The notion seems so obvious that it usually goes unquestioned by courts and commentators. However, as Scott and Triantis (2004, 1446) point out, that is at least in part a historical accident: "The dominance of the compensation principle is now unquestioned, but [an] inquiry into its historical roots suggests that the elevation of compensation to a universally applicable norm results more from mistaken path dependence than from a sustained and systematic appreciation of the merits of the rules governing contract damages." Once we get beyond the contract/market differential, the case for the "make-the-victim-whole" remedy is pretty weak. The decision to breach can be viewed as the exercise of an option to abandon with the remedy being the implicit price of that option. By looking at the pricing of explicit termination options, we can get some insight into how the implicit option could be priced. The evidence from the explicit pricing of the termination option indicates that the price need bear no relation to the amount of money that would fully compensate the counterparty if the option were exercised.

If the damage remedy should be the contract/market differential, there remains a timing question. Should the differential be reckoned at the time of the repudiation or breach? Or should it be reckoned at the time of the trial, or at any other date? I explore this question looking at cases from American and foreign (England and Israel) jurisdictions.

The UCC allows for the recovery of profits to a lost-volume seller. In earlier work (Goldberg (1984 and 2006, ch. 12)), I have argued that this made no sense when the question is framed as pricing the buyer's termination option. I reprise that argument here and then consider a recent case in which a court was confronted with the question of whether Michael Jordan was a lost-volume seller.

Two cases in which a book publisher accepted a manuscript but then refused to publish it came to very different remedies. In both instances the contract was the standard publisher's form. Also in both instances the court concluded that measuring damages would be too speculative. One court concluded that the author should receive only nominal damages (six cents); the other that the author should receive restitution for the time spent writing the manuscript (over $300,000). The remedy, I argue, should be viewed as pricing of the publisher's option to abandon if new information on the marketability of the book were to become available.

The final chapter in Part I concerns the dividing line between a penalty clause and a liquidated damages clause. Judge Posner, who is uncomfortable with the notion that a clause agreed to by sophisticated parties should be unenforceable, nonetheless held in *Lake River Corp. v. Carborundum Co.* that a minimum quantity clause was a penalty and therefore unenforceable. Properly framed, the clause was neither a liquidated damage nor a penalty clause. The defendant wanted the flexibility to adapt as new information became available. Providing that flexibility was costly to the plaintiff and the minimum quantity clause determined the implicit price of that flexibility.

In Part II, I try to rehabilitate the much-maligned "tacit assumption" approach to the question of whether consequential damages should be recoverable. In these cases the option characterization of breach is inapposite. If, for example, a carrier were to fail to deliver goods on time, usually the reason would not be because the carrier chose to delay. The failure might result in substantial losses for the shipper and the issue would be whether the carrier should be responsible for those losses. When parties do take this into account, the contracts generally disclaim responsibility for consequential damages. The ubiquity of disclaimers casts doubt on the default remedy which is much more likely to find the loss compensable. I will examine two significant cases adopting the tacit assumption approach. In the United States, New York is one of the few jurisdictions in which the tacit agreement approach is still alive; in *Kenford Company v. Erie County* the Court of Appeals rejected claims to recover consequential damages following the decision by the County not to build a domed stadium. In England, the House of Lords limited recovery for the late redelivery of a time-chartered vessel in *The Achilleas*.

Part III considers the excuse doctrines from a number of angles. The first chapter criticizes an approach to excuse doctrine proposed by Professor Eisenberg that would expand the scope of excuses. The next chapter considers what should happen once the performance has been excused. Should there be any restitution of money paid? Should there be compensation for expenditures that had been made in reliance upon the now-excused contract? In England until 1943, the law had been that we leave the parties where they were at the time of the excusing event. There would be neither restitution nor compensation for reliance. A decision by the House of Lords and subsequent legislation changed the law so that there would be restitution and there might be compensation for reliance. The UCC rules are similar. I argue in that chapter that the earlier rule of leaving the parties where we found them is the better default rule.

The final chapter in Part III concerns a different problem. After the parties have entered into a contract, one of them might become concerned about the ability of the counterparty to perform. If it were to continue to perform, it would run the risk that the other party would breach and would not be able to compensate for expenses incurred. If, on the other hand, it did not continue its performance it would run the risk that a court might find it to be the breacher. It could avoid this choice if it had a right to demand assurance that the other party would perform. Prior to passage of the UCC, American law did not provide a right to demand assurance, although the parties could contract for such a right. The UCC provides for the right (2-609) and the Restatement (Second) has adopted a similar position. In *NorCon v. Niagara Mohawk*, the New York Court of Appeals purported to take a cautious path finding only a limited right to demand assurance in non-goods cases. However, they chose a poor vehicle. The rationale for a default rule that recognizes a right to demand assurance is that parties haven't bothered to think about the problem when designing their agreement. In this instance, however, the assurance issue had been fought over for years; the agreement provided for as much assurance as the public utility regulators would allow.

Part IV deals with the problem of the enforceability of something that is not quite a contract. I will pass on the problem that receives the most attention on this front – promissory estoppel. That is not because it is unimportant; rather it is because I have nothing interesting to add to the conversation. Instead I will consider two other issues. The first is the enforceability of agreements to agree or memoranda of understanding (MOU), in particular the treatment of what Judge Leval labeled a "Type II" agreement – an agreement to negotiate in good faith. In *Brown v. Cara*, the Second Circuit found that the parties had created a Type II agreement and remanded to determine whether the defendant's failure to complete the transaction had been in good faith. My intention in digging into this case was twofold. First, I wanted to see how parties would argue a Type II case. Unfortunately, there was virtually no argument on the issue at all. Second, I wanted to see how hard it would have been to write a clearly enforceable contract. In fact, it would not have been difficult.

The second issue is the revocability of an offer. The issue arises in Contracts casebooks in the context of a subcontractor attempting to revoke an erroneous bid after the general contractor has won the job, but before the general and sub have agreed. Generations of law students have been confronted with the conflicting views of Judges Hand and Traynor. While Traynor's decision was perceived as a significant innovation, even providing the basis for a new section of the Restatement, it turns out to have had virtually no impact beyond the scope of bidding for public construction projects. Even in those, the cornerstone of Traynor's analysis – reliance – proved problematic.

Reliance-talk permeates contract law and scholarship. One party relies on the other's promised performance, or its statements, or its anticipated entry into a formal agreement. It is the centerpiece of the Fuller-Perdue (1936) triumvirate of interests to protect. Reliance, they argued persuasively, is tremendously important. And many scholars were persuaded. Saying that reliance is important, however, says nothing about what we should do about it. The leap from the proposition to implications for doctrine – a leap made by Fuller-Perdue and many followers – does not follow. The Fuller-Perdue framework does nothing to resolve the Goldilocks problem: is the protection of reliance too much, too little, or just right?

Too often court decisions or scholarship forward arguments of this form: people want to be able to rely upon X and if the law does not take that reliance into account then something bad (inefficiency for some, injustice for others) will occur. Principles of contract doctrine can then be invoked, rejiggered, or even amended, so that the reliance is properly accounted for. The discussion, I believe, typically fails to ask the most basic questions: what do parties do and why do they do it? Much of this book concerns how parties choose to protect their reliance and the implications for both contract doctrine and interpretation.

PART I

Direct damages

2. The reliance-flexibility tradeoff and remedies for breach

Contract performance takes place over time, and the nature of the parties' future obligations can be deferred to take account of changing circumstances. One or both of the parties might want to rely on the continuity of the arrangement while, at the same time, maintaining the flexibility to adapt as new information becomes available. If the two parties were under single ownership, the owner could determine the appropriate tradeoff between flexibility and reliance. If they were not, the coordination would be done by contract and the contract would define the tradeoff. On the one hand, the parties want to adapt as new information becomes available. But on the other hand, if one party has relied on the continuation of the relationship, the counterparty's adaptation to that new information might cause it considerable harm.

There are many ways parties might deal with the reliance-flexibility tradeoff. One party might, for example, be given discretion over the quantity decision. I have analysed that problem in Goldberg (2006, ch. 5) and consider one manifestation of it in Chapter 7 below. Here I want to confine attention to a particular response to changed circumstances, namely termination of the agreement. When designing their relationship, the parties might include an option to terminate for one or both parties. The option might be unconditional or it might be exercisable only in certain circumstances. The counterparty might want to impose a hurdle to protect its reliance upon the continuation of their arrangement. The more it would be hurt by termination, the greater the price it would want to put on the option to abandon. If the contract made the termination option explicit, exercising that option would not be a breach of the agreement.

In effect, one party sells discretion (or flexibility) to the other. The "price" would reflect the value of flexibility to one party and the cost of providing that flexibility to the other. The price need not be explicit. As some of the illustrations below will demonstrate, the contract structure will determine an implicit price of flexibility. Breach is, of course, a special case of the option to terminate – if the contract did not address termination, then the remedy for breach would be the default price of the option to abandon. Once this is recognized, it is clear that the price of that option need bear no relationship to the legal remedies for breach embodied in the UCC or Restatement. Rather than starting with doctrine and working out, my approach is to begin with the design problem and work backward to doctrinal considerations. By observing how parties do resolve the reliance-flexibility tradeoff we can get some insights into how the default remedy rules might be constructed. In particular, it calls into question the notion that the remedy should make the promisee whole. The benefit of the bargain, so routinely invoked by courts and commentators, does not fare well.

To illustrate the variety of means for pricing the option to abandon, I will describe a number of different instances in which reliance is important and one or both parties has the option to abandon. The illustrations include the venture capital contract, the illusory contract, the breakup fee in a corporate acquisition, the pay-or-play contract in the movie industry, and severance pay. Despite the fact that the reliance interest in these examples is substantial, the exercise price can be quite low. Indeed, in some instances, the price is zero. I will then turn to the implications this has for contract remedies.

I. ILLUSTRATIONS

A. Venture Capital Contract

Consider first the venture capital contract. The venture capitalist (VC) provides funds to an entrepreneur whose project typically has a high risk of failure and, even if successful, a long period before the project will yield positive returns. The VC does not commit to funding the entire project. Instead, the VC will phase payment, allowing it to terminate its obligation as new information on the likely success of the project becomes available. The VC pays for this option upfront in the share price. The option to abandon is generally accompanied by a right of first refusal. If the entrepreneur found an alternative supplier of funds, the VC would have the right to continue funding on the same terms proposed by the third party. The option to terminate – to not throw good money after bad – is valuable to the VC. But it is costly to the entrepreneur who would be sitting with an incomplete project and no viable funding source to complete it. The entrepreneur would be especially vulnerable if the VC were to use the option to rewrite the deal on more favorable terms. That is, when the option to abandon is triggered, the VC could say that it would only fund the next round if the terms were altered in its favor.

So, what protection of the entrepreneur's reliance would the contract exhibit? In virtually all venture capital deals the answer would be that the VC would pay nothing at the time the option is exercised. All the entrepreneur has is an unenforceable understanding that if the business performs as expected, the VC will invest in another round. The first refusal right makes it unlikely that an alternative source of funds would appear; any third party would recognize that since the VC has better information, if it chose not to match, this would likely be a poor investment. The entrepreneur's protection of its reliance would take two forms. First is the VC's self-interest: If the information produced has been positive, it will be in the VC's interest to proceed. Delay or abandonment hurts it. Second, if the VC's threat to terminate is perceived as an opportunistic attempt to renegotiate, its reputation will suffer. For present purposes, the key point is that although the entrepreneur relies on the VC's future funding, it would rarely, if ever, receive compensation if the VC were to exercise the termination option.

B. The Illusory Contract

In some instances, the reliance-flexibility tradeoff can be accomplished despite the parties deliberately making their agreement legally unenforceable. That is, one party might be encouraged to make investments in reliance on the continuation of its relationship notwithstanding the fact that it would have no legal recourse if the other party were to terminate. If a contract said in effect, "I will do it if I want to," it would be deemed illusory and lacking consideration. For example, the standard franchise agreement between Ford and its dealerships pre-1940 took this form. The unenforceability was not an accident of careless drafting. Ford knew what it was doing. (Kessler, 1957, 1150–52) Ford had only promised to fill future orders if it chose to do so. In *Bushwick-Decatur Motors, Inc. v. Ford Motor Co.*, the district court described a Ford franchise agreement in detail: "The Sales Agreement, by its term Article (9)(c) was terminable at any time, at the will of either party, and does not bind defendant to sell or deliver, or plaintiff to buy, nor does it impose any liability on defendant if it terminates or refuses to make sales to the other party. The Sales Agreement was to be observed by the parties only so long as was mutually satisfactory." (*Bushwick* 1, 920–21)

The court found the agreement to be illusory, despite the claimed reliance of the dealer on alleged oral statements by Ford representatives:

> [T]he oral contract "in substance" provided … that defendant's settled policy was "Once a Ford dealer, always a Ford dealer"; that by the dealership

> contract "the plaintiff had become a member of the great Ford family; that the plaintiff would remain a Ford dealer as long as it wanted to"; that the Ford policy, settled for many years, "was a guarantee of this; and that the plaintiff need have no hesitation whatever in investing all available funds in the promotion of the sale and servicing of Ford products as such investments would be perfectly safe." … [T]he agreement was reaffirmed [numerous times and] "at all such occasions, plaintiff was encouraged to enlarge its facilities, increase its sales force and expand its business, in reliance on the assurances given by the defendant that plaintiff was 'in' as a Ford dealer as long as it wanted and should have no concern over the wisdom of making long term commitments and long term plans." (*Bushwick* 2, 678)

Neither Chrysler nor General Motors went to the extreme of making their agreement unenforceable. However, by making the agreement terminable on very short (say, fifteen days') notice, they essentially accomplished the same thing. Their agreements were enforceable, but only for the brief period. The auto manufacturers wanted their dealers to make investments in reliance on continuation of the relationship, and by and large dealers did so. The dealers relied on the expectation that their satisfactory performance would assure renewal of their franchise. Dealers wanted more but, absent legislative intervention, they could not get the producers to give explicit protection to their reliance. On their eventual success in obtaining legislation, see Macaulay (1966).

The General Motors–Fisher Body contract, subject of much academic interest, provides another illustration. In 1919, the two entered into a ten-year agreement in which Fisher agreed to produce and General Motors agreed to purchase almost all of GM's closed automobile bodies. Despite the considerable reliance by both, the agreement was unenforceable. While General Motors promised to place orders for substantially all its bodies, Fisher only promised to tell GM whether it would accept the orders. It did not promise that it would fulfill them. "In the event that the FISHER COMPANY accepts the orders specified in the schedules from time to time furnished by GENERAL MOTORS, it shall proceed to make and deliver the automobile bodies called for by said schedules …" The reliance of each was protected in part by the consequences if either walked away. Both would have suffered significant losses since neither had an adequate alternative – the high switching costs, arguably, constrained the parties and protected the reliance of each. The contract price, however, was zero.

Kellogg's contract with a supplier of packaging material for its cereal provides a more current illustration of a clearly unenforceable agreement. (*Kellogg Co. v. FPC Flexible Packaging Company*) The contract was for three years. The "quantity clause," such as it was, read as follows:

"Kellogg generally encourages its employees to obtain required goods and services from suppliers who have entered into formal agreements with Kellogg, and Kellogg agrees to use reasonable efforts to *communicate the existence* of this Agreement to such employees with a general need to obtain the Products and Services within the scope of this Agreement." (emphasis added) Either party could terminate the Agreement with 120 days' notice. While the agreement was, obviously, too open-ended to be enforceable for any future orders, it would have been enforceable for any orders that had already been executed. It, like the Fisher Body contract and the Ford franchise contracts, was backward-enforceable, but not forward-enforceable. Nonetheless, it likely provided sufficient assurance to encourage the supplier's reliance on continuation of its dealings with Kellogg.

C. Breakup Fees

In a corporate acquisition, there can be a temporal gap of many months between execution of the contract and its actual closing. During that period a lot can happen which might result in the buyer wanting to terminate the deal. The terms governing the buyer's option to terminate are the subject of extensive bargaining. The buyer is particularly concerned about the accuracy of the seller's representations (adverse selection) and post-execution behavior (moral hazard). The buyer also would like the ability to walk away from the deal if external forces result in a decline in the value of the seller or if it is unable to arrange financing.

However, once the contract has been executed, the seller can have a substantial reliance interest in the deal closing. The seller's reliance has two components. First, there is the simple reliance on the agreed price. It does not want to give the buyer a free option to buy at the contract price only if the market stays the same or goes up. Second, once the contract is executed, the stand-alone value of the seller's business might be adversely affected. Key personnel might start looking for new jobs; investment decisions are postponed; relations with old customers, suppliers, and bankers might be impaired; and a failure to close might send a negative signal about the viability of the company. The greater the seller's reliance on the deal going through, the more protection (the higher the effective option price) it will try to get.

The acquisition agreement requires that all the closing conditions be met; if not, the buyer would have a zero-price option to walk away. Not every inaccuracy, however trivial, would allow the buyer to walk away; typically, the walk-right is conditioned on the inaccuracies that individually, or in the aggregate, constitute a material adverse effect (MAE). In addition, the closing can be contingent on a broader condition: Between the exercise and closing date, there cannot have been a material adverse change (MAC). The greater the seller's reliance, the more likely it is that the MAC will be hedged in by exceptions making it more difficult for the buyer to walk. The exceptions generally put the risk of exogenous change on the buyer, with the seller bearing the risk of endogenous change (its behavior reducing the value of the combined firm) and its inaccurate statements. In their study of MAC clauses, Gilson and Schwartz (2005, pp. 349–50) considered the following exceptions:

> (1) changes in global economic conditions; (2) changes in U.S. economic conditions; (3) changes in global stock, capital, or financial market conditions; (4) changes in U.S. stock, capital, or financial market conditions; (5) changes in the economic conditions of other regions; (6) changes in the target company's industry; (7) changes in applicable laws or regulations; (8) changes in the target company's stock price; (9) loss of customers, suppliers, or employees; (10) changes due to the agreement or the transaction itself; and (11) a miscellaneous category. The agreements also were coded for two qualifications to the explicit inclusions or exclusions of the traditional MAC definition. These qualifications would make a specified inclusion or exclusion inapplicable if the MAC either specifically affected the target company or had a materially disproportionate effect on the target company.

Some buyers, particularly private equity firms, include explicit breakup fees in their agreements. If completely unconstrained, these would put the risk of a decline in value from exogenous causes entirely on the seller. Or the breakup fee could be conditional. The agreement in *Hexion Specialty Chemicals, Inc. v. Huntsman Corp.* provides a good illustration. Because the value of the target firm had fallen, the buyer wanted out. The buyer's option had, in effect, three different prices. If it could prove that there had been a MAC, it could walk away at a zero price. If the buyer used its best efforts to obtain financing but failed, it would pay a termination fee of $325 million. Finally, if the deal failed to close because of a "'knowing and intentional breach of any covenant,'" damages would be uncapped. Citing a number of bad acts by the buyer and its lawyers, the vice chancellor found that the breach of a covenant was intentional. After losing at trial, the buyer settled for $1 billion.

The buyer's right to terminate is not an afterthought; it is a significant element in the deal and is often the subject of considerable negotiation. The option price – or, as *Hexion* illustrates, the option *prices* – would reflect the seller's reliance.

D. Pay or Play and Severance Packages

Next, consider a movie studio contracting with an actor to appear in a movie to be filmed in the near future (say, six months later). That was the situation in the casebook favorite featuring Shirley MacLaine's dispute with Twentieth Century Fox following the cancellation of the film project *Bloomer Girl*. A lot can happen in the period between signing the contract and commencing filming. The script might be disappointing; the genre might become less attractive; a similar film might be released; a director incompatible with the actor might sign on; a more attractive actor might become available; the actor's reputation might be tarnished in the interim; and so forth. As the primary claimant on the project's earnings, the studio has the incentive to make adaptive decisions that enhance the expected value of the project. The right to terminate the actor before filming commences would be valuable to the studio. The actor enters into the contract in reliance on the project going forward and on her being in the film. Her reliance is the opportunity cost of accepting this project and foregoing other possible offers that might come along in the intervening months. The studio's flexibility and the actor's reliance are protected by a pay-or-play clause. The studio maintains the right not to make the movie and, if it does choose to make the movie, to do so without this actor. The price of this option depends on the marketability of the actor. For a major talent, the pay-or-play option would kick in upon entering into the contract and the compensation would be the so-called fixed fee. Major talent typically receives a percentage of the gross offset against a fixed fee. The fee might be in the \$20 million range. If the share of the gross were 10 percent, the gross would have to reach \$200 million before the contingent compensation would kick in. For lesser talent, the option might not be triggered until a subsequent event – perhaps the appearance of a bona fide alternative offer for the actor. Until that point, the actor would be committed to the project, but the studio would have a free option to terminate.

If the studio were to terminate, the agreement might impose some limitations on the actor's behavior. In a typical pay-or-play contract, the talent would have no duty to mitigate, but it would have to offset any earnings. That is explicit in the union contract of the Director's Guild: If the director is employed by a third party during the contract period, the employer "shall be entitled to an offset of the compensation arising from such new employment for such remaining portion of the guaranteed period against the compensation remaining unpaid. …" However, "the Director shall have no obligation to mitigate damages arising from his or her removal. …" (Selz et al. (1997, 34))

The pay-or-play clause is a variation on a severance package (except the actor is not an employee). An employment agreement might give the employer the discretion to terminate the agreement at its convenience ("no cause") and, if so, it might specify what compensation, if any, would be required. The structure of these contracts can vary in subtle ways. Consider, for example, the multi-year contracts of two coaches in major college sports programs: John Calipari at Kentucky and Rich Rodriguez, then at West Virginia. The coach and the university both have a substantial reliance interest in the relationship. If either chose to terminate without cause, that party would have to bear some consequence, but both wanted to retain that option. The two contracts each chose a somewhat different way to protect reliance. If Kentucky terminated Calipari, it would pay liquidated damages of $3 million per year for each remaining year on the contract. That was somewhat less than he would receive if he had not been fired and if he collected at least some of the incentive payments. Calipari would be required to "make reasonable and diligent efforts to obtain employment." If he were to succeed, then the damages would be "reduced by the amount of the minimum guaranteed annual compensation package of the Coach's new position." That is, he would have a duty to mitigate and there would be a partial offset. If, on the other hand, Calipari chose to terminate early, he would owe as liquidated damages an amount that decreased over time – $3 million if the termination were in the first year, declining to $500,000 in the fourth year and nothing in year five. The Rodriguez arrangement was simpler. If either he or the school terminated without cause, there would be a one-time payment of $2 million. Rodriguez would neither have to mitigate nor offset any earnings.

The point of these examples is that the option to terminate the agreement can create value, and the price of that option reflects the counterparty's reliance. I say "reflects," since, as some of the preceding examples show, there can be considerable reliance but little or no compensation if the option were to be exercised.

II. THE DAMAGE REMEDY

If a contract does not explicitly allow for termination, what then? The default rule is that termination would amount to a breach and the promisor would be liable for damages (or specific performance). The promisor has an option and the exercise price of that option would be the damage remedy. That framing has generated much criticism –

indeed, hostility. It is inconsistent with the dominant view as described by Farnsworth (1998, § 12.8) in his treatise:

> The basic principle for the measurement of those damages is that of compensation based on the injured party's expectation. One is entitled to recover an amount that will put one in as good a position as one would have been in had the contract been performed. At least in principle, a party's expectation is measured by the actual worth that performance of the contract would have had to that party, not the worth that it might have had to some hypothetical reasonable person. Damages based on expectation should therefore take account of any circumstances peculiar to the situation of the injured party, including that party's own needs and opportunities, personal values, and even idiosyncrasies.

An alternative formulation is the "indifference principle" as described by Craswell (1988, 636): "The stated goal of contract damages is 'to put the plaintiff in as good a position as he would have been in had the defendant kept his contract.' In economic analysis, this is usually translated as … the amount necessary to leave the plaintiff absolutely indifferent, in subjective terms, between having the defendant breach and pay damages or having the defendant perform." For an enthusiastic endorsement of the indifference principle, see Eisenberg (2005).

Oliver Wendell Holmes famously said that the "duty to keep a contract at common law means a prediction that you must pay damages if you do not keep it – and nothing else." (Holmes, 1897, 462) Note that while Holmes makes the option explicit and sets the option price as the damage remedy, he says nothing about what the damage remedy should be. The notion that a contract is merely an option to perform or pay damages has elicited much criticism. The decision to terminate is not viewed as a choice, but as a wrong. The option formulation has often been linked with the concept of "efficient breach." I find that terminology unfortunate. It ignores the fact that the parties could determine ex ante the consequences of termination of their relationship. The parties are concerned with efficient adaptation to changed circumstances and new information. "Efficient breach" should be considered in that context. If the contract were silent on the consequences of one party's decision to terminate (breach), then there might be circumstances in which termination would be the appropriate (efficient) response.

To some commentators breach is immoral, and the amorality of Holmes's option notion grates. Some, like David Friedmann (1989), would treat a contract breach as a transgression against another's rights. Friedmann (1989, 2) argues that "a party is generally bound to perform his contractual promises unless he obtains a release from the promisee."

For Friedmann, expectation damages would not be adequate. The remedy, he insists, should not be monetary damages, but specific performance. The specific performance remedy, I should note, also establishes an exercise price for the option – it just does it differently. Instead of establishing the price directly, it requires the party seeking termination to purchase the right from the counterparty at a negotiated price. The promisee would have the right to refuse.

After pages of argument against allowing the promisor to walk away (on ethical and efficiency grounds), Friedmann takes almost all of it back:

> As a normative matter, parties in a contractual setting should be left free to define the ambit of their rights, and it is open to them to stipulate that the promisor will be allowed to terminate the contract subject to the payment of damages. The efficient breach theory assumes, however, that, even if they have not done so and even if they intended to confer on the promisee a broader entitlement, the law will nevertheless defeat their joint intention by granting the promisor the option to breach. (23)

The parties should be free, that is, to choose what, if anything, should happen if one party wants to terminate. His entire attack is on a default rule, and he appears quite content to allow parties to contract out in any way they see fit. His argument boils down to the notion that specific performance should be the default remedy, not expectation damages – the promisee should have a veto. Ironically, Scott and Triantis (2004, 1477–86), taking the options framework, reach the same conclusion. Their rationale is quite different. Framing the question in terms of options makes it clear that the option price need bear no relationship to the standard damage remedies of contract law – expectation, reliance, or restitution. Rather than privileging any of the three, Scott and Triantis recommend the "none of the above" alternative. Specific performance would be a forcing default rule that would, perhaps, induce the parties to contract around it and make the option price explicit. (Specific performance would only be their default rule for contracts between sophisticated businesses. For consumer contracts, their default rule would give the consumer a free option to cancel an order.)

I regard the Scott and Triantis proposal as a form of academic shock treatment. The expectation damages remedy is so firmly entrenched in the minds of judges, lawyers, contracts professors, and even first-year students that a bold proposed change was necessary to get their attention. The fundamental point is that the contract law remedy is, in effect, the implied termination clause. As Epstein (1989, 108) asserts: "Damage rules are no different from any other terms of a contract. They should be understood solely as default provisions subject to variation by contract. The operative rules should be chosen by the parties for their own purposes, not by the law for its purposes."

However, the notion that termination is a wrongful act makes the remedy default rules stickier than others. As Scott and Triantis (2004, 1435) note: "Although most of contract law provides default rules from which parties are free to contract away, remedial defaults carry heavier presumptive weight than other provisions." The stickiness of the expectation damage remedy is, as Scott and Triantis observe, in part a historical accident, but it also has great rhetorical power. If a breaching party were perceived as having wronged the promisee, then corrective justice would seem to require that, like a tort victim, the promisee should be made whole. That provides an anchor for doctrinal argument and friction for moving away from the default remedies. Reframing the problem as a matter of transaction design and recognizing the reliance-flexibility tradeoff show why the benefit of the bargain remedy is too simplistic. Holmes's framing as the promisor having a choice between performing or paying damages was, in large part, a response to the notion that default rules should be derived from ethical norms rather than commercial needs. Reviving Holmes's aphorism would at least nudge the rhetoric in a more useful direction.

Much scholarship, particularly economic analyses of remedies, proceeds on the implicit assumption that the parties are incapable of pricing termination themselves and that the policy options are limited to money damages (expectation, reliance, restitution) or specific performance. By framing the problem as one of pricing the termination option, it is clear that in a wide variety of contexts the efficient rule (i.e., one which sophisticated parties would voluntarily choose) bears no relation to the ones featured in the lawyer's rhetoric and the economist's models. To be sure, there are classes of cases in which a default remedy of expectation damages would be efficient. I argue elsewhere that there is a strong case for protecting the contract-market differential, which I have labeled the narrow expectation interest. (Goldberg, 2006, ch. 10) Scott and Triantis (2004, 1479–80) make a similar argument. But beyond that, there is little reason to believe that there would be any relationship between the option price and the default remedies of law or the remedies modeled by economists.

A standard criticism of contract remedies is that they systematically undercompensate promisees. The option framework suggests that in many instances the current law overcompensates. In particular, making the promisee whole means that if the buyer were to breach, the remedy should include lost profits. The expectation damages would be the difference between the price and the but-for costs, whereas the reliance remedy would exclude lost profits. Analysis of decided cases suggests that courts rarely award reliance damages, but that is misleading. In a study nearly two decades ago, Gibson (1997, 915) found that "in 467 of the cases *most likely* to produce reliance damages, only fourteen (2.9 percent) did so." That would seem to indicate the unimportance of the reliance remedy. However, if instead we look at it from the contract design perspective, the picture is different. The General Motors standard form said GM "may at its option immediately terminate all or any part of this order, at any time and for any reason, by giving written notice to Seller." If it did so, the seller's remedy would be the equivalent of the standard reliance remedy. GM would pay for all items that had already been completed under the purchase order and the costs of work-in-progress less the value of any goods the supplier could resell to third parties. There would be no recovery for overhead and other elements of lost profits. (Goldberg (2014, 1065)) This is, in effect, the reliance damage remedy. Ben-Shahar and White (2006, 959) found similar language in other automobile supplier contracts. I suspect that similar language would be found in many contracts between manufacturers and their suppliers.

Empire Gas Corp. v. American Bakeries Co. provides a good illustration of overcompensation. American entered into a four-year requirements contract to buy propane and conversion units from Empire. Conversion units would enable American to have its trucks switch between propane and gasoline. Empire did not manufacture conversion units; it bought them in a competitive market and provided them to customers as an accommodation. American reneged, buying none, and Empire sued. The jury determined how many conversion units would have been sold (2,242) and how much propane would have been purchased, but for the breach. Given these numbers, it then determined the profits that would have accrued had American complied. For the conversion units alone, the lost profits were 36 percent of the projected sales. The jury found an additional $2 million in lost profits for the foregone propane sales, despite the fact that propane was sold in a competitive market and the contract price was determined by a meeting competition clause ("purchase propane motor fuel solely from Empire … as long as Empire … remains in a reasonably competitive price posture with other major suppliers."). In effect, the remedy set a substantial option price for the right to purchase at the market price in two competitive markets (conversion units and propane fuel).

The *Empire Gas* decision did not make clear how the lost profits on the propane were reckoned. Because of the meeting competition clause, the contract-market price differential would have been zero. The expert must have assumed that Empire was a lost-volume seller. Had the contract not been breached, the damage calculation presumed that Empire would have been able to sell all American's needs and it would not have had to cut back at all on its sales to others. The court does not, however, invoke the lost-volume measure (UCC 2-708(2)). I will discuss the lost-volume-seller problem in Chapter 4 and explain why from an option perspective, the remedy is perverse. My point here is that in *Empire Gas* there is no discussion at all of why the contract would establish a high option price for the privilege of buying at the market price in two competitive markets.

Rodriguez v. Learjet, Inc. provides a second illustration of the over-generous compensation that would result from awarding lost profits. The contract to purchase a new airplane included a series of progress payments; in the event that the buyer terminated, Learjet would keep the payments already made. The buyer terminated shortly after entering into the agreement and sued for return of its initial payment of $250,000, asserting that the payment was an unenforceable penalty. Learjet defended by arguing that it was not a penalty. To show this, Learjet argued that it was a lost-volume seller, and it demonstrated that it had the capacity to sell this plane and another; it proved to the court's satisfaction that it had suffered lost profits of over $1.8 million. Therefore, the measly $250,000 was not a penalty and the court enforced it. The value of getting approval of its progress payment schedule (a schedule of option prices) apparently exceeded the one-time gain of $1.8 million. The implicit option price of the lost-volume-profit remedy clearly exceeded the explicit option prices in Learjet's schedule of nonrefundable progress payments.

I do not expect contract law to abandon the benefit-of-the-bargain approach. I do hope, however, that focusing on the contract-design questions will have some effect. The lost-volume-seller problem is one example. The notion that lost profits in general should routinely be enforceable is another. The unenforceability of penalty clauses, discussed in Chapter 7, is yet a third. My modest hope is that the analysis might nudge doctrine a bit in the right direction by requiring a high standard of proof for the lost profits on the one hand, and by facilitating the limitation of damages on the other.

3. Assessing damages: now or then?

It is generally uncontroversial that one element of the damage remedy for a breach of contract is the contract price-market price differential. There can be serious disagreements on the rationale for this remedy and on its implementation, particularly whether there are additional damage claims (e.g., lost profits), the relationship between the money damages and cover, and at which time the damages should be measured. In this chapter I want to focus on the last question. If one party breaches (or repudiates), there are a number of dates that could be chosen for ascertaining the market price. The generally accepted rule is "time of the breach" although courts sometimes have chosen alternatives like the date at which performance was to be completed or the date the decision was rendered. The existence of a firm rule is more important than the content of the rule. Otherwise, the parties would invoke the rule more favorable to them at the time of the trial and the court would have little guidance in choosing between the proffered measures.

Courts in the United States and elsewhere have found application of the principle difficult. One court noted that "one of the most difficult interpretive problems of the Uniform Commercial Code … [is] the appropriate time to measure buyer's damages where the seller anticipatorily repudiates a contract and the buyer does not cover." (*Cosden* (p. 1066)) I want to analyse the problem by focusing on four cases. The first two deal with anticipatory repudiation. The others do not on their face appear to raise the question. The first ostensibly concerns whether the subject matter of a contract was sufficiently unique to allow for an award of specific performance. The second was framed by the Israeli Supreme Court as an unjust enrichment claim for restitution. When the doctrinal underbrush is cleared away, both raise the question of whether the plaintiff would have the choice of basing its damage claim on the price at the time of breach or at some future date.

I. COSDEN OIL & CHEMICAL CO. V. KARL O. HELM AKTIENGESELLSCHAFT

Cosden, a producer of polystyrene, promised to deliver the product over a period of time to Helm, a trader. It delivered some, but because of production problems, it cancelled the remaining orders. Anticipating the problem, Helm engaged in self-help, withholding payment for the polystyrene that had been delivered. Cosden sued for payment and Helm counterclaimed for the failure to deliver the remainder of its order. The jury found that Cosden had anticipatorily repudiated and found that Helm had suffered damages of around $630,000 from which it subtracted the roughly $360,000 that Helm had failed to pay. The main issue on appeal was which date should be used to determine the market price. This mattered, since the price of polystyrene had risen between the time of the repudiation and the delivery date.

In *Cosden*, the court considered three dates: "Cosden argues that damages should be measured when Helm learned of the repudiation. Helm contends that market price as of the last day for delivery-or the time of performance-should be used to compute its damages under the contract-market differential. We reject both views, and hold that the district court correctly measured damages at a commercially reasonable point after Cosden informed Helm that it was cancelling the [order]." (1069)

The economist's notion of "rational expectations" suggests that the price of an asset today is the best estimate of its price in the future. If it were otherwise, clever people would engage in arbitrage. So, it would appear that parties should be indifferent to which of the three prices was used, as long as the decision was made when the contract was entered into. That proposition has to be qualified. The relevant price at any of the three dates is not the *current* price. That may sound cryptic, so let me first give a simple example. Suppose that the inflation rate in the economy is very high. Then if the inflation-adjusted price (the real price) of a commodity had remained unchanged, the nominal price today would be substantially below the price of the same commodity a year hence. However, the price today for delivery of that commodity a year hence would be equal to the expected value of the commodity a year from today – the price would take into account the expected rate of inflation. A homogeneous product to be delivered on two different dates should be viewed as two different products. So, to simplify, if the original contract called for 10 tons of polystyrene to be delivered on March 31 (call it P3/31), the relevant market price would be the price of P3/31 as of the "time of the breach." In effect, the contract should be viewed as an asset and the problem is to ascertain the value of that asset at the time of the breach.

At any of the alternative times of the breach, the relevant market price would be for polystyrene to be delivered on March 31. Polystyrene prices happened to have risen between the date of repudiation and the date of performance, so the actual values differed. Not surprisingly, the parties, deciding after the fact, chose the price most favorable to their position. In practice, in many (most?) instances, prices for the precise product/date combination might not be available and compromise will be necessary. The court appears to have done so in this case by choosing the *current* market price at each of the three alternative times of the breach. That is, if the time of the breach was found to be February 1, the court appears to have chosen the spot price on February 1 rather than the February 1 price for delivery on March 31.

Of the three alternatives, the court's choice was the proper one. The anticipatory repudiation doctrine gives the innocent party a reasonable period of time during which it can decide whether it should accept the repudiation. It should have enough time to weigh alternatives. The repudiation does not become a breach until it is accepted (or should have been accepted). For commodities traded in thick markets, the time period might be measured in minutes – for others, like polystyrene, the period would be longer. For a time charter, discussed in the next section, the period would be longer still. The court, noting that the UCC treats cover as the "preferred remedy," puts this in terms of giving the innocent party an opportunity to cover. "When a buyer chooses not to cover, but to seek damages, the market is measured at the time he could have covered – a reasonable time after repudiation." (1072)

Rather than treating cover and damages as alternative remedies as the UCC does, it is more useful, I believe, to treat cover as *evidence* of the price at the time of breach. There should be no presumption that the buyer would cover. If the market price had risen, the buyer should consider whether it still makes sense to buy the product. If the buyer is a trader, as was the case here, the cover concept loses its meaning. Helm engaged in numerous transactions; it would make no sense to label any particular trade as the cover transaction. In this case, both parties attempted to identify specific trades as the cover transaction. Cosden argued that Helm's trades in early February were cover and Helm claimed that its trades in late February were cover, since prices had risen. The jury properly denied both.

The essential take-away is that the damages are the change in the value of an asset – the contract – at the time of the breach. Had the House of

Lords recognized that principle, the results in the next case would have been different.

II. GOLDEN STRAIT CORPN V. NIPPON YUSEN KUBISHIKA KAISHA (THE GOLDEN VICTORY)

The matter of the proper date for reckoning damages arose in a very different context in *The Golden Victory*. In July 1998, the owner of the Golden Victory chartered the tanker to a Japanese company for seven years. The charter included a clause that was "invariable in time charters for tankers likely to visit the Gulf" (719):

> If war or hostilities break out between any two or more of the following countries: USA, former USSR, PRC, UK, Netherlands, Liberia, Japan, Iran, Kuwait, Saudi Arabia, Qatar, Iraq, both owners and charterers shall have the right to cancel this charter. Either party, however, shall not be entitled to terminate this charter on account of minor and/or local military operation or economic warfare anywhere which will not interfere with the vessel's trade.

The language is not unique. A similar term is included in the New York Product Exchange (1993) form, with the names of the countries to be filled in at the time of chartering. (clause 32). The hire rate was initially set at $31,500 per day, increasing by a formula that was not included in the decision. In addition, the owner would receive a share of the profits over the base rate. The charterers repudiated in December 2001 and three days later the owners accepted the repudiation. In a September 2002 interim declaratory award, the arbitrator found that there had been a repudiation and that the earliest contractual date for redelivery would have been in December 2005. The damage measurement issue was not decided until October 2004. That gap turned out to be significant. The second Gulf War began in March 2003; had the contract still been in effect, the war clause would have been triggered and the charterer would have exercised its right to terminate.

The owner claimed that the terminal date for measuring damages should be December 2005. The charterer argued that, since it would have terminated in March 2003, it should only be liable for damages through March 2003. The arbitrator agreed, as did the judges in the commercial court, the appeals court, and, finally, in the House of Lords (in a 3–2 split). In justifying this result, Lord Carswell invoked language from a decision a century earlier: "Why should he listen to conjecture on a matter which has become an accomplished fact? Why should he guess when he can calculate? With the light before him, why should he shut his eyes and grope in the dark?" (431 citing *Bwllfa and Merthyr Dare Steam Collieries (1891) Ltd. v. Pontypridd Waterworks Co.*)

The arbitrator took evidence from experts on whether in December 2001 the war was merely a possibility or was probable or inevitable. There was considerable discussion of *The Mihalis Angelos* in which the charterers cancelled three days early because there was no way that the vessel could be available at the time and place specified. The court held that the charterers had breached. However, it held that there were no damages because the failure to meet the deadline was "predestined." The majority took this as an indication that they could consider events subsequent to the repudiation in assessing damages. The owner argued that the "loss is crystallised at the date of repudiation and an arbitrator or court should not look at such events in making the assessment. The only exception to this rule was where the subsequent event could be seen at the crystallisation date to be inevitable or 'predestined.'" (714)

Lord Bingham, in his dissent, noted that if the damages had been calculated at the time the liability decision was made, the Gulf War would not have occurred and, presumably, the arbitrator would have had no difficulty awarding damages for the last two-plus years of the charter. Could the charterer then have come back to the arbitrator and asked for a refund for the last two years? Presumably the arbitrator and the majority would have rejected such a claim, perhaps invoking "finality." But why make the remedy depend on the length of the damages phase of the proceedings? War was only one of the many risks that might have impacted the value of the charter. Suppose that there had been no war (wishful thinking). If the market price for charters collapsed, should the charterer's damages be increased to take into account the latest conditions? If not, which post-breach, pre-decision factors should a court take into account when reckoning damages? Indeed, if one took seriously the court's question, "with the light before him, why should he shut his eyes and grope in the dark?" then why not wait until the judicial process is complete and determine damages after their Lordships have spoken?

As in *Cosden*, the charter was an asset of the owner and the problem was to determine the value of the asset at the time of the repudiation. The complicated pricing formula – indexing and profit sharing – made that more complicated, but the complications were independent of the timing question. Lord Mance (Court of Appeals) recognized that the contract was an asset, but failed to understand the implications: "But the element of uncertainty, resulting from the war clause, meant that the owners were never entitled to absolute confidence that the charter would run for its full seven-year period. They never had an asset which they could bank or sell on that basis." (543–44) That's half right; the value of all assets is entirely determined by the future and the future is, by definition, uncertain. That does not mean that the assets can't be valued. The majority suggested that the war clause made the duration of the charter (and therefore its value) uncertain: "Where there is a suspensive condition such as a war clause, however, the duration of the charter was always uncertain, depending on a contingency of the occurrence of an event which was by definition within the contemplation of the parties." (715) By that reasoning, every contract with a force majeure clause would be at risk.

Valuing the asset would, by necessity, take into account the possibility that the war clause would come into play and that one of the parties would exercise its cancellation option. If at the time of the repudiation, war was a low probability event, the discount would have been minor; and conversely, if the repudiation was at the beginning of March 2003, the value of the asset would be close to zero. A simple analogy might be helpful. Suppose a company is litigating a patent claim. If it were to win, the share value would be $100 and if it were to lose, the share value would be zero. If the chance of winning is 50:50, the value of the stock on the eve of decision is $50. Post-decision it would be $0 or $100. Varying the probabilities would alter the stock price; if winning were "predestined," the stock price would approach $100 and if it were exceedingly unlikely, it would approach zero. The likelihood of an event at the time of the breach, whether remote or predestined, is one of the determinants of the value of the asset.

The Lords' failure to comprehend this point is illustrated in Lord Brown's opinion:

> Shift the facts here and assume that the arbitrator had found, as at December 2001, a probability (or even merely a significant possibility) of (perhaps imminent) war breaking out in the Gulf, but that in fact, by the time damages finally came to be assessed, not only had war not broken out but all risk of it had disappeared – or, indeed, the assessment might not have taken place until the whole nominal term of the charterparty had expired. On the view taken by the minority of your Lordships, the damages award would have had to reflect a risk which never in fact eventuated, a conclusion in the circumstances, greatly to the owner's disadvantage. Yet that inescapably is the logic of the minority's approach. (724–25)

And that is how it should be. Markets take into account the risk, incorporating the best information at the time of the repudiation. If the likelihood of the particular event changes over time or, as in this instance, comes to pass, the market will reflect those changes. If the news turns out to be better than had been anticipated (Brown's no war scenario), the measured damages at the time of the breach would have been below the measurement at the time of the decision. And if the news turns out to be worse, as in the actual case, the measured damages at the time of breach would exceed those at the time of the decision. Whether the losses were probable or predestined would be determined by the market, not by the judges.

Counsel for the shipowners was Nicholas Hamblen. Shortly thereafter as a judge he faced the same issue and distinguished it, holding that the repudiation of a wheat contract terminated the transaction and that the fact that the seller would have been able to invoke the prohibition clause did not affect the outcome. (*Bunge SA v. Nidera BV*) However, other English courts have followed *The Golden Victory*; see *Novasen SA v. Alimenta SA, Flame SA v. Glory Wealth Shipping PTE Ltd., and Fulton Shipping Inc. of Panama v. Globalia Business Travel S.A.U.*

III. KLEIN V. PEPSICO

The case's ticket to the casebooks is its treatment of the specific performance remedy. Specific performance would be available if the goods are unique or "in other proper circumstances." Klein asked for, and the trial court granted, specific performance, holding that the subject matter of the transaction (a G-II airplane) was unique. However, the decision was overturned on appeal. While the ostensible issue was the uniqueness of the airplane, the underlying concern was the time at which the damages would be determined. Nothing in the decision indicated that the court considered this question.

Klein was in the market for a used corporate jet. He entered into a contract with Pepsico for a Gulfstream G-II. (The transaction was somewhat more complicated with an intermediary involved, but we can ignore that.) Pepsico reneged and the court found it liable. Klein did not have a special interest in this particular plane; he was buying with the intent to resell. Surprisingly, the court did not put any weight on this. One of the hallmarks of uniqueness, after all, is that the buyer has some specific reason for wanting this particular item. The classic examples of items meriting specific performance are heirlooms and real property. In both instances there is at least a presumption of idiosyncratic value which would not be captured by a standard money damages remedy. Since Klein intended to resell, there should have been no reason to believe that idiosyncratic value was relevant.

The market for used G-II's was not a thick one, but there were some around. Klein's expert testified that there were twenty-one other G-II's on the market, but only three were roughly comparable. Klein made bids on two other G-II's after Pepsico refused to deliver. Klein also invoked the "other proper circumstances" standard, arguing that he didn't purchase another G-II because prices had started to rise. Instead he purchased the newer model, a G-III. The trial court accepted Klein's two arguments but was overturned by the Court of Appeals. That court rejected Klein's argument, noting that "price increases alone are no reason to order specific performance." (80) It is not clear why the court classified Klein's purchase of a G-III as "instead of" the purchase of a G-II. Klein had not argued that it was a substitute – if it was, that would have precluded his arguing for specific performance. Since Klein was a buyer and seller of airplanes, there is no reason to believe that any particular purchase was a substitute for the Pepsico plane. Could monetary damages have made Klein whole? Apparently yes. According to the Court of Appeals, the trial judge "repeatedly stated that money damages would make Klein whole." (80) Why then was Klein willing to spend money and two years litigating the issue? And why ask for specific performance for delivery of an airplane two years after the seller failed to deliver?

Not mentioned at all in the opinion is what was happening with this particular G-II in the interim. The plane was not mothballed awaiting the determination of its owner. Pepsico kept the plane and operated it for two years. In the normal course of events, an additional two years of wear and tear would mean that the value of the plane had declined, so that the plaintiff (who did not have a non-financial interest in the plane) would normally have opted for the damage remedy – the contract-market differential at the time Pepsico refused to deliver. Specific performance would not entail giving Klein physical possession of the plane. He would get the *financial equivalent*, what is known as monetary specific performance or a constructive trust. That is, he would be treated as if he had received the plane and was selling it at its current market price. If the market price of the G-II had increased in the post-breach period, Klein would prefer the specific performance remedy for the same reason that Helm preferred to measure damages at the time of the trial. In fact, the price of a used G-II had increased. Had the market price of G-IIs followed the normal pattern, decreasing because of depreciation and obsolescence, Klein would no doubt have asked for the standard damage remedy – the price differential at the time of the breach.

A legal system that relies on monetary damages as the predominant remedy, Anglo-American common law regimes, would focus on the time of breach. Systems in which specific performance is the preferred remedy (e.g., Germany, France, Israel) could emphasize the time of decision. In effect, this would treat the asset as having been transferred to the non-breaching party who holds it until the date of decision. I think that approach is less attractive than the time-of-the-breach measurement, but it is at least a plausible way of monetizing specific performance. As long as the rule is understood, ex ante, it should not matter much which is adopted. When contracting, the parties do not know the future course of prices, so they do not know which rule would be in their interest if a breach occurred. Allowing the promisee to choose the remedy (money damages versus specific performance) after the facts are known would create the same problem as allowing Helm to wait until the delivery date to determine which date should be designated as the time of the breach.

IV. ADRAS BUILDING MATERIAL V. HARLOW & JONES GMBH

In *Klein*, the plaintiff wanted the specific performance remedy because the market price had risen after the breach. In an Israeli case, the situation was reversed, the price having fallen since the breach. Israel's contract law is governed by statute and the preferred remedy is specific performance, not monetary damages. In a decision that is excruciatingly painful to read (perhaps it reads better in the original Hebrew, but I doubt it), the Supreme Court denied the normal remedy (specific performance) and opted for a restitution remedy of disgorgement. The tone of the majority's opinions is exemplified by S. Levin's pronouncement: "the economic school of law ignores in cases like this the fact that we are dealing with people with moral feelings and not with robots." (241)

The basic facts are simple enough. Harlow was a German trading company that sold steel, among other products. It entered into a contract to deliver 7,000 tons of steel to Adras for DM 620 about one month before the Yom Kippur War. There seems to be agreement that the parties contemplated a particular batch of Polish steel that was in the port of Hamburg, but the steel was essentially generic. Harlow delivered to Adras about 5,000 tons but reneged on the rest, selling it to third parties for about DM 800. Adras sued for the contract-market differential on the roughly 2,000 tons that Harlow failed to deliver. It won in the district court. On appeal, however, the Supreme Court, while holding that Harlow had breached, denied compensation because Adras had not "terminated" the contract. Since the price of steel had returned to DM 620 by the time the case was heard, the Court ruled that Adras could not prove a loss.

Adras did not sue for almost two years after the breach and even then the Supreme Court held that filing suit did not amount to termination.

The statute says that damages are the contract-market differential at the time the contract is terminated. The Supreme Court then granted an additional hearing on whether the law of unjust enrichment could apply if there existed a contract, and if so, how would this affect Adras's claim. To summarize the chronology, the contract was entered into on September 6, 1973, Harlow breached on April 11, 1974, Adras brought the claim on January 26, 1976, the district court decided the case on October 17, 1980, the Supreme Court's first decision was October 10, 1982, and the final decision was on February 11, 1988. From this chronology, it is unclear which date the court used to conclude that the market price had returned to the original contract price. According to Judge Barak, "the Court's basic starting point … should be that there was a contract between the parties *which continues to exist* since it was not lawfully terminated." (257, emphasis added) If the contract was not terminated, which date matters for assessing damages? 1976? 1980? 1982? 1988? None of the above? All of the above? I confess that I do not understand how a contract can be breached but not terminated, yet that distinction is what created all the confusion.

The seller's refusal to deliver was unequivocal; all the judges agreed that there had been a fundamental breach. The judges agreed that the steel was not unique. Judge Barak, the strongest proponent of the restitution view, acknowledged that the steel in question "complied with the contract terms in quantity and quality but had no special identificatory sign. (276) But, he continued, "it is clear on the facts that the steel stored in Hamburg was meant to be sent to the appellant in order to perform the contract and that the respondent diverted the steel for its own benefit and all this in order to increase its profits by breaching the contract." (277) Despite an extraordinary amount of verbiage in the five opinions, none bothered to say whether the contract included a delivery date. Viewing the case through an American lens, if there had been a delivery date, it had long since passed and that date would have established a termination date. If there were no termination date, then there would have been an anticipatory repudiation and the UCC says that the aggrieved party may "for a commercially reasonable time await performance by the repudiating party." (UCC 2-610(a); the Restatement Second 350 (f) is similar) It would not have been possible for Adras to wait three years (or more) keeping the contract open. Calculating contract damages would have been straightforward – the contract/market differential at the time of the breach. That, recall, was what the district court had decided and the Supreme Court had rejected.

The aggrieved party's apparent ability to postpone termination and to wait indefinitely complicates the picture. If the waiting resulted in the price falling back to the contract price, as happened, there would be no contract damages. To bypass this difficulty, the court invoked the restitution statute. The majority evidenced a particular fondness for the restitution concept. Judge Barak made this clear: "According to my approach, the general principles of unjust enrichment apply like a vulture which spreads its wings over all the other laws, regardless of whether they do or do not contain provisions concerning unjust enrichment and regardless of whether or not these unjust enrichment provisions deal with an existing contract or with a contract that was terminated." (p. 262) He backed off, a little, later in his opinion confining his decision to "situations in which the contract between the parties is still alive, leaving for the future the further question of the case where the contract has been terminated because of the breach." (p. 267)

The morally culpable breacher, having been unjustly enriched, must disgorge its profits. That is the restitution remedy. What is the profit in this case? It is the difference between the contract price and the price paid by the third party. The market price at the time of the breach is what a third party would be willing to pay. We do know what that is because the third party did pay DM 800. So, what the majority labels "profit" turns out to be the market/contract differential at the time of the breach.

That fact has escaped notice by the commentators. For example, in his otherwise perceptive critique of the decision, Dagan (2000, 118) uses an illustration in which B promised to sell a non-unique good to A for $100,000, and A's "expected profit" was $5,000. B sells instead to C who "desperately needs the promissory resource" for $125,000. The expectation interest, he says, is $5,000 and the disgorgement interest is $25,000, hence the divergence. No, the expectation interest is the market-contract differential and there is good evidence of the market price – what a willing buyer, C, agreed to pay. The expectation interest and the restitution interest in this illustration are both $25,000.

Goodhart (1995) presented a stripped down hypothetical based on *Adras*. Rather than having years pass, everything takes place within two weeks: "The Highlight Power Co buys a cargo of fuel oil from the Global Oil Corp for delivery on 1 February. There is a sudden international crisis. The price of oil shoots up. Global resells the oil to another purchaser at a much higher price and delivers it to the new purchaser on 20 January. The crisis ends as quickly as it began. The price of oil falls back and Highlight is able to purchase oil from a different supplier at the original price for delivery on 1 February." (3) He questions the *Adras* solution because "[w]hat has happened is that the subsequent and unforeseen fall in the price of oil has enabled Highlight to mitigate its loss to zero. There seems no adequate reason why the reduction or elimination of a loss as the result of the plaintiff's mitigation should open the way to a claim for restitutionary damages." (10) Mitigation is irrelevant. Unlike *Adras*, there is no reason to question the time of termination here, it was the moment the seller sold to the new buyer (20 January). The value of the asset at the time of the breach was the contract-market differential; the subsequent course of prices should be irrelevant. (Of course, if Global had only promised to deliver oil of certain specifications by 1 February, and it did so, then there would have been no breach.)

In *Adras*, the court reinstated the original remedy under a new name. The standard expectation damage remedy (the contract-market differential at the time of the breach) had been rejected in the Supreme Court's prior decision; it resurfaced as profit to be disgorged under the unjust enrichment standard. In effect, in the words of a dissenting judge, the decision gave Adras "two bites of the cherry." (251) It could receive the monetary damages at the time of the breach or at some future date when it decides to terminate, whichever is larger. Barak appears to agree: "Normatively, I see nothing wrong with the claimant's having the option of bringing two alternative claims with the aim of being awarded the highest damages it can prove." (273)

If the market price had risen post-breach, then the buyer's claim would have been the same as Klein's, a claim for monetary specific performance. Given the Israeli preference for specific performance, that would have been a plausible outcome. The fact that the price had fallen meant that Adras did not want performance; it wanted standard, good old Anglo-American contract damages. The court, having ruled that out, got there by an alternative route – invoking unjust enrichment and restitution.

The decision would appear to give the non-breaching party a valuable option; either take the greater of the damages measured at the time of the breach or at the time of the decision. Standard option theory suggests that the value of that option increases with time, so delaying termination adds to the option's value. However, this result rests on an unstated assumption. What can the seller do after it has breached, but before the buyer terminates? For the majority, all it could do is watch its liability stay the same or increase. But suppose that the price had fallen below the original contract price. Could Harlow show up on Adras's doorstep with 2,000 tons of steel and demand payment of the contract price? In the American case, the window for the seller to change its mind is generally small, but the possibility that the price would fall is a risk that the buyer would bear if it were to fail to accept the repudiation. Unless Israeli law is asymmetric, binding the seller, but giving the buyer the option to wait, the seller would retain the option to retract or "unbreach." That is, by not terminating the agreement, the buyer would run the risk that prices would fall, as they did in this instance, and the seller would then choose to perform, making the buyer worse off than had it immediately terminated. This does raise a semantic point: if the buyer has not yet terminated and if the seller is free to perform until the buyer terminates, then why classify the seller as a breacher?

This was a court so interested in celebrating the "great vulture" of unjust enrichment that it had lost track of what it was doing. The disgorgement remedy turned out to be nothing more than the standard monetary damage remedy. The peculiarity in Israeli law that seems to allow an aggrieved party to put off termination indefinitely appears to give it a valuable option; but if the seller can change its mind prior to the termination, then that option is largely illusory. The court's opinion, lengthy as it is, is silent on this.

SUMMING UP

Although the issues came up in different jurisdictions and were in different doctrinal boxes, the four cases all raised the same point – at what date should damages be reckoned? Should post-breach events be taken into account? For anticipatory repudiation, the answer should be negative. If the aggrieved party would have a legitimate claim for specific performance, but it could only get the monetary equivalent, then the question would be at what point must that party choose between the two remedies? Should it be at the time of the breach (money damages) or the time of decision (monetary specific performance). In both *Klein* (district court) and *Adras* (Supreme Court), the court appears to give the plaintiff a choice at the time of the trial so that the plaintiff would know which was the more favorable and would choose accordingly. In both instances, the courts failed to recognize that they were providing such a choice and did not consider whether affording the plaintiff such a choice would be justified. Instead they considered doctrinal questions which bore no relation to any possible justification. Was the Pepsico plane "unique"? When, if ever, was the Harlow-Adras contract terminated?

4. The lost-volume-seller problem and why Michael Jordan wasn't one

I have a certain fondness for the "lost-volume-seller" problem since it was the topic of the first article I published after moving to a law faculty. I elaborated on the subject in my last book, so here I can just summarize the basic points. The problem arises when a buyer cancels an order (breaches) and the seller resells the product at the contract price. The buyer would argue that the resale was in mitigation and therefore the seller has suffered no damages. However, the seller would argue that it would have sold the second item regardless of whether or not there had been a breach, and it should, therefore, be compensated for the profits it would have received had it sold both to the breaching buyer and the new buyer. I argued that the seller's claim conflates two questions: was there a loss and, if so, should the seller be compensated. Even though the answer to the former is typically positive, I argued that the answer to the latter should be negative.

I. THE LOST-VOLUME SELLER

The concept has proved sufficiently confusing that courts sometimes consider it even when it clearly does not fit. If it were legally impossible for the seller to make the second sale, then there could, by definition, be no lost-volume profit. That has not stopped the courts. Consider *Tigg v. Dow Corning*, in which a high-powered panel stumbled. The unanimous decision was written by then Circuit Judge Alito with Ed Becker also on the panel. In the first half of the opinion, the court concluded that the parties had entered into an exclusive contract and that Dow Corning had breached a duty to use best efforts. The best efforts "obligation is intended to protect the original seller, who in an exclusive arrangement depends solely upon the buyer to resell the goods." (1125) It then considered Tigg's claim that it was a lost-volume seller:

> Accordingly, Tigg cannot contend at the same time that it could have sold additional adsorbers and control stations to others even if Dow Corning had

> fulfilled its purchase obligations. It therefore appears to follow that Tigg was not a lost-volume seller. However, we will not (and do not) go so far as to hold that Tigg was not a lost-volume seller. We need only conclude that the district court could not find as a matter of law that Tigg *was* a lost-volume seller. At the very least, the court was obligated to submit this factual question to the jury. (1130)

The court had already stated the one relevant fact. The court had found that the contract was an exclusive dealing contract; so, as long as the contract was in force, Tigg was precluded from selling to anyone else. If Dow had not breached, Tigg could not have sold to anyone else. That is what "exclusive" means. "So long as Dow Corning did not breach, Tigg was obligated to sell to Dow Corning and only Dow Corning." (1126) There could be no second sale so there could be no lost-volume profits. There should be nothing left for the jury to determine. The same point comes up in Michael Jordan's claim against Worldcom, discussed later in this chapter.

In the lost-volume cases, the contract and market price are the same, so if a buyer were to cancel an order there would appear to be no damages. The claim is that the seller should be compensated because he would have had the additional sale and his lost "profit" would be the difference between the contract price and his "but for" costs. For a retailer, that would be the gross margin – the retail minus wholesale price. The retailing cases play a prominent role in the literature and pedagogy with *Neri v. Retail Marine* playing a major role. In practice not so much. Since *Neri* was decided in 1972, there are only four recorded cases involving claims by retailers against consumers and the retailers and customers each won two: *Modern Marine v. Balski* (boat, seller wins); *Lake Erie Boat Sales, Inc. v. Johnson* (boat, buyer wins); *Van Ness Motors, Inc. v. Vikram* (car, seller wins); *Schiavi Mobile Homes, Inc. v. Gironda* (mobile home, buyer wins).

If the buyer walked away and the dealer sold the boat at the same price, the rule focuses on whether the seller would have sold another boat. If so, the seller has lost his "profit" (the wholesale–retail differential) on the second boat and it would be entitled to a damage award of the lost profits. The analysis gets more complicated when the seller's ability to sell the second boat is questioned. Could the second buyer have bought only this boat? Would the retailer be able to sell additional boats at the same cost? These and other complications are irrelevant if the problem is reframed in terms of the option price.

If the seller would not have been able to sell another unit, perhaps because the supply was limited (for example, because this model was so attractive) it could not get another boat from the manufacturer, then there would be no damage. So goes the rule. When framed as setting an option price, the remedy makes no sense.

When placing an order, the customer wants some flexibility (the option to change her mind) and the seller wants some protection of its reliance on the order. The remedy prices the option as the gross margin. For cars and boats, it would be in the 12–15 percent range. In effect, the customers agree to pay $3,000 for the option to pay an additional $17,000 to buy a boat with a retail price of $20,000. Leaving aside the question of whether any consumer would have any idea that she had made such a commitment, we can ask whether an *informed* consumer would be willing to pay such an option price. The answer almost certainly is: No. The UCC's remedy overprotects the seller's reliance which is, typically, trivial. The dealer, after all, can take into account the likelihood that a certain percentage of his orders would result in cancellations. The likelihood that a buyer would walk away is one of the risks of doing business; the dealer can adjust its inventory policy taking into account the expected rate of buyer cancellations. The rate is predictable. Moreover, it can be influenced by the seller's decisions. In particular, the seller can set an explicit option price – say, a non-refundable deposit. Under some conditions a consumer would agree to a substantial deposit. If, for example, the model is a hot seller, manufacturers might have to allocate the boats amongst their dealers; even if a dealer had potential buyers for more than, say, twenty boats a month, it could not sell to all of them. The option price as reckoned by the lost-volume formula would be zero – the dealer could not have sold another boat. That, however, is precisely the situation in which the customer might rationally choose to pay a substantial option price (post a nonrefundable deposit). Conversely, if demand were slack, the Code remedy would result in an option price equal to the gross margin, whereas the contract would likely set an option price at, or near, zero. UCC § 2-708(2) gets it backward.

Cases outside the retailing context are a bit more common. The aggrieved seller claims that had there been no breach, it would have been able to produce and sell all the other units anyway. So, its loss would be the difference between the contract price and its "but-for" costs, the costs it would have incurred had it produced the units the buyer refused to take. Costs not associated with production of these units – research and development, advertising, marketing, most plant and equipment, some labor – would not count; they would be part of the lost profit. Lost profit, especially for high-tech products, could therefore be a significant part of the contract price – for example, in *Teradyne v. Teladyne*, the lost profits amounted to about 75 percent of the contract price. Interpreting this in the option framework, the buyer would be paying \$75 for the option to purchase the product for an additional \$25. That is the contract that the remedy creates. Such a deal makes little business sense, especially if the seller has ample capacity to meet the needs of this buyer and others (which must be so if the seller is indeed a lost-volume seller). As in the retail context, the presumption would be that the option price would be greater if the seller faced significant output constraints – the remedy again is perverse.

Unfortunately, the UCC elevates economic misunderstanding into a statutory command: "If the measure of damages provided in subsection (1) is inadequate to put the seller in as good a position as performance would have done then the measure of damages is the profit (including reasonable overhead) which the seller would have made from full performance by the buyer." (UCC 708(2)) The sparsity of reported cases suggests two plausible explanations, one happy, the other not. Parties might have included options in their agreements, perhaps in the form of deposits or liquidated damages, and when disputes arose, courts might have honored them. However, in at least one case, *Davis v. Diasonics*, a \$300,000 deposit was rejected by the court. Ironically, the plaintiff's win on that point turned out to be a bigger loss; after years of litigation and the concomitant litigation costs, the court found lost-volume damages of \$450,000. So, even if courts are skeptical about liquidated damages, breaching buyers might be happy not to press the point. The less happy explanation is that the lost-volume remedy is so firmly entrenched in the minds of litigators and judges that it is routinely embodied in settlements or decisions, not even warranting recognition. The damage remedy for the propane gas not taken in *Empire Gas* (discussed in Chapter 2) illustrates this possibility.

I won't speculate as to which version is closer to the truth. My emphasis on the option framework is not idiosyncratic; Scott and Triantis (2004, 1483) come to the same conclusion. My hope is that by encouraging courts and litigators to think in option terms, practice and interpretation might be nudged in the right direction. Interpretation could narrow the scope of § 2-708(2) by finding other remedies "adequate"; courts could be more aggressive in enforcing deposits and liquidated damages when confronted with lost-volume claims.

II. MICHAEL JORDAN, LOST-VOLUME SELLER, AND MITIGATION

Well, what does this all have to do with Michael Jordan? He had a lucrative endorsement contract with WorldCom. After WorldCom went bankrupt, it rejected his endorsement contract and Jordan raised the lost-volume argument in support of his claim. The decision of the bankruptcy court has been gradually making its way into the Contracts casebooks. See, for example, Dawson, et al. (2013, 68), Macaulay, et al. (2010, 77), George and Korobkin (2012, 535) and Cunningham (2012, 97). The case raised two issues: (1) could Jordan claim that he was a "lost-volume seller" and (2) should Jordan's claim be reduced because he failed to mitigate (or, more precisely, he failed to take actions that would have reduced the measured damages). The former question was easy enough; the latter is a bit more complicated, since the mitigation doctrine itself is badly muddled. The bottom line is that the lost-volume argument was irrelevant and Jordan's recovery should not have been contingent upon whether he had attempted to mitigate the damages.

In 1995, Michael Jordan signed a ten-year endorsement deal with WorldCom. He, along with the Looney Tunes characters, did a number of commercials for the WorldCom subsidiary, MCI, and Jordan became a major spokesman. WorldCom subsequently went bankrupt. (To make matters confusing, the court referred to the debtor as both WorldCom and MCI; to simplify, view them as interchangeable.) WorldCom filed for bankruptcy on August 30, 2002 but did not reject the Jordan contract until July 18, 2003. Jordan filed his claim on August 14, 2003. The endorsement deal did not allow Jordan to enter into deals with other telecom companies, but otherwise was not exclusive. Jordan's contract was for a lot of money and not much work. In addition to a $5 million signing bonus he was to receive a base compensation of $2 million per year. There were three other components of Jordan's compensation. If he brought in referrals, he would receive a percentage of the resultant sales. He would receive a royalty on telephone debit cards bearing Jordan's likeness and on any long-distance revenues from such cards. Finally, he would receive 100,000 stock options per year, with the total value capped. In return for this compensation, Jordan was to make himself available for four days per year for no more than four hours per day. Otherwise, he was free to enter into as many non-telecom endorsement deals as he desired. Jordan had sixteen other endorsement deals when he entered into the contract and still had many of them (e.g., Nike,

Gatorade, and Hanes) when the debtor formally rejected the Jordan contract in July 2003.

He received payment for the first six years. After the contract was rejected, Jordan filed a claim for $2 million for each of the last four years. The debtor conceded liability for the first two payments, but contested the others, claiming that Jordan had a duty to mitigate by entering into an alternative endorsement agreement and that Jordan had failed to do so. In response, Jordan raised a lost-volume-seller argument, which the court correctly rejected. It then held that Jordan had failed to mitigate. The court required a further hearing to determine the extent to which the mitigation would have offset Jordan's claim. The parties then settled, reducing his unsecured claim to $5,925,000.00. (Joint Stipulation Resolving Claim No. 36077 (September 28, 2007))

Before turning to the analysis of the decision, we should ask whether the contract anticipated the possibility that WorldCom would terminate the agreement without justification. The answer is Yes, it did. But, No, that would not have worked in this situation. The relevant clause read:

> Jordan shall have the right to terminate this Agreement … in the event of the occurrence of any of the following:
>
> 1. If WorldCom defaults on its payment obligations …
> 2. If WorldCom breaches a non-financial material provision of this Agreement and fails to cure such breach … or,
> 3. If WorldCom becomes insolvent, has its assets assigned for the benefit of creditors or is adjudicated bankrupt and is unable to meet its obligations under this Agreement when they become due.
>
> Any termination pursuant to the agreement shall be effective upon the giving of written notice; provided however, that all compensation due and owing to Jordan *shall immediately become due and payable*. (emphasis added)

If WorldCom breached, all of the future payments would immediately become payable. That's simple enough. Under clauses (1) and (2), Jordan's obligation would cease and WorldCom would owe the full amount. Jordan would have no requirement to mitigate. What if WorldCom were to become bankrupt? Clause (3) would seem to yield the same result. It would, that is, if it were enforceable. But it isn't. Under bankruptcy law, that clause, known as an ipso facto clause, is unenforceable. The reason, I am told, is that this claimant should not be advantaged vis a vis other claimants. The bankruptcy context, therefore, precluded reliance on the contractually provided remedy. The bankruptcy judge, not being bound by the contract language, had to determine whether Jordan's post-rejection behavior would limit his recovery.

Jordan invoked the lost-volume-seller concept to support his position. He argued that to be a lost-volume seller he need only show that he had the capacity to take on additional business. But, he claimed, he had no obligation to do so. Since the contract only bound him to perform sixteen hours of work per year, it is obvious that he had ample capacity to take on many deals. Rejecting this argument, the court asserted that proving capacity would not be enough. "[T]o recover lost profits under this theory, a non-breaching party must prove three things: (1) that the seller of services had the capability to perform both contracts simultaneously; (2) that the second contract would have been profitable; and (3) that the seller of service would have entered into the second contract if the first contract had not been terminated." (*WorldCom*, 687) "Lost volume" really meant lost volume. It required more than capacity (in this instance Michael Jordan's time). It required an actual subsequent sale of Jordan's time, and that did not happen. Indeed, as we shall see, the court emphasized Jordan's disinclination to pursue an additional endorsement. "Jordan has not shown he could and *would have* entered into a subsequent agreement. Rather, the evidence shows that Jordan did not have the "subjective intent" to take on additional endorsements." (687)

The lost-volume defense was doomed. Why even try? It was an attempt to avoid the mitigation Catch 22. The mitigation defense, as framed by the court, put Jordan in an awkward spot. Suppose that after learning of the bankruptcy, Jordan entered into a new endorsement deal with the same terms. In response to Jordan's claim, WorldCom would assert that the new deal mitigated Jordan's damages and that he was owed nothing. If, on the other hand, Jordan did not make a reasonable effort to obtain a new deal, he would have failed to mitigate and would lose again. His only path to recovery would have been to show that he had made a reasonable, but futile, effort to get a new deal. Not surprising then that Jordan's counsel attempted a Hail Mary to avoid the Catch 22.

Jordan's capacity argument was plausible, but poorly packaged. The issue was not "lost volume." Rather, the argument should have recognized the partial exclusivity in the deal. Jordan had ample capacity to take on as many other non-telecom deals as he wanted without impairing his ability to perform the WorldCom contract. WorldCom had the exclusive right to use Jordan only in the telecom market and only for sixteen hours per year. For the other 8,744 hours, he was free to do whatever he wanted. He was free to endorse any non-telecom product, free to unretire from basketball, revive his baseball career, and do anything else except endorse a competing telecom company. Engaging in any of these activities would not be mitigation. The only thing he could do to mitigate would be to enter into an endorsement agreement with a different telecom company. If he did get such an engagement, then, as the court should have held in *Tigg v. Dow Corning*, the lost-volume argument would have been unavailing since the contract would have precluded his doing both deals.

Should Michael Jordan have tried to take on a new telecom endorsement? Jordan argued that mitigating by taking a deal with a different telecom company would have been a bad business decision. His advisors argued that switching to another telecom after having served as MCI's primary spokesman would make him appear a mercenary and would harm his reputation.

> The evidence in this case establishes that when Jordan decided not to pursue another endorsement opportunity with a telecommunications provider following WorldCom's bankruptcy, that decision was based on several reasonable business judgments made by Jordan and his advisors as they both attempted to minimize the harm to Jordan's reputation arising from WorldCom's collapse and to implement their overall business strategy. First, Falk and Polk believed that Jordan's credibility as an endorser would be destroyed for every company that he represented if he agreed to an endorsement contract with another telecommunications company following WorldCom's collapse because, under the circumstances, "he would have been seen as a mercenary just going for the highest dollar." … [Falk testified] that the allegations of fraud associated with WorldCom's bankruptcy were "extremely embarrassing" to Jordan … . Polk [testified] that the scandal surrounding WorldCom's collapse and bankruptcy was "very embarrassing" to Jordan and that he would not have advised Jordan to accept another telecommunications endorsement because he believed that entering into another endorsement would harm his reputation … . Portnoy [testified] that she spoke with Jordan about the WorldCom bankruptcy, that the situation was "horrible" and that because Jordan was WorldCom's main spokesperson they were concerned about his reputation. (Michael Jordan's Memorandum in Support of His Motion for Summary Judgment, p. 16, July 7, 2006)

In addition, Jordan's agent testified that "Jordan had implemented a strategy of not accepting new endorsements because of a belief that new deals would jeopardize his ability to achieve his primary goal of National Basketball Association ('NBA') franchise ownership." (687) Jordan had two business reasons for not pursuing an additional telecom endorsement deal; doing so might make his endorsements less credible (and therefore less valuable) and cutting back on endorsements generally might increase the value of his non-endorsement activity (getting an NBA franchise).

The court improperly framed the mitigation requirement as "any similar deal," where similarity was defined entirely on the basis of being a quality endorsement. "Similarity," for this court, did not mean a telecom deal. It meant *any deal* that would pay Jordan a reasonable amount of money for a reasonable period of time. "MCI's expert stated that similar endorsement opportunities existed between 2003 and 2005 had Jordan chosen to pursue them, based on a measure of Jordan's popularity and familiarity with the public. ... Polk testified that had Jordan wanted to do product endorsements during 2003 and after, he could have obtained such deals." (691) By holding that Jordan would have been able to enter into other "similar" (non-telecom) deals, the court did not have to confront Jordan's argument that pursuing another telecom deal would have been a poor business decision. The court failed to recognize the possibility that under the contract Jordan was free to take on as many, or as few, non-telecom deals as he desired. A non-telecom deal, regardless of how similar the dollar value, could not have been in mitigation.

The court did, however, put a lot of weight on Jordan's ownership aspirations. It found that Jordan would not have pursued *any* new endorsement business. Since Jordan "had already implemented a business strategy of not accepting new endorsements," (692) the court concluded that he had already decided not to do anything that would mitigate the damages. It is this last argument that I want to pursue.

When parties enter into a long-term agreement, they typically give up some of their freedom to respond to new information in a manner that would be optimal for them. That is the price they must pay to get the benefits of a long-term commitment. Each party sacrifices some flexibility for their mutual benefit. If one party were to breach, should the other party be bound to continue to follow a path that is no longer in its interest? At one extreme, the party would be completely unconstrained by the contract and free to follow its own interests. Alternatively, at the formation stage, each party might recognize that in the future, for some reason, it might not be able to perform. In that event, it might want some assistance from the counterparty to reduce its liability, even if that might entail the counterparty foregoing its own interest following the breach.

How are these two interests to be balanced? Gergen (2009, 1399) asserts that the courts have favored the plaintiff's ability to avoid any additional obligation: "the law permits a party to withhold or refuse performance in response to breach to avoid suffering a loss that damages may not adequately compensate even if the response inflicts a disproportionate loss on the defaulter." He might be overstating; the language of the employment termination cases suggests a stronger emphasis on the employee's need to mitigate. Still, I would argue, Gergen is surely right in emphasizing the priority of the plaintiff's post-breach interests. Should the law always favor the plaintiff? No. We are "only" attempting to determine a default rule. Parties would be free to contract around it. Jordan did. But in the bankruptcy context, the default rule was a mandatory rule.

Following a material breach, the raison d'etre for the non-breacher sacrificing flexibility is no longer relevant – there are no future mutual benefits. Consider a manufacturer who is losing money on a particular product. If the contract is not breached by the counterparty, the manufacturer would remain on the hook. His short-term interest (unconstrained by his contractual obligation) would be not to continue production and to do something else with his assets. But by entering into the long-term agreement, he promised the counterparty that he would continue to produce (or be held liable for damages). That promise was valuable to the counterparty who relied on the promise and would have suffered if the manufacturer were free to follow his short-term interest. If, however, the counterparty did breach, it would no longer be relying, and there would be no reason for the manufacturer to ignore his short-term (unconstrained) interest.

How does that apply to Michael Jordan? If, as he contended, Jordan no longer desired to do endorsements, would he be bound to continue seeking endorsements for the remainder of the ten-year term? The notion that he must mitigate implicitly assumes that the constraint still exists. Jordan entered into a ten-year agreement in which he gave up the flexibility to take on different telecom endorsements or determine that he no longer wanted to endorse WorldCom. That commitment was valuable to WorldCom as evidenced by the price. But WorldCom's reliance became irrelevant when it breached or, as actually happened, it rejected the contract in bankruptcy. No longer would there be a reason for Jordan to ignore his short-term (unconstrained) interest. Whether that meant he would take on more endorsements, fewer endorsements, or try to extricate himself from the endorsement business should not matter.

I want to add one more related argument on Jordan's behalf. There is a difference between the non-breacher who does nothing (Jordan) and one who does something (Jordan signing with another telecom). There is an even bigger difference between these cases and cases like *Luten Bridge*, where mitigation consisted of ceasing to perform activities that were no longer in the breaching party's interest.

Compare two cases invoking the "different and inferior" criterion – a variant on the "substantially similar" standard in *WorldCom*. In both instances, a movie studio invoked the pay-or-play clause and cancelled a film project. (For more on the cases see Goldberg (1998) and Goldberg (2006, ch. 15)) In *Parker v. Twentieth Century Fox*, the studio offered Shirley MacLaine a second picture which differed in some material aspects from the first: a non-musical versus a musical and it modified her approval of the director and screenplay. She refused and the studio argued that because she had failed to mitigate, it owed her nothing. The majority rejected that argument, holding that the second offer was different and inferior, and therefore she did not have to accept the substitute project. In an earlier case, cited by both the majority and dissent in *Parker*, *de la Falaise v. Gaumont-British Picture Corp.*, Constance Bennett performed two radio plays in the time slot vacated by the cancellation of the picture. The studio argued that the earnings from the two radio plays should be offset against the fee owed her. The court concurred, saying that a radio play was different, but not inferior. It is hard to imagine how one could conclude that Shirley MacLaine's alternative was inferior, while Constance Bennett's was not. The difference, unremarked by the courts, was that Constance Bennett had taken the new deal, whereas Shirley MacLaine had not. The pay-or-play deals concerned the actor's responsibility with regard to the contractually defined *time* slot. In the exclusive dealing context, the concern would be with the *market* slot – telecoms for Jordan, adsorbers for Tigg.

A plausible explanation for the disparate treatment is the distinction between not acting (MacLaine, Jordan) and acting (*Luten Bridge*, Bennett, Jordan signing with another telecom). The distinction is, and ought to be, significant. The standard Director's Guild agreement (see Goldberg (2006, 298)) makes the distinction explicit. If the studio decided not to use a director with a pay-or-play agreement, the director would have no duty to mitigate; but if he took another project in the time slot, those earnings would be offset against his claim. The nature of the project (different or inferior) would be irrelevant. Indeed, as the trial judge in *Parker* asserted, had MacLaine earned anything in the time slot, including as a seamstress, those earnings should have been offset against her claim. (Goldberg (2006, 286)) Whether there should be an offset is an issue that the parties could contract over. Jordan's deal (clauses 1 and 2), for example, did not require him to offset if WorldCom terminated without cause. Recall that in the two coaching contracts discussed in Chapter 2, John Calapari's contract required that he use "reasonable and diligent effort" and if he succeeded he would have to offset earnings while Rich Rodriguez's required neither any effort to find a new job nor any offset if he succeeded in doing so.

A plausible way of summarizing the rule would look like this. If a party happens to engage in an activity which could be characterized as mitigation, then a reasonable default rule is that any earnings would be offset against the damage claim. There should, however, be no affirmative duty to undertake the activity. The non-breaching party's duty to avoid adverse consequences should be limited to cases like *Luten Bridge* in which the claimant continued to perform an activity that the breacher no longer wanted and was of no value to the non-breaching party. If, for example, Jordan showed up for the sixteen hours, WorldCom would not have been liable for his expenses.

To sum all this up: (1) the lost-volume argument was irrelevant; (2) even if there were a duty to mitigate, the court erred by not restricting its focus to the relevant market slot – telecoms; (3) the breach (rejection) should have allowed Jordan to pursue his own interest as he perceived it at the time of the breach – the court should have honored his stated interest in cutting back on his endorsement activity; (4) had it restricted its attention to telecoms, the court should have given weight to Jordan's concern that by switching, he would harm his reputation by appearing to be a mercenary; I think that inquiry would easily have come out in Jordan's favor, but the court might choose to treat it as a fact question; and (5) on a more general level, whether the earnings from performance of the non-breacher should be offset against the damage claim is separable from the mitigation question; it is only a matter of default rules and in many instances parties contract out of them.

5. Six pennies for your thoughts: *Freund v. Washington Square Press*

The sad tale of Philip Freund's futile litigation against Washington Square Press shows up in many Contracts casebooks. After the publisher reneged on its agreement to publish his book, he sued and won. But it was a Pyrrhic victory as the court gave him only nominal damages – six cents. The case stands for the proposition that damages will not be awarded if they are too speculative. I confess that I have never understood how one is supposed to draw the line between "too speculative" and the merely uncertain. The line appears to have moved since the *Freund* decision in favor of plaintiffs. Farnsworth (§ 12.15) says that the requirement has been relaxed to "reasonable certainty" and that "[d]oubts are generally resolved against the party in breach on the rationale that one 'who has wrongfully broken a contract should not be permitted to reap advantage from his own wrong by insisting on proof which by reason of his breach is unattainable.'" (Farnsworth (§ 12.15, citing *Locke v. U.S.*)

Why should we care about *Freund*? It still has some precedential value, however watered down that might now be. Beyond that, the case does illustrate a few things. First is a recurring theme of this book: you can't trust the courts to provide an accurate rendition of the facts. In this case you can't even trust the Court of Appeals' characterization of what went on in the courts below. Second, while I hope that *Freund* is an outlier, it does illustrate a lawyering skill that is often lacking: proving damages. I do not only mean the conceptual problem; I include the basic computational questions as well. Third, even in a simple form contract, an adhesion contract if you will, there can be interpretation problems. In this instance, both the "without prejudice" and "reversion" clauses created some ambiguity. Fourth, the ambiguity was a self-inflicted wound. It would have been easy enough for the publisher to resolve the problem, ex ante; the puzzle is why it didn't do it.

Freund had three theories of damages and all were rejected. The theory that has received most attention from commentators and treatise writers was his claim for lost future royalties. The Court of Appeals held that: "His expectancy interest in the royalties – the profit he stood to gain from sale of the published book – while theoretically compensable, was speculative. Although this work is not plaintiff's first, at trial he provided no stable foundation for a reasonable estimate of royalties he would have earned had defendant not breached its promise to publish. In these circumstances, his claim for royalties falls for uncertainty." (861) It appears that the court was actually deciding the issue. Appearances, however, can be deceiving. The issue was not up for appeal, a fact that the court did acknowledge in a footnote. (859) As it turned out, not only was the royalty issue not before this court, it was never ruled on by any court. True, Freund did make a half-hearted effort to prove lost royalties, but when he submitted his damage claim to the trial court, he omitted any mention of the possible lost royalties.

By its apparent rejection of the lost royalties claim, the court has misled commentators. In criticizing the result, Professor Eisenberg, for example, argued that Freund should at least have been able to prove a minimum level of sales, had the court remanded on that issue:

> For example, in *Freund*, although total book sales might not have been determinable at an amount that was more likely than not, there must have been some amount of book sales, and therefore some amount of royalties, that was more likely than not. (Indeed, the publisher would almost certainly have made projections showing some likely minimum amount of sales before it decided to publish the author's book.) …
>
> * * *
>
> Of course, the record in *Freund* does not show how the baseline measure would have applied to the facts, but that is only because the Court of Appeals reversed the award of damages without remanding for a new trial on that issue. It is hard to imagine, however, that the author could not have established some damages under the baseline measure by showing the minimum sales of comparable books to libraries, theatrical bookstores, and general bookstores. (1998, 1056–57)

In addition to the damage issues, Freund's case raises some other questions. The first is peculiar to this case. When the Press offered to return the manuscript, it conditioned it on Freund's signing a release. The litigation never made clear why a release was asked for and what it meant. The second relates to book publishing contracts in general. The contract called for an advance and allowed the author to keep the advance if the publisher decided not to publish the book. This was a form contract produced by the publisher; why not simply say that the advance was an option (or liquidated damages)? We will come back to those questions, but first we will recount Freund's story.

Freund was a prolific author, still active up to the end. Shortly after his death at age 98, his final volume of a multi-volume treatise on the history of theatre was published. In addition to his history of the theatre, he published numerous novels, poems, and plays, and produced a number of television scripts. At trial he testified that he had published about thirty-five books (A16). He also had been a publisher; he testified that he had established Pilgrim House shortly after graduating from college in the 1930s and that the press continued in operation until 1955. (A23) He claimed at trial that he "continued to be a publisher to the present day." (A39) It is not clear what he meant by that, but his claim to be a publisher was necessary for him to be qualified as an expert to get his estimate of the costs of publishing into the record.

Freund signed a contract dated May 3, 1965 with Washington Square Press to write a book entitled *Modern British and American Drama: A Critical Review*. At the time, he was 56 years old. Here are the relevant clauses of the contract:

> 3A. The Author agrees to deliver to the Publisher not later than July 1, 1967 a complete typewritten script of the Work in duplicate … . If the script shall not have been delivered within three (3) months after said date, the Publisher may, at its option, terminate this agreement … and may recover from the Author all monies which it may have advanced to the Author upon the Work.
>
> 3B. If the script delivered shall not, in the sole opinion of the Publisher, be suitable for publication, the Publisher shall have the right to terminate this agreement by notice in writing to the Author given within sixty (60) days after such delivery and, in such event, neither party shall have any further rights or obligations hereunder, provided that any amounts actually paid to the Author prior to the delivery of the rejected script shall remain the property of the Author.
>
> 4. The Publisher agrees to publish the Work within 18 months after manuscript receipt in hardbound edition at its own expense … . The paperbound edition shall follow no later than two years after hardbound publication.
>
> 8A. The Publisher shall pay to the Author or to his duly authorized representative an advance of $2,000.00 against all the Author's earnings under this agreement payable as follows:
>
> $1,000 on demand after January 1, 1966 and $1,000 on delivery of the manuscript, which total sum of $2,000 shall be non-returnable.
>
> 16A. If the Publisher shall fail to publish the Work within [18 months after manuscript receipt] … this agreement shall terminate and the rights herein granted to the Publisher shall revert to the Author. In such event all payments theretofore made to the Author shall belong to the Author without prejudice to any other remedies which the author may have.

> 16D. If a petition in bankruptcy shall be filed by the Publisher, or if the Publisher shall be adjudicated bankrupt by any court, … or if the Publisher shall liquidate its business for any cause whatsoever (*except liquidation in connection with the transfer of all or a substantial part of the business to a transferee intending to carry on the publishing business*), this agreement shall terminate automatically without notice. (A207-215, emphasis added)

The royalty clause (8B) set the rate at 10 percent of the retail price for the first 10,000 hardbound copies sold. It established different (higher) rates for sales beyond that. Paperback books had a lower royalty rate (8C).

In August 1967, the Press agreed to a substitution. Instead of the book on American and British drama, Freund would submit a book titled *The Theater of Eugene O'Neill*. Freund submitted a nearly complete manuscript in September 1967, delivering the final half chapter in December 1967. The delay was to take into account the opening on Broadway of an O'Neill play, "More Stately Mansions." (A118) After sixty days had passed without the Press terminating the agreement, the manuscript was deemed accepted. (3B) On December 31, 1968, the Press was acquired by Simon & Schuster. (A228) It ceased production of hardbound books and, therefore, would not publish Freund's book. Freund was not made aware of this until he inquired in March 1969. The editor-in-chief, Daniel Kurland, sent Freund a termination letter on March 7, 1969.

> In accordance with our telephone conversation, this letter will serve to revert to you all publishing rights licensed to us under our publishing agreement of May 3, 1967 [sic] for the above work (later restricted to an analysis of O'Neill), and we relinquish all claims to any share of the proceeds which you may derive from any future license of such rights.
>
> You, in turn, release us from any further obligation under that agreement except for the return of your manuscript, which will immediately follow our receipt of a copy of this letter signed by you. (A216)

Freund replied three days later noting that it was "a very legal-looking document you've sent me" and noting that he had consulted a lawyer who recommended that he not sign the release. (A217) The release, or lack thereof, played a big role as events played out. There are two ambiguities involved. What claims was Freund supposed to relinquish and what was meant by "return of your manuscript?" With regard to the former, the "without prejudice" clause (16A) suggested that Freund would be entitled to the standard remedy for breach of contract. (The appellate court found that the "without prejudice" clause was standard in author contracts.) (A247) As I understand it, even if the "without prejudice" clause gave the author a remedy, the release effectively would vitiate its impact. The net result would have been to extend the publisher's option from 60 days (3B) to 18 months (4, 16A). I do not understand why a publisher would choose a combination of a without prejudice clause and a release rather than a more direct path. It is, after all, the publisher's form contract.

There was no attempt at trial to clarify the meaning of "without prejudice." Only in its brief at the Court of Appeals did the defendant finally propose a meaning:

> Plaintiff author would have had the right, under the final clause of Art. 16A, which provided that the reversion to plaintiff following termination was "without prejudice to any other remedies which the Author may have", to have claimed any part of the "advance" which might have been unpaid, or to seek reimbursement of any expenses or losses (for example, in connection with pre-publication promotion) incurred in foreseeable reliance on the contract, or for payments that might have been due on account of other contracts, or for copyright infringement, defamation, invasion of privacy or unfair competition. Here, no such claim was warranted, and none was made. (p. 13)

Missing in this definition was any reference to the author's right to pursue a damage remedy for breach of contract. At trial, the defendant's counsel took the stand to assert that he had offered to return the manuscript. When pressed on what claims were to be released, he bobbed and weaved before finally stating that "[m]y speculation would be that the man who wrote the letter didn't know and that he was acting gratuitously and not under advice of counsel." (A178)

Kurland's letter appeared to offer a quid pro quo. If you sign the release, we will return your manuscript. What, if anything, did that mean? The contract language seems clear that the intellectual property would revert to Freund regardless of whether he signed a release. A subsequent publisher might be reluctant to go forward if there appeared to be a cloud on the title. The release requirement could perhaps mean that the Press would give Freund a document asserting that he had the right to sell the manuscript. In the litigation the cloud on title issue was not mentioned. For Freund, the bigger issue was physical. The Press had the physical manuscript and he didn't. Recall that back in the 1960s manuscripts had to be typed. Freund submitted the ribbon copy to Washington Square Press and kept a carbon for himself. At trial he testified:

Q Did you take any steps whatever to have your O'Neill manuscript published by anyone?

A There was no way in which I could. I didn't have the manuscript. A carbon cannot be submitted to a publishing house. It's considered a discourtesy, and I expected that Simon and Schuster would fulfill the contract when they saw I meant business about it getting published, because they had broken other contracts with me, as you know.

Q You say there were no ways that you could – at all times you had a full carbon copy in your possession; isn't that a fact?

A I wouldn't say it is full, because I made certain polishing changes on the final manuscript which I don't have on the copy, but one cannot send out a yellow-page manuscript like this of 740 pages to a publisher. It has to be the first copy. Furthermore, I didn't have the manuscript. It would have been illegal of me to submit that.

Q Professor Freund, did you type the manuscript that you submitted to Simon and Schuster yourself?

A Yes. (A150)

If this is correct, even if Freund's IP claim was unassailable, the publisher's possession of the physical manuscript would have precluded Freund's shopping the manuscript elsewhere.

Freund initially filed suit in July 1970. (A234) The only relief he asked for was specific performance – that the defendant be ordered to publish the book. (A239) The case was heard on May 25, 1971 and decided on July 16, 1971. Finding that the defendant had breached the agreement, the court nonetheless denied Freund's plea for specific performance. Supervising the performance, said the court, would be too difficult. However, the judge gave Freund a second bite of the apple. He "direct[ed] that the defendant return to the plaintiff the manuscript presently in its possession and that the plaintiff need not sign any waivers or releases in connection therewith. I further set the matter down for a trial on the issue of monetary damages, if any, sustained by the plaintiff by reason of the breach of contract." (A222) The judge, like everyone else associated with the case except the defendant, thought that the release mattered.

The damages trial took place in October 1971 and the decision was handed down on December 22, 1971. Freund proffered three theories: (1) his tenure at Fordham University was deferred thereby delaying his promotion; (2) the lost royalties; and (3) the cost of replacement – how much it would cost him to publish the book. He won only on the third claim at trial. The appellate court affirmed, with two dissenters arguing that he should get only nominal damages (six cents). The Court of Appeals, as noted, agreed with the dissenters.

The tenure claim suffered from a number of flaws. The biggest is the one that all three courts recognized. Freund did receive a promotion when he applied for it and there was no indication that it was delayed by the failure to publish the book. Even assuming that hurdle could be overcome, there were serious problems. The contract was breached in March 1969, shortly after Freund's sixtieth birthday. Since retirement at age 65 was mandatory, he had only a small window for the increased earnings. (Freund's witness' assertion that a full professor could work for an additional three years was unchallenged.) (A73) To prove the loss, Freund should have had to show the present value of the different earning streams with and without publication. No such effort was made. Freund did manage to put his earnings into the record. (His starting salary of $8,000 in 1966 was greater than the starting salary of lawyers at the top New York law firms.) The only other data introduced to prove his future earnings were the average salaries in a single year for associate and full professors at Fordham (all departments, all vintages). (A69–A72) There was no attempt to use these numbers (or any other numbers) as a basis for calculating the earning differential. At the end, his counsel simply asserted a number. "The plaintiff has testified as to what his salary was. Father Trivitt, his superior and the head of the department at Fordham, testified as to what a reasonable expectation of his salary would have been. The aggregate sum of this would probably have been in excess of $15,000." (A199)

Moreover, Freund was not in a traditional academic department. His appointment was in the Department of Communication Arts. (A84) At the time of his appointment, the department had never had a tenure-track faculty member. (A81–A84). He had been in a non-tenure track role for five or six years and was only put on the tenure track in 1966, *after* the book contract had been signed. (A118) Whether one adopts my assumption-of-the-risk test (see Chapter 8) or a foreseeability test, the claim for this element of damages would fail. A book publisher should not be expected to take into account the possibility that an author would subsequently take a tenure-track appointment in a department that had never had a tenure-track faculty member and take responsibility for the failure to receive tenure.

Freund did make a brief proffer of evidence regarding lost royalties. As weak as his argument was, his counsel further undercut it with an odd strategic choice. Freund testified: "A book like this has an automatic sale to college libraries, of which there are, of course, about 1,500 in the country, and public libraries, of which there are about 2,500 in the country. So that it would have an almost automatic sale, not to the public, but to about 4,000 outlets." (A130) He continued by noting that the book would probably have a retail price in the $10–$12.50 range. With a 10 percent royalty, that would suggest a royalty of about $4,000, less the $2,000 advance.

Then it gets weird. His lawyer introduced a line of questioning designed to show that the book might not have sold well. The most charitable interpretation is that she intended to show that the Press deliberately chose not to publish because it would have lost money. If that was her intention, however, she never followed up. In 1968, Louis Sheafer published the first of his two-volume biography of Eugene O'Neill. (Volume 2 appeared five years later and won him the Pulitzer Prize in 1974.) After acknowledging the appearance of Sheafer's book, counsel asks: "Professor, in your capacity as a publisher would you undertake the publication of a book on a topic that has already been explored thoroughly?" (A134–135) After he noted that "it would certainly have a more limited sale initially" (A135) she continued: "So that, as publisher, is it a poor risk to publish something after someone else had published a scholarly work on the same subject for the same audience?" (A135) He then agrees with her that the sales would be handicapped. (A126) She then concludes this line of questioning: "Professor, I asked you the question, would you, as a publisher, undertake the publication of this manuscript now." (A137) Poor Freund is a bit flummoxed, answering both as publisher and author: "Well, I'd like to undertake it because it would enable me to get a full professorship which I would love to retire with because I have pension benefits thereby, besides gratification. Naturally, having spent two years working on it, I would like to see it in print. I don't want to throw it away. Yes, I would personally, but I wouldn't necessarily enter upon it in the hope of making profit thereby." (A137)

This would appear to be a nice gift to the defense. However, the defense has a different purpose. It wants to show that if Freund had self-published the book, he would have made money. It argued that Freund failed to mitigate and had he done so by self-publishing, there would have been no damages. "If he did publish the book now, that is, if he did spend this money, then it would result in a profit to him. So there is no damage at all, and that's why I asked the question." (A141) Freund's response to the question should have undermined his royalty claim: "It might result in profit, it might not. It might sell 50,000 copies, it might sell 2,000 copies, it might sell none. It's a risky business. You know, publishing is risky."(A141)

Thus, the only evidence on possible future sales was (1) Freund's assertion that many libraries would carry the book, (2) the claim that the publication of Sheafer's book would have adversely affected sales, and (3) Freund's admission that sales could have been most anything because publication is a risky business. Not a lot for a court to go on. And, as we shall see, Freund's counsel chose not to pursue this element of the claim.

Freund's final theory was that he should recover the "cost of completion." What would it cost Freund to get the book published by someone else (in this case, him). The defense argues that he should have self-published in mitigation and, had he done so, he would have made enough money in his role as publisher to eliminate any possible damage claim. Freund argues that any duty to mitigate did not require him to publish and, in any event, the release issue precluded his publishing elsewhere. The proof of the cost of production was in two steps. Freund called Washington Square's production manager to ascertain the cost of production of a "740 page typewritten manuscript with print order of 5,000 copies, including cost of design, typesetting, plates and art work." (A49) The witness tried to dodge the question but eventually concluded that the cost would be about $9,000. Freund testified as an expert (given his background as a publisher) that the cost would be about $11,500. (A159) There was additional testimony on the cost of producing the paperback edition.

In her summation, Freund's counsel asked for $30,000 in damages. "The plaintiff's costs of publication at this point would be ... between nine and eleven thousand dollars for the hard-cover edition, $6,500 for the soft-cover edition, and $15,000 in salaries which – the difference between what he would have had as a – what he had as an assistant professor and as possibly a full professor." (A203–4) Note two things. First, the numbers don't add up. Even with the lower bound on costs, the total would be $30,500. Second, there was no claim for lost royalties. The trial court was never faced with that question.

Freund's counsel gave two reasons for his not publishing the book himself after Simon and Schuster had informed him of its decision. "He did not elect to publish because he wanted Simon and Schuster's name on the book; he wanted the prestige, the position of Simon and Schuster on the book; and, in addition, he didn't have the manuscript." (A202) Simon and Schuster provided a brand name, an indication of quality that would be beneficial to Freund. Perhaps more important, Simon and Schuster had a substantial distribution network. Freund, in effect, was buying both quality certification and distribution services. This point will have particular relevance when considering *Chodos v. West Publishing* in the next chapter.

The trial court rejected Freund's tenure-based claim on the ground that "there was no evidence in this case, whatsoever, showing that, had plaintiff elected to submit his application for promotion at an earlier time, it would have been granted or denied." (A7–8) The court held that "the natural and probable consequence of this breach is the amount of money it would cost plaintiff to publish, in hard cover." (A8) It then took the two estimates of the cost that were in the record (Freund's estimate somehow lost the last $500) and split the difference, awarding $10,000. Proof of damages for the non-publication of the paperback fell "short of a preponderance because it is conjectural and a recovery therefor cannot obtain herein." (A9) There was no mention of the royalties.

The appellate court noted that Freund had received his promotion, so there were no damages on that score. The dissent added that the failure to obtain a promotion was not a foreseeable consequence of the breach. (A252) The majority also stated that royalties were too conjectural, even though it had not been asked. (A246) The majority justified the cost of completion remedy in two ways. First, it analogized a construction contract in which the builder failed to complete the house or used the wrong materials. Oddly, it cited *Jacob & Youngs v. Kent* which *denied* replacement costs and it did not bother to explain why this case should be distinguished. (A249) Second, it cited the UCC; after noting that 2-708 is inapplicable, it stated that in 2-710 incidental damages are recoverable. It did not, however, say why these costs should be classified as incidental.

The dissent rejected the cost of completion remedy: "The quantum of damages in a construction contract alluded to by the majority is capable of measurement. However, damages from the non-sale of an unpublished book – where the contract speaks of the author's remuneration in terms of royalties – are clearly unascertainable." (A254) This is a non sequitur. Projecting the costs of a non-published book should be no more difficult than projecting the costs of an unfinished construction project. I think what the court meant was that the cost of publication was a poor measure of the lost royalties, which it did find to be unascertainable.

Freund's brief to the Court of Appeals made clear that he was neither contesting the trial court's rejection of two of his claims nor had he contested the claims in the prior round: "The plaintiff did not cross appeal with respect to the lower court's denial of damages to him on the question of failure of promotion or loss of possible royalties. Consequently, the question of the failure to be promoted by reason of the defendant's breach of contract and damages for the future royalties which might have accrued to plaintiff had the book been published were never before the Appellate Court." (11)

In its brief to the Court of Appeals, the defendant argued that awarding the cost of completion would have substantially overcompensated Freund. The estimated cost was based on the assumption that 5,000 copies would be printed. Assuming that all had been sold and that the retail price was between $10 and $12.50, the royalties would have been between $5,000 and $6,000. Subtracting the advance would result in a net of $3,000 to $4,000. The Court of Appeals did not pick up on this argument. It nonetheless rejected the construction analogy.

> In our view, the analogy by the majority in the Appellate Division to the construction contract situation was inapposite. In the typical construction contract, the owner agrees to pay money or other consideration to a builder and expects, under the contract, to receive a completed building in return. The value of the promised performance to the owner is the properly constructed building. In this case, unlike the typical construction contract, the value to plaintiff of the promised performance – publication – was a percentage of sales of the books published and not the books themselves. Had the plaintiff contracted for the printing, binding and delivery of a number of hardbound copies of his manuscript, to be sold or disposed of as he wished, then perhaps the construction analogy, and measurement of damages by the cost of replacement or completion, would have some application.
>
> Here, however, the specific value to plaintiff of the promised publication was the royalties he stood to receive from defendant's sales of the published book. Essentially, publication represented what it would have cost the defendant to confer that value upon the plaintiff, and, by its breach, defendant saved that cost. The error by the courts below was in measuring damages not by the value to plaintiff of the promised performance but by the cost of that performance to defendant. Damages are not measured, however, by what the defaulting party saved by the breach, but by the natural and probable consequences of the breach to the plaintiff. In this case, the consequence to plaintiff of defendant's failure to publish is that he is prevented from realizing the gains promised by the contract – the royalties. But, as we have stated, the amount of royalties plaintiff would have realized was not ascertained with adequate certainty and, as a consequence, plaintiff may recover nominal damages only. (861–62)

So, Freund was left with his $2,000 advance, an award of six cents, and possession of a manuscript that was no longer marketable. Sheafer's second volume had appeared by the time the case was decided and there was no longer a market for another book on O'Neill. None of the courts paid attention to the $2,000 advance. Three aspects of the advance should be recognized. First, it was surprisingly large – 25 percent of his academic salary. To put this in context, it was greater than the advance I received for this book, nearly half a century later. Second, the relevant question regarding lost royalties was not whether there would be any sales (as Professor Eisenberg suggested), but whether the sales would have generated royalties exceeding the $2,000 advance.

Third, the combination of an advance with the reversion to the author if the publisher chooses not to publish gives the publisher an option. There could be a number of reasons why a publisher might value the option to change its mind after having accepted a manuscript. This case illustrates two. Here the publisher changed its business plan following the merger; it chose to no longer publish any hardbound books. If the marketability of a book were to change following acceptance, the publisher might want the freedom not to go forward with publication (much like the pay-or-play clause described in Chapter 2). The publication of Sheafer's first volume might, for example, have discouraged a publisher. The price of the option was the advance plus whatever was meant by the "without prejudice" clause. Perhaps the publisher chose to include the clause with the expectation that it could be negated by a release. That seems to me an unnecessarily convoluted way to arrive at a sensible outcome.

In *Freund,* because future sales were too conjectural, the plaintiff did not even assert a claim based on projected royalties. Instead the plaintiff raised other possible theories for recovery which the courts rejected, so Freund ended up with only nominal damages. In a later case in the Ninth Circuit, the court started from the same premise – sales projections would be too uncertain for ascertaining damages. However, rather than award nominal damages, the court found an alternative theory to give a ridiculously large award to the author. That case is the subject of the next chapter.

6. *Freund* through the looking glass: *Chodos v. West Publishing Co.*

Like Philip Freund, Raphael Chodos delivered a manuscript to a publisher. As in Freund's case, the publisher was purchased by another publisher and a decision was made not to publish the manuscript. Like Freund, Chodos sued and won. In both instances future sales were too uncertain to justify an award of lost royalty income. However, there their paths diverge. Freund, as we saw in the previous chapter, received six cents. Chodos received $300,000. Moreover, he was bitterly disappointed that it was not a whole lot more. Sometimes when you delve into a case you feel like you have arrived in an alternate universe where the laws of nature do not apply. *Chodos v. West Publishing Co.* is one such case.

It could have been even worse. The jury instructions allowed the jury to consider Chodos's damage claim for $1.44 million. West ended up arguing in favor of upholding the $300,000 judgment apparently because it believed that the Court of Appeals would find Chodos's claim credible. How could this have happened? One contributing factor was the Court of Appeals' endorsement of a restitution remedy. A second was the court's (and the parties') misapplication of that remedy. The prior problem however, was one of contract design. Had the contract been properly designed, the author would not have had a claim. The design was not a matter for negotiation. Like Freund, Chodos did not negotiate; he simply accepted the publisher's standard form agreement. I will elaborate below on what I believe would have been the appropriate structure. No surprise, it would involve making explicit the publisher's option to publish. Before doing that, however, I should first recount the tale, including the multiple levels of litigation.

In the late 1980s, Chodos, a California lawyer, conceived of the idea of writing a book on the law of fiduciary duty. In 1995, he pitched the idea to Bancroft-Whitney, a publisher of legal books, which approved the project. The signed contract was on the publisher's standard form for a work for hire. He would receive no advance and his compensation would exclusively be in the form of a royalty of 15 percent of the gross revenues. He was informed that a typical successful work would normally generate about $1 million in gross revenues over a five-year horizon. In addition, Chodos anticipated that the book would generate business for his law practice. He completed the work in 1998. He claimed to have spent about 3,600 hours on the project.

Bancroft-Whitney had been owned by Thomson Legal Publishing. In 1996, it was merged with West Publishing Company and became a division. In 1998, in an internal reorganization, West instituted a new marketing structure for this type of product, one or two volume publications priced below $500 (classified as "Tier II"). Prior to the reorganization, the book would have been marketed by field representatives. Under the new scheme, the marketing would consist of a mass mailing to 25,000 California attorneys. West's management determined that it would lose money if it published the book; a "business case template" projected a $20,000 loss over a five-year period. In early 1999, West informed Chodos that "[t]here is no question about the high quality of the work, but based on our analysis of the potential sales of the publication, unfortunately [West] must decline to publish [the Work] … The decision not to publish was made after significant deliberations concerning the market potential and the fit within our current product mix." (Def. Brief 2001, 13)

Chodos then filed suit. In his initial complaint, he alleged that West had breached its contract. He then amended the complaint, asserting that the contract was illusory and that he should be compensated in quantum meruit. It was illusory, he argued, because West maintained the right not to publish the book; it could publish if it wanted to, but did not commit to do anything. Reckoning that his legal fee was $400 per hour, he asserted that he should be compensated for his time at that rate, resulting in a claim of almost $1.5 million. West countered, arguing that the contract was not illusory because of the implied covenant of good faith. It then argued that the decision not to publish was made in good faith and it had not, therefore, breached the contract. Moreover, if the court were to find that there had been a breach, the damages would be ascertainable so that the remedy would be the normal damage remedy, not quantum meruit. The lower court granted West's motion for summary judgment and dismissed the case.

A Ninth Circuit panel reversed with Judge Reinhardt writing the opinion for a unanimous court. The agreement was not illusory, it held, agreeing with West that the implied covenant of good faith made the contract enforceable. However, it disagreed with West as to whether the refusal to publish was made in good faith. West claimed that good faith required only that it make a reasonable business decision and that its conclusion that publication would result in a loss justified its decision not to go forward. However, the court, relying on contract language, concluded that West could only exercise its good faith judgment with respect to the quality of the manuscript. The "acceptance clause" said that West could decline to publish if it found the work unacceptable in form and content. Business prospects were irrelevant. The court held:

> Chodos thus labored to complete a work of high quality with the expectation that, if he did so, it would be published. He devoted thousands of hours of labor to the venture, and passed up substantial professional opportunities, only for West to decide that due to the vagaries of its internal reorganizations and changes in its business strategies or in the national economy or the market for legal treatises, his work, albeit admittedly of high quality, was for naught. It would be inequitable, if not unconscionable, for an author to be forced to bear this considerable burden solely because of his publisher's change in management, its poor planning, or its inadequate financial analyses at the time it entered into the contract, or even because of an unexpected change in the market-place. Moreover, to allow a publisher to escape its contractual obligations for these reasons would be directly contrary to both the language and the spirit of the standard Author Agreement. (999)

It concluded: "Because West concedes that the manuscript was of high quality and that it declined to publish it solely for commercial reasons rather than because of any defect in its form and content, we hold as a matter of law that West breached its agreement with Chodos." (1000)

The subsequent discussion of the possible remedies available to Chodos for the breach is notable for the complete lack of any concern for the possible function of a remedy. The court first cites an earlier California decision on the election of remedies:

> It is well settled in this state that one who has been injured by a breach of contract has an election to pursue any of three remedies, to wit: He may treat the contract as rescinded and may recover upon a quantum meruit so far as he has performed; or he may keep the contract alive, for the benefit of both parties, being at all times ready and able to perform; or, third, he may treat the repudiation as putting an end to the contract for all purposes of performance, and sue for the profits he would have realized if he had not been prevented from performing. (1001)

The court then, citing another California case, *Oliver v. Campbell*, claimed that the availability of the restitution remedy depended on whether damages were ascertainable:

> The remedy of restitution in money is not available to one who has fully performed his part of a contract, if the only part of the agreed exchange for such performance that has not been rendered by the defendant is a sum of

> money constituting a liquidated debt; *but full performance does not make restitution unavailable if any part of the consideration due from the defendant in return is something other than a liquidated debt.* (1001, emphasis added by the court)

The issue as framed by the court was whether the 15 percent of the gross royalty payment constituted a "liquidated debt." If so, quantum meruit would be unavailable. The court concluded that it was not a liquidated debt because "it was not a certain or readily ascertainable figure." (1002)

> The mere existence of a fixed percentage royalty in a contract does not render that royalty a "liquidated debt," if the revenues to which that percentage figure is to be applied cannot be calculated with reasonable certainty. Here, it is impossible to determine even now what those revenues would have been had West not frustrated the completion of the contract. Had West honored its contractual obligations and published the treatise, the revenues would have depended on any number of circumstances, including how West chose to market the book, and how it was received by readers and critics. Accordingly, under *Oliver*, Chodos is entitled to sue for restitution for the time and effort he reasonably invested in writing the manuscript … . We express no opinion as to how restitution should be calculated in this case, nor do we intimate any suggestion as to the appropriate amount of such recovery. (1002–3)

The court added in a footnote that even if the royalties were deemed a liquidated debt, Chodos might still be able to argue that he anticipated additional benefits from publication in the form of enhanced professional reputation and increased client referrals. Since these were not liquidated debts, restitution might be available on that ground. (1003)

If the "debt" is not sufficiently certain, the non-breaching party can recover in quantum meruit. The court appears to be setting a high threshold for certainty, one that has the potential to displace the standard contract remedy as the norm. While Reinhardt's opinion declined to suggest how to calculate the restitution, the parties both interpreted it as the cost of performance. Chodos said $1.44 million; West said $67,200. The jury gave a verdict for $300,000 with no explanation. I will argue below that both sides made a fundamental error which resulted in their overestimating the damages. But first, I will summarize the dispute as framed by the parties.

At trial, the jury was instructed to determine "the amount, if any, you deem necessary to compensate the Plaintiff for the value of the time and effort he reasonably invested in writing the manuscript, including the extent, character and value of Plaintiff's services." (Def. Brief, 2003, 11) Chodos interpreted this as the opportunity cost of his time. West interpreted it as the reasonable value of the services performed. The final jury instruction allowed the jury to consider both.

Chodos's theory was simple enough. West should pay him for the time he expended on the project at the rate at which he sold his time, his opportunity cost. He claimed to have worked on the manuscript for 3,600 hours and that his hourly rate as a practicing lawyer was $400 per hour. West's strategy was twofold. First, it sought to discredit Chodos's numbers. Second, it brought in an expert to determine how much West would have had to pay on the open market to produce the manuscript.

West attacked Chodos's assertion that he had spent 3,600 hours working on the manuscript:

> Chodos had no proof that he actually devoted 3,600 hours to his manuscript. The evidence at trial actually made it doubtful that Chodos ought to recover based on a claim of 3,600 hours or a rate of $400 per hour. For example, Chodos conceded (1) that there were months that he did not work on his book at all; (2) some of the time he claimed was for time spent exercising or practicing tai chi; (3) some of the time he claimed was while he was driving; and (4) he could not state the specific amount of time he spent on the book on any single day. Chodos conceded that he never tracked the time he spent working on his manuscript. (Def. Brief, 2003, 18)

Chodos responded by first noting that he did not keep time records because the anticipated compensation under the contract did not require him to do so. He did not deny the claim that some of the hours claimed were not directly related to the writing task. Instead, he argued that counting them was legitimate:

> Nor is there anything inappropriate in Chodos including, in his estimate of time and effort invested in writing the manuscript, time when he was getting and drinking coffee or doing physical exercises or driving his car. There is nothing about any of these activities which precludes thinking hard about the book; and whatever West and its managers may think to the contrary, the most important and valuable time and effort an author can invest in writing a manuscript is the time and effort he spends thinking hard about the ideas to be discussed in it (rather than typing out units and characters in order to meet the per unit/character count standard). (Pl. Reply Brief, 2003, 11)

In addition to attacking Chodos's claim for the number of hours devoted to the book, West also questioned the price. Chodos, it argued, did not sell his time at a uniform rate of $400 per hour:

> As for his hourly rate claim, Chodos conceded (1) that he had no established hourly rate as an author; and (2) that during the time in question he sold his services as a practicing lawyer on varying terms including at $300 per hour,

> $350 per hour, $360 per hour, and on a blended contingency and flat-fee basis. Chodos further testified that he performed other work in the legal profession, such as giving professional lectures and publishing other legal works for no compensation at all or, in one instance, for what he estimated as $1,000. Thus, the jury had evidence that Chodos performed work of a legal nature for a variety of wages other than $400 per hour. (Def. Brief, 2003, 18)

Chodos testified about how many hours he worked as a lawyer before, during, and after he was writing the manuscript:

> [H]e explained that like most lawyers he had about 1500 hours a year of professional time to sell, and that he was able to and did earn more than $600,000 each year from his professional activities both before and after he wrote the book, except that during the period he was writing the manuscript and for a while after West repudiated the publishing contract, his professional earnings were greatly reduced because of the book's demands on his time. (Pl. Brief, 2003, 7–8)

Neither party followed up on this. As a rough estimate of the hours he worked on the book, they could have subtracted his actual billed hours from 1,500 for each year. In the post-completion period, they could have focused on how many additional hours he claimed he would bill in order to make the investment worth his while. Any estimates along these lines would have been contestable, but, for whatever reason, neither party saw fit to pursue this line of inquiry.

Even if West had prevailed on discrediting Chodos's numbers, the resultant award would most likely have been substantial. The number of hours and the price of his time could only be reduced by so much. West did have its expert witness testify that it should have taken only 1,500 hours to write the manuscript. (Def. Brief, 2003, 10) Still, even with a reduced rate of $300 per hour, that would have yielded an award of $450,000.

West's alternative theory, the so-called open market theory, was that restitution should be based on how much Chodos should have been paid if West had bargained for his service in the open market. Its expert, a senior vice president with over thirty years in the publishing business, argued that compensation should not have been on an hourly basis. He analysed the sales of twelve books he deemed similar to Chodos's and concluded that the most a publisher would pay Chodos for writing a single-volume, single-subject book would be $34,619. (Pl. Brief, 2003, 9) He also considered two alternative valuation methods that were established in the publishing industry. One was a per unit basis, either per page or per word. Usually, he testified, "he would normally allow an hour per page for the case summaries, and one-and-one-half hours per page of text." (Pl. Reply Brief, 2003, p. 12) The other was based on what a comparably situated author would have been paid. The expert concluded that under the former, Chodos would receive $67,200; under the latter, he would receive $34,619. (Def. Brief, 2003, p. 18) Chodos characterized this testimony as a "hearsay-based, publisher-skewed, after-the-fact, fabricated-for-purposes-of-litigation estimate." (Pl. Reply Brief, 2003, p. 6)

Chodos argued that the open market concept had a significant flaw. The parties' evaluations ex ante were too far apart to make a deal for the author's time:

> But so far as this case is concerned, no such market exists or could exist, because Barbre's [West's witness] testimony – and common sense – make it ineluctably clear that the sellers in such a hypothetical market (successful practicing lawyers) and the buyers (huge corporate law book publishers) necessarily have different and irreconcilable criteria for measuring the value of an author's time and effort. The successful practicing lawyer wants to receive the amount he could otherwise sell his time and efforts for to clients; the publisher wants to pay only a small fraction of a conservative estimate of the gross revenues it anticipates receiving from sales of the book. Accordingly, there is not, and cannot be, any "going price" or "comparable charge" for the services of successful practicing lawyers in writing legal books.
>
> * * *
>
> Of course, everyone knows what West was actually willing to pay, and what it actually promised to pay: 15% royalties, on an estimated $1,000,000 of sales, plus a promise to use its resources and marketing expertise to publish the book …
>
> * * *
>
> But the fatal flaw in this notion is that successful practicing lawyers like Chodos, who can sell their time for $400 per hour, would never agree to sell their time to West or any other legal publisher for $25 per hour. That is why, to the extent there is any "open market," practicing lawyers and publishers regularly contract, not on the basis of hourly fees, but rather on the basis of royalties plus referrals. (Pl. Reply Brief, 2003, 6)

Chodos's primary argument was that he had entered into the deal with the expectation that royalties would only be a small component of his compensation. His main source of revenue, he anticipated, would be the millions of dollars he would receive from the additional referrals resulting from the publication. (Pl. Brief, 2003, 14) Over 90 percent of his anticipated benefits were independent of West's expected benefits.

What happened to the manuscript? Unlike in *Freund*, the book was published. Chodos self-published the book. It is still available on

CD-ROM from the Blackthorne Legal Press. Chodos showed the book to the jury in order to indicate the magnitude of his work. West attempted to introduce data on its sales to indicate the marketability of the book. Chodos objected and the court sided with Chodos. In its brief, West did note that Chodos's "claim for $1.44 million is grossly out of proportion with the modest five figure sales that his book earned in the commercial marketplace." (Def. Reply Brief, 2003, 3) Other than that, there is no evidence as to the book's sales.

Thus, the court was faced with two different theories: Chodos's opportunity cost theory; and West's open market theory. The trial court submitted both theories to the jury:

> You are to determine the amount, if any, you deem necessary to compensate the plaintiff for the value of the time and effort he reasonably invested in writing the manuscript, including the extent, character and value of plaintiff's services. In assessing the reasonable value of the plaintiff's time and effort, you may evaluate what he would have been paid if the parties had bargained for plaintiff's services in the open market. (Pl. Brief, 2003, 14)

The trial court instructed the jury to return a general verdict fixing the total amount Chodos should receive; the jury returned a verdict of $300,000. Chodos appealed, arguing that it "was a figure unconnected to any testimony or argument in the record, and manifestly arrived at as an improper compromise – not between conflicting facts, but between conflicting legal theories." (Pl. Brief, 2003, 24) West was pleased with the outcome. It argued that "[t]he district court correctly instructed the jury. ... Substantial evidence supported the jury's $300,000 verdict and its damage award should be upheld." (Def. Brief, 2003, 10) It tactfully refrained from suggesting what evidence did support the verdict. Just to recapitulate, West initially decided not to publish because it expected it would lose around $20,000. After years of costly litigation it ended up grateful that it only had to pay $300,000.

The Court of Appeals upheld the verdict in an unpublished opinion. ("This disposition is not appropriate for publication and may not be cited to or by the courts of this circuit except as provided by Ninth Circuit Rule 36–3.") The court concluded:

> It was within the competence of the jury to determine the value of Chodos's services based on West's testimony on the hourly or per unit compensation that West would have offered to have the treatise written and Chodos's testimony on what a practicing attorney would have accepted to produce the treatise. The district court's "open market" jury instruction, which gave the jury discretion to do so, was not in error. (474)

It might have been useful if the court explained why. It didn't. Perhaps the judges recognized that the contract damage remedy that they had rejected was a lot more certain than the restitution remedy they had imposed.

I do not want to get bogged down in the intricacies of California restitution law. I would have thought that one element of a claim for unjust enrichment would be that the defendant had been enriched. That does not seem to be essential according to the California precedents as summarized by Chodos: "Where a plaintiff performs services for the defendant at the latter's request, he may recover in quantum meruit for the reasonable value of those services, without regard to any of the provisions of the failed contract. … In such a suit for restitution, the plaintiff is entitled to the full amount of the reasonable value of his efforts and services, even though – because of the defendant's repudiation of the contract – they turn out to have been of no actual value or benefit to the defendant." (Pl. Brief, 2003, 17–18) The cases cited for this proposition differ from this case. In one set of cases the defendant received nothing. However, the ex ante expected value of the plaintiff's costs were less than or equal to the defendant's expected benefit. (See *Earhart v. Low*) In the second set of cases, the defendant's ex post gain was substantially greater than the ex ante expected gain, and the quantum meruit claim assured the defendant that it would not have to share the upside. (See *Maglica v. Maglica*)

Chodos fit neither pattern. Ex ante, as Chodos observed in his brief, the cost to Chodos greatly exceeded the benefit to West. Ex post, West received nothing. Chodos had expended a considerable amount of effort. In other unjust enrichment cases the plaintiff suffers the loss and receives nothing in return. For example, if Smith paints Brown's barn, at the end of the day Smith has suffered a loss and has nothing to show for it. For Chodos it is different. Chodos spent many hours producing the manuscript, but in the end he did have something of value – the manuscript. Remarkably, neither party, nor the courts, followed up on this.

There are, I suppose, no hard and fast rules to determine the appropriate amount for restitution. If Chodos is to be compensated for the cost of producing the manuscript (his time), then he should have to net out the benefit he received from producing the manuscript. How much is the manuscript worth? He was free to market it to any other law text publisher. There is no evidence on whether he attempted to do so. If he did, apparently he failed. He did, as noted above, self-publish the book and apparently the sales were modest. The value of the manuscript to Chodos was not confined to the potential royalties, as he had made clear. The bulk of the value was its role in marketing Chodos – generating referrals, and so forth. So, to properly calculate the restitution it should have been necessary to net out Chodos's gains – the projected future sales of the book *and the future increase in business* resulting from its publication. Ironically, the Court of Appeals ordered the quantum meruit remedy because it found sales too hard to measure; but to properly reckon restitution, it would have to do the same and more – it would also have to prove future referral income. Fortunately for Chodos, West's counsel failed to recognize this.

The Court of Appeals erred in the first instance by asserting that the damages were too difficult to ascertain. If we only focus on the loss and ignore the fact that Chodos still had a publishable manuscript, then projection of royalties would not be that difficult. I will suggest three plausible approaches. First, Chodos claimed that he had been told that a book of this sort would gross about $1 million in five years and that would yield a royalty of about $150,000. Second, West provided evidence of the sales of other books from the same category. These sales could be used to project Chodos's sales. Third, West did some internal calculations which led it to conclude that the book would not be profitable. Those projections could have been used. None of these is perfect, but any of them would have been adequate. If the market for the book had changed prior to the breach (as in *Freund*), then this should have been taken into account. There was, however, no reason to believe that the market for books on fiduciary duty had changed in the three years after the contract had been formed.

Chodos would have asked for consequential damages as well – the lost future referrals. The Court of Appeals in a footnote even hinted at the possibility that these would be recoverable. "It might also be reasonably argued that West's publishing of Chodos's treatise was an additional element of consideration to which Chodos was entitled, since substantial benefits other than the royalties he would have received might have accrued to him as a result of publication, including enhanced reputation and additional client referrals." (1003) The claim is similar to Freund's claim for the loss due to the delay of his tenure. However, in Freund's case, the publisher was unaware of the possible effect; here, it was obvious from the start that Chodos expected the marketing benefits would be a significant element of his compensation. It was clearly foreseeable, just as Kenford's land appreciation was foreseeable. (See Chapter 9) Nonetheless, as in *Kenford*, there should not be recovery for this element. There is no reason to believe that the publisher would have assumed this risk.

Of course, Chodos still had a marketable manuscript and that should be taken into account when reckoning damages. One could argue that all that Chodos lost was time. But for the breach, the book would have been published earlier. The loss would be the difference in value of two otherwise identical earning streams, differing only by the dates at which they started. Whether the fact that Chodos did not (could not?) get another major publisher to publish the book could, perhaps, be thrown into the mix. Chodos might argue that this publisher's reputation and distribution network were superior to the alternatives. Accepting this sort of argument could produce a peculiar argument in which the author argues, "Gee, you're wonderful" and the publisher counters with, "Shucks, I'm just an average guy." There seems no reason in principle to believe that this particular publisher is so superior to the next best alternative, which brings us back to the loss being the delayed stream of earnings. Once we recognize that the author is left with a potentially valuable asset, it becomes extremely difficult to determine damages (and, lest we forget, restitution).

That brings us back to the contract design question. This is the publisher's standard form. Why not anticipate this mess and structure the contract to avoid it? The publisher wants two options. First, it wants the ability to reject a manuscript on quality grounds. The standard form gives it that right and it allows the publisher to claw back any advances. There is one notable instance in which Joan Collins kept her substantial advance ($1.2 million) for an admittedly unpublishable manuscript. "Random House agreed to an unusual clause that Miss Collins's agent, the late Irving (Swifty) Lazar, sought for his luminous clients: Anticipating that their prose might be found wanting, Mr. Lazar had insisted that they be paid upon completion of their manuscripts, regardless of whether the publisher thought that the writing had merit." (Hoffmann, NYT 1996) Second, after a manuscript has cleared the quality hurdle, there remains the issue of marketability. Circumstances might have changed since the contract was signed and the publisher would desire the option not to publish. To exercise that option, the publisher would pay a predetermined amount and return the manuscript to the author. The simplest way of doing this would be to make the advance the option price. If we, the publisher, choose not to publish, you, the author, will keep the advance and be free to market the manuscript elsewhere. There would be no breach, simply the exercise of an option.

So, why don't they do that? I suppose that part of the answer is, "if it ain't broke, don't fix it." Chodos acknowledged that he could not find "any published California decisions, or any published federal decisions applying California law, which construe or interpret author-publisher agreements." (Pl. Brief, 2001, 14) Only a handful of New York cases were cited by either party or by the courts. If the contract rarely, if ever, winds up in litigation, then why bother to change it, however poorly it is designed? Still, I don't understand why parties would continue using a form that has the potential to produce extreme damage remedies when it would be simple to draft the form so that the optionality is made clear and the exercise of the option not to publish would not be characterized as a breach. If sellers do persist in utilizing a form contract which would treat the decision not to publish on commercial grounds as a breach, then I would be content with measuring damages by projected royalties and not offsetting by the value of the manuscript that the author retains. If publishers are foolish enough to draft their standard forms so that they are open to such an interpretation, let them suffer the consequences. But, restitution? A bridge too far.

7. Cleaning up *Lake River*

When considering the distinction between liquidated damages and a penalty clause most modern casebooks begin with Judge Posner's decision in *Lake River Corp. v. Carborundum Co.* The litigators framed the case in terms of the liquidated damages/penalty clause distinction. If a stipulated damage remedy in the agreement could be characterized as liquidated damages, it would be enforceable. But if a court found it to be a penalty, it would not. A lot of scholarly writing, including that of Judge Posner, has questioned the logic behind the penalty clause bar in contracts between sophisticated parties. Nevertheless, the doctrine has survived. Indeed, in some states, notably Illinois, there is a presumption in favor of finding a disputed clause to be an unenforceable penalty.

In *Lake River*, the defendant, Carborundum Corporation ("Carborundum"), had agreed to pay for bagging a minimum quantity of its product over three years, but only had about half that amount bagged. The plaintiff, Lake River Company ("Lake River"), argued that the minimum was a liquidated damage clause and should be honored. The defendant claimed that enforcing the clauses would yield an award in excess of actual damages and therefore, the clause should be treated as a penalty. Judge Posner, despite his hostility to the penalty clause bar, accepted the defendant's version and threw out the disputed clause.

Properly understood, the language in question was neither a penalty nor a liquidated damage clause. That question should never have arisen. The contract gave the buyer considerable discretion as to when and how much it would use the seller's services. By granting the buyer flexibility, the seller provided a valuable service and incurred some costs in providing that service. The minimum quantity clause was a key factor in defining the obligation and in pricing the service. Even if one were to cling to the stipulated damages framework, the analysis would demonstrate that the stipulated damages were not necessarily excessive. Given the proper understanding, a reasonable court could easily have found a valid liquidated damage cause. Of course, a single case study cannot show that the doctrine is wrong, but the debunking of a famous decision is at least a step in that direction.

The facts as presented in the opinion are misleading. The role of the suspect clause cannot be understood without other contract language absent from the opinion. Its absence is a symptom of the problem – the litigators failed to appreciate the underlying economics of the transaction and their framing of the issues reflected that.

In Section I, I will summarize the trial judge's opinion and the arguments made in the respective parties' briefs. In Section II, I will present Judge Posner's opinion. His argument, which largely tracks Carborundum's, was that enforcement would dramatically over-compensate Lake River, and, therefore, the minimum clause would be an unenforceable penalty. In Section III, I will introduce two clauses in the contract that were ignored by all the participants, but which put the suspect clause in perspective. I will then show how, if the issue had been properly framed, the over-compensation question disappears. I will first show why the clause helped define the contractual obligation and had nothing to do with stipulated damages. I will then show that even if the clause were viewed as defining stipulated damages, the estimate would have been reasonable (or at least not unreasonable); it should fall in the liquidated damages category. Finally, I will consider a thorny doctrinal problem, raised only obliquely in *Lake River*: if there is an anticipatory repudiation of a contract containing a stipulated damage remedy or a minimum quantity, should the promisee's mitigation (technically, avoidance) be taken into account in assessing the promissor's liability?

I. THE CASE PRE-POSNER

The story, as recounted in the briefs and the opinions, is a simple one. Carborundum entered into a three-year contract with Lake River which would bag and distribute Ferro Carbo, an abrasive powder. In order to prevent possible contamination with other products, Carborundum insisted that Lake River install a new bagging system costing $89,000 to be used exclusively for Ferro Carbo. (1286) The clause in controversy (Paragraph 4) was a minimum-quantity guarantee:

> In consideration of the special equipment [i.e., the new bagging system] to be acquired and furnished by LAKE-RIVER for handling the product, CARBORUNDUM shall, during the initial three-year term of this Agreement, ship to LAKE-RIVER for bagging a minimum quantity of [22,500 tons]. If, at the end of the three-year term, this minimum quantity shall not have been shipped, LAKE-RIVER shall invoice CARBORUNDUM at the then prevailing rates for the difference between the quantity bagged and the minimum guaranteed. (At 1286)

Because the demand for Ferro Carbo had declined, Carborundum only bagged about 12,000 tons in the three years, 55 percent of the minimum. Had Carborundum shipped the minimum, it would have paid $533,000. Carborundum actually paid $292,000, leaving a shortfall of $241,000, which Lake River argued it was entitled to as liquidated damages. Carborundum refused, precipitating the litigation. The price for Lake River's services turned out to be about $24 per ton ($533,000/22,500). To assure payment, Lake River engaged in self-help (unsuccessfully), asserting a lien over 500 tons of Ferro Carbo valued at $269,000 in its possession. (1286) The market unit price of the Ferro Carbo, therefore, was $538 per ton ($269,000/500), making Lake River's services 4–5 percent of the market price ($24/$538). Both the trial judge and Judge Posner found that it was not entitled to assert that lien; that issue need not concern us.

The trial judge found that the purpose of Paragraph 4 was to stipulate damages and that it passed muster:

> Paragraph 4 of the contract was inserted in order to estimate damages which would be sustained by Lake River in the event the contract was not fulfilled. In other words, paragraph 4 was in the contract as an attempt by Lake River to assure a certain return on its investment in the special equipment to be purchased, and Carborundum knew this. (*Lake River, trial*, 4)

The clause was valid, the court argued, because

> At the time that the parties entered into the Agreement, the amount of injury which would be suffered by Lake River in the event of a breach by Carborundum was uncertain in amount and difficult to measure, given the unpredictability of the timing or amounts of shipments of product by Carborundum to Lake River, and the inability to predict with any degree of accuracy the flow of revenue under the contract. The minimum quantity agreed to between the parties was not unrealistic or unreasonably large. (4–5)

These findings were designed to satisfy the Illinois standard, which Judge Posner characterized in this way:

> To be valid under Illinois law a liquidation of damages must be a reasonable estimate at the time of contracting of the likely damages from breach, and the need for estimation at that time must be shown by reference to the likely difficulty of measuring the actual damages from a breach of contract after the breach occurs. If damages would be easy to determine then, or if the estimate greatly exceeds a reasonable upper estimate of what the damages are likely to be, it is a penalty. (1289–90)

In their briefs, both parties accepted this framing of the question as the proper characterization of the stipulated damages. Carborundum's argument that the clause was an unenforceable penalty had two prongs. First, it used the testimony of Lake River's contract negotiator, James Passerelli, to show that Lake River did not intend to provide a reasonable estimate of damages – indeed, it was entirely unconcerned with damage measurement. Second, it argued that application of the clause in certain contexts would be punitive because it would result in an assessment far exceeding actual damages. (Def. Brief, 13, 17)

Passerelli's testimony was characterized, not entirely accurately, as follows: "In fact, Passerelli testified that Lake River's *sole purpose* for inserting the provision in the contract was to force Carborundum to perform the agreement." (14, emphasis in original) Passerelli's actual testimony reads as follows:

> QUESTION: When you put the minimum quantity provision in the contract you were merely trying to assure a return on investment and you were not attempting to estimate the damages that Lake River would sustain if Carborundum breached the contract, were you?
>
> ANSWER: That's correct. …
>
> QUESTION: Indeed what you wanted to do was to assure that either Carborundum would go through and perform the contract as it had agreed or that Carborundum would be forced to pay Lake River as if it had gone through with the contract?
>
> ANSWER: That's correct.
>
> QUESTION: Indeed, what you provided in the contract was that if Carborundum breached the contract it would have to pay 100 percent of the amount that it would have paid if it had gone through with the contract, isn't that correct?
>
> ANSWER: I believe that is correct, yes. (13–15)

The testimony did not say anything about "forcing" Carborundum to *perform*; it was only forced to *pay*. It did, however, suggest that the purpose of the clause was unrelated to any damage projections. This led Carborundum to point out that "by Lake River's own admission, Paragraph 4 was not inserted to provide a fair estimate of damages to be paid as an alternative to performance." (15) Lake River's response to this was a rather lame attempt to downplay Passerelli's legal sophistication: "[t]he minimum guarantee provision was not inserted as a determination of the legal damages Lake River would incur as a result of a breach by Carborundum, since Passerelli, who negotiated the Agreement, was unfamiliar with the concept of legal damages." (Pl. Brief, 11) Ignorance is not much of a defense, especially when the agreement was negotiated by a senior employee and signed by the president. Lake River was trapped by the framing of the issue as penalty versus liquidated damages. Otherwise, it could have turned the testimony to its advantage by agreeing that it had not intended that the clause be related to damages, but that it had another purpose entirely.

Second, Carborundum argued that enforcement of the clause would, in certain circumstances, result in overcompensation. It began with a *reductio ad absurdum*:

> [I]f Carborundum had not delivered one pound of the Product, pursuant to the literal terms of Paragraph 4, Lake River could bill Carborundum $533,700.00. Simple mathematics reveals that Lake River would have received an almost 600 percent return on its $89,404.00 investment for equipment that has a useful life beyond the term of the Agreement. It is patent that there is absolutely no relationship between the amount of damages that could be estimated at the inception of the Agreement and the amount provided in Paragraph 4. (15–16)

It went on to argue that Lake River had underestimated costs so that, if there had been full performance, Lake River would have lost money. An award of $241,000 would, therefore, have given Lake River a large windfall. (17) Lake River conceded that it had underestimated costs, but claimed that it still would have made a modest profit had Carborundum fully performed. (Pl. Brief at 14) The trial court found that if Carborundum had delivered the contract minimum "Lake River still may not have made a profit on the contract." (4) The accuracy of the profit projections doesn't matter for our purposes and the issue did not surface in Posner's opinion. If it had mattered, he surely would have been justified in accepting the trial court's finding as not clearly erroneous.

I will argue in Part III that the economic rationale for Paragraph 4 was that it was meant to constrain Carborundum's discretion regarding its use of Lake River's facilities. Lake River did at least hint at an argument of this sort:

> [T]he Agreement was structured so that Lake River would have to stand ready to perform throughout the Agreement's term, even though Carborundum's actual shipments might be considerably reduced. Under the circumstances of reduced shipments, such as actually occurred here, expenses which Lake River might have saved had Carborundum been forthright about its intent not to perform were in fact continuously incurred throughout the contract term. (Pl. Brief, at 10)

The "forthright about its intent" language is typical of the over-the-top rhetoric of both sides. Lake River also claimed that Carborundum had "agreed to a higher minimum volume in return for a lower unit price." (2) I am suspicious of this statement since in its extensive recounting of the negotiations, Lake River did not identify any instance in which the contract price was reduced in exchange for an increase in the minimum volume. (8–11)

Both parties agreed that the contract had been breached and that the breach was Carborundum's failure to send the minimum amount of Ferro Carbo to Lake River. Had Lake River's counsel understood the transaction, he would have identified a different breach. At the end of the three years, the contract had been fully performed, save for Carborundum's failure to pay. That failure was the only breach. After summarizing Judge Posner's opinion, I will elaborate on that point.

II. POSNER'S DECISION

What has made the case so attractive to casebook authors was that Judge Posner was playing against type. Although he did not believe the rule against enforcement of penalty clauses made sense when dealing with agreements negotiated by sophisticated business parties, he felt bound by Illinois law. (1288–89) He concluded that Paragraph 4 was an unenforceable penalty clause because, if the liquidated damages were awarded, Lake River's total compensation would always exceed what it would have earned had Carborundum met the minimum quantity. He began with a variant on Carborundum's argument:

> Suppose to begin with that the breach occurs the day after Lake River buys its new bagging system for \$89,000 and before Carborundum ships any Ferro Carbo. Carborundum would owe Lake River \$533,000. Since Lake River would have incurred at that point a total cost of only \$89,000, its net gain from the breach would be \$444,000. This is more than four times the profit of \$107,000 (20 percent of the contract price of \$533,000) that Lake River expected to make from the contract if it had been performed: a huge windfall. (1290)

Carborundum, in making the same point, had failed to subtract the cost of the bagging system, but that doesn't really matter since either number will do. The significant difference between the two formulations is more subtle. Carborundum, recall, asked what would happen if it had failed to deliver even one pound; its breach would not have occurred until the three years had expired. Posner's hypothetical involves a breach, or anticipatory repudiation, on day one. That raises a different issue, one that I will consider below.

Posner then made calculations of Lake River's profit for various quantities short of the 22,500-ton minimum. The expected cost at the minimum quantity was $533,000 less the 20 percent profit that Lake River had projected (although, as noted above, Lake River would not have actually earned profits, because the cost projections were overly optimistic). He then assumed that the only fixed cost was the bagging system and that the variable costs were roughly proportional to the quantity. So, for the actual output of 55 percent, Lake River's expected profit would be $19,000 for the service provided plus $241,000 in damages – over twice its expected profit had Carborundum performed. (1290–91) For all quantities below the minimum, Lake River's net would exceed the profits had Carborundum met its minimum contract obligation. Moreover, he pointed out, his calculations assumed that the bagging system had no value apart from the contract. If it had some value, he noted, the numbers would get even worse. (1291)

Before turning to the contract itself, I should note that this calculation exaggerates the discrepancy. Distinguishing fixed and variable costs can be problematic, but it is safe to say that the bagging system was not the only fixed cost. Unless the 20 percent profit was meant to be the payment for all the other fixed factors (management salaries, the building, the warehouse, etc.), fixed costs over the life of the contract were undoubtedly higher. One obvious variable cost was the bagging material, but responsibility for that was assigned to Carborundum in clause 3. Still, if Lake River were guaranteed $533,000 regardless of the quantity bagged, then, for any quantity below the minimum, Lake River would appear to do better than if it had produced the minimum. So, if we read the Illinois penalty clause language narrowly, the minimum payment of Paragraph 4 must always result in a compensatory payment in excess of Lake River's damages, and it should lose. The numerical illustration, right or wrong, adds nothing, save an exclamation point.

III. FRAMING THE DISPUTE

Posner's opinion did not consider any possible explanations for why the minimum payment might have been included in the contract. Although the contract itself was attached as an appendix to Lake River's brief, (App. 13) neither the parties nor the courts invoked any of the other contract language. Two clauses are of particular importance, providing the context that was lacking in the briefs and the written opinions.

Without them it is hard to understand why Carborundum would agree to a minimum:

> 1.Scope of Agreement. From time to time during the term of this Agreement, CARBORUNDUM shall ship to LAKE-RIVER's packaging plant located at Berwyn, Illinois, quantities of CARBORUNDUM's product known as "Ferro Carbo" (called "Product"). CARBORUNDUM agrees to purchase from LAKE-RIVER and LAKE-RIVER agrees to furnish to CARBORUNDUM all terminal services necessary for the orderly conduct of CARBORUNDUM's business in the marketing and distribution of the product. …
>
> 2.c. Shipping. LAKE-RIVER shall load and ship the bagged product for CARBORUNDUM's account and according to CARBORUNDUM's shipping instructions. For scheduling purposes, LAKE-RIVER shall not be required to bag more than four hundred (400) tons of product each week. LAKE-RIVER shall ship bagged product from storage or from current production by trucks or box cars as CARBORUNDUM shall direct. Trucks and box cars shall be loaded in accordance with instructions issued by CARBORUNDUM. Sufficient dunnage shall be furnished by LAKE-RIVER for CARBORUNDUM's account to properly protect bagged product in transit. Shipping documents shall be prepared and distributed by LAKE-RIVER as directed by CARBORUNDUM. (Pl. Brief, Appendix. 13–14)

Consider first clause 2.c. Buried in the middle of a paragraph about shipping instructions is the only explicit contractual constraint on Carborundum's claim for Lake River's services. It could not ask Lake River to bag more than 400 tons in any week. (I have no idea why the maximum obligation was located in the middle of a clause dealing with other, largely mechanical, matters.) So, had Carborundum shipped the maximum each week, Lake River would have bagged over 60,000 tons – about three times the contract minimum. However, the contract language itself is not entirely consistent with the parties' description of the contract. Lake River's brief, for example, cites the testimony of a Carborundum executive saying that the "equipment he recommended be purchased had the capacity to bag 10,000 tons per year," (Pl. Brief, 15) roughly half the contractual maximum and one-third greater than the contractual minimum. Even though the facilities would be designed to handle 10,000 tons per year, Lake River was obligated to stand ready to handle twice that amount; meeting that obligation might have entailed considerable extra costs. Or, perhaps, this was simply a drafting error. Regardless, it seems clear that Lake River had committed itself to being ready to bag up to 400 tons per week every week for three years. The contract gave Carborundum considerable discretion regarding the timing. However, Lake River overstated Carborundum's flexibility, arguing that

Lake River faced "*complete uncertainty* as to when Carborundum would ship the Product for bagging." (Pl. Reply Brief, 5, emphasis added)

Returning to clause 1, what is it that Carborundum promised to do? This was neither a full-output nor a requirements contract; Carborundum only said that it would deliver Ferro Carbo "from time to time." The contract was for two things. First, Lake River would bag and distribute some product if Carborundum delivered it. However, Carborundum did not promise to deliver any product. Second, Lake River promised that it would stand ready to bag a certain amount of Ferro Carbo at a fixed price (subject to adjustment for labor costs), and it would stand ready for three years. Carborundum remained free to buy bagging and distribution services from anyone. Carborundum's option is the crucial feature of the contract. If for any reason Carborundum decided not to send product to Lake River, it wouldn't have to. So, if it received a better offer, had lower costs at its other facilities, or if demand for its services fell off, it would have no obligation to use Lake River's services.

We do not know what was in the minds of the contracting parties. The best evidence we have is the written document. It may have been poorly drafted, but, however inartful the language, the obligations of both parties were plain. The contract can be rephrased to make the structure clearer: Carborundum agrees to pay a flat rate of $533,000 over the course of the three years (subject to the labor cost adjustment) for the right to have 22,500 tons bagged during that period. Any additional tonnage will be billed at the rates set forth in the price schedule. The timing of the payment of the $533,000 depends on when Carborundum uses Lake River's services. Carborundum does not, however, commit to when, or if, it will send any product for bagging. It simply has an option. That option is constrained; it cannot require Lake River to bag more than 400 tons in a week.

Lake River provided a valuable service by standing ready to bag Carborundum's product. The minimum quantity/minimum payment served three functions. First, it provided consideration – absent the first clause of Paragraph 4, this would have been an illusory agreement. Second, given that Carborundum would have been free to take its business to a lower-cost provider during the three years, the minimum payment drastically reduced the incentive to do so. In effect the clause set the price on the first 22,500 tons at $0. (As it turned out, $0 was too high.) Only for quantities greater than the minimum would Carborundum find it potentially profitable to shop.

Third, it priced the service Lake River provided. Carborundum paid for three years' worth of access to Lake River's bagging facilities at a predetermined pricing formula and that is what it received. It could decide whether to exercise its option (that is, use the facilities) after it learned more about market conditions. The price of that flexibility has nothing to do with damage estimates. The flexibility had value to Carborundum and it was costly to provide for Lake River. The price, like that for other services, would fall somewhere between the expected value to the former and the expected cost of the latter. The price was not quoted explicitly. The higher the minimum, the greater the implicit price of the flexibility. Perhaps Carborundum paid too much for the flexibility, but there is no reason to second-guess the consideration paid for provision of a valuable service.

When we recognize that the contract was one giving Carborundum substantial discretion for three years, then it is clear that Posner's characterization of the contract as still being executory is incorrect: "Lake River was the victim of a breach of a portion of the contract that remained entirely unexecuted on either side. Carborundum had not shipped the other 10,500 tons, as promised; but on the other hand Lake River had not had to bag those 10,500 tons, as it had promised." (1287) But, as Lake River's counsel asserted, it had fully performed; there was nothing left to execute. For three years it had stood ready to bag up to 400 tons of Ferro per week. "Carborundum's argument that Lake River incurred no expenses as a *result* of the breach ignores the reality that Lake River's expenses, as required by the Agreement, were all incurred *before* the breach – which occurred at the end of the Agreement's term on September 1, 1982." (Pl. Brief, 10)

Even if we were to treat the suspect clause as one stipulating damages, the expected damages are not confined to those Judge Posner recognized. As Lake River noted, "the *quid pro quo* Lake River received for giving Carborundum control over the timing of product shipments was a guaranteed minimum amount of revenue." (Pl. Reply Brief, 7) The district court and Lake River emphasized the uncertainty of the revenue stream as a justification for the minimum. But the timing itself is not the problem. In order to afford Carborundum flexibility in determining the tonnage to be bagged, Lake River had to incur costs (explicit or otherwise) in addition to the bagging machine costs mentioned in the contract and in Judge Posner's opinion. To stand ready to perform, Lake River might have to maintain a larger facility or labor force than otherwise; or it might have had to maintain sufficient capacity to remain ready to meet this obligation; or, perhaps most important, it might have had to forego an attractive alternative. Lake River did note some of the additional costs, although it failed to mention the opportunity costs:

> Under the Agreement, Lake River was required to spend more than $89,000 to purchase bagging equipment, was required to set up a brand new bagging operation to be used exclusively for Carborundum's Product, and was required to incur all of the fixed costs associated with setting aside the necessary space (including plant depreciation, corporate overhead, taxes, and utilities such as light and heat). Lake River was also required to have sufficient manpower available to run the bagging operation, but could not efficiently allocate such manpower between the Carborundum project and its other projects in light of the uncertainty over the timing of product shipments by Carborundum. (Pl. Reply Brief, 6)

If we treat payment for the minimum quantity as stipulated damages, with this understanding of the contract, it should be clear that damage estimation would be extremely difficult *ex ante* and measurement would be extremely difficult *ex post*. For example, determining what opportunities were foregone (or, *ex ante*, could be foregone) by Lake River because it had to stand ready to bag 400 tons per week for three years with a fixed price schedule would be a complex (if not futile) exercise. The clause should certainly meet the Illinois criterion concerning "the likely difficulty of measuring actual damages." (1289) So, even if we treat the minimum payment clause as subject to the penalty clause bar, a better understanding of the contract would make the liquidated damages characterization more plausible.

One doctrinal device for avoiding the penalty clause rule is to treat the payment as an "alternative performance." (Farnsworth (1998, § 12.18 n. 44)) Take-or-pay contracts, in which the buyer agrees to pay for a minimum whether it actually takes that quantity, have routinely been enforced. Posner attempted to distinguish this contract from a take-or-pay agreement (1292), even though neither party had raised the issue in its briefs. He distinguished, apparently, on the basis of the relative magnitude of the fixed costs: "If, as appears not to be the case here but would often be the case in supplying natural gas, a supplier's fixed costs were a very large fraction of his total costs, a take-or-pay clause might well be a reasonable liquidation of damages." (1292) The high fixed cost, or more precisely, the specificity of an asset, is not the essential feature of take-or-pay contracts. Asset specificity is, at most, a sufficient, but not necessary condition. The key feature is that the seller incurs costs by granting discretion to the buyer. A take-or-pay arrangement (say, between a coal mine and a power company) and this contract perform the same role in the same way. The party with discretion (Carborundum or the power company) has to pay the opposite party (Lake River or the coal mine) for the costs it could incur by affording that discretion. Both set a non-linear pricing formula: a fixed price independent of usage, a zero marginal price up to the minimum, and a positive marginal price thereafter.

IV. THE ANTICIPATORY REPUDIATION HYPO

The contract, as I noted above, was fully performed by Lake River. But what if the contract were in fact breached prior to the end of the three-year period? Recall that in Judge Posner's hypothetical, the contract was breached on the first day. There is a fundamental difference between the case in which the three-year term had expired and one in which one party repudiated prior to expiration. How should we treat an anticipatory repudiation or the premature total breach of a long-term contract? The major difference is that once the contract is recognized as abandoned, Lake River's resources would be freed up. Carborundum should still be responsible for paying for the minimum quantity; it had breached its promise to pay. However, the damages could be offset by the value of the resources freed up by the termination.

Posner claimed that Lake River raised this argument: "Lake River argues that it would never get as much as the formula suggests, because it would be required to mitigate its damages." (1291) I assume that this was raised in oral argument because it was not in the briefs. He rejected the argument because, he claimed, it would undercut the virtues of liquidated damages. (1291) However, if Lake River's counsel was responding to the premature breach scenario, it would be a sensible response. If Lake River no longer had to assure that it could bag 400 tons per week, it could have used its capacity for other purposes. So, while Carborundum would still be responsible for the minimum payment in the event of an anticipatory repudiation, the law *might* require it to offset against that payment revenues received from utilizing the freed up capacity elsewhere.

I said *might* in the previous paragraph purposefully since the law regarding damages for the anticipatory repudiation of a long-term contract is a bit of a mess. Even if it is a contract for goods falling squarely in the take-or-pay/alternative performance box, courts struggle with the problem. (See *Tractebel Energy* and *Roye Realty*) The problem is compounded when the contract is for a service (like bagging); contract law has been somewhat less inclined to offset in "to do" contracts, the reason being that it could have been possible to do the additional work while still performing the contract.

The problem is further compounded if the disputed clause is characterized as being for stipulated damages, rather than as an essential element of the agreement defining the limits on Carborundum's discretion. As a matter of sound economics and policy, there should be no difference. However, if the stipulated damage remedy is viewed as exclusive, one could argue that there should be no offset following an anticipatory repudiation. That is Judge Posner's position. I do not believe that the law requires identical treatment of a breach and an anticipatory repudiation, but I am content to leave it as a recommendation: in the event of an anticipatory repudiation, the default rule should be to offset the promisee's benefits against the stipulated damages.

V. CONCLUDING REMARKS

The preceding suggests five conclusions. First, what was at stake in this contract was the provision of a service – setting aside capacity – which was valuable to the buyer and costly for the seller to provide. The primary purpose of the minimum quantity clause was to price that service, not to define a remedy. Second, even if a court did somehow choose to read the clause as a stipulated remedy, the difficulty of measuring the costs incurred by setting aside capacity would have made the clause a plausible liquidation of damages. Third, the doctrinal boxes led to the obscuring of the simple economics of the transaction. Absent an economic framework, the litigators could not make the argument cleanly, although bits and pieces of it did appear in their briefs. Fourth, there is a big difference between a failure to hit a minimum target in a completed contract and a repudiation of that contract. For the latter, it is plausible that the damages should be offset by the non-breacher's gains from redeploying the freed-up assets. Finally, while we cannot generalize from a single data point, this analysis provides one more bit of ammunition against the penalty clause bar for contracts between sophisticated parties.

PART II

Consequential damages

8. The "tacit assumption" and consequential damages

When I first taught Contract Law and came to the subject of consequential damages, I took a look at the UCC. I was taken aback by the UCC comment: "the 'tacit assumption' test for the recovery of consequential damages is rejected." (UCC 2-715, Comment 2.) When considering whether the parties intended that the promisor be responsible for a particular claim by the promisee, it did not seem unreasonable to me to ask whether the parties had implicitly allocated the risk. That was how I read the case that set out the tacit assumption approach in the United States, Holmes's decision in *Globe Refining Co. v. Landa Cotton Oil Co.* "It is true," said Holmes, "that, as people when contracting contemplate performance, not breach, they commonly say little or nothing as to what shall happen in the latter event, and the common rules have been worked out by common sense, which has established what the parties probably would have said if they had spoken about the matter." If the promisor were to fail to perform, he continued, "the extent of liability ... is likely to be within his contemplation, and, whether it is or not, should be worked out on terms which it fairly may be presumed he would have assented to if they had been presented to his mind." (543)

That seems pretty benign. But the reaction to it has been anything but benign. In his screed against *Globe Refining*, Larry Garvin summarizes some of the commentary:

> It is fair to say that the contracts clerisy long ago rejected *Globe Refining*, a rejection if anything rendered more emphatic over time. Consider, for example, Samuel Williston. In his magisterial contracts treatise, he stated that asserting the tacit agreement theory "is to assert a fiction which obscures the truth and invites misapprehension which may lead to error." Or Arthur Corbin, who criticized Holmes's history and declared that foreseeability "does not require that the defendant should have had the resulting injury actually in contemplation or should have promised either impliedly or expressly to pay therefor in case of breach." Or Allan Farnsworth, who observed that it "has been generally rejected as overly restrictive and doctrinally unsound." Or Karl Llewellyn, who wrote that Holmes's "*Globe Refining* opinion started out after the mirage of 'perfect compensation, not a penny more,' and came out with as

> harsh a result as could a commercial woodenhead." Or Article Two of the Uniform Commercial Code, which expressly casts it aside. Or the Restatement (Second) of Contracts, which does the same. Or the Restatement of Contracts, which does the same, albeit less bluntly. Or, for that matter, most English courts and commentators, whose early opinions and statements provided practically all of the doctrinal support for *Globe Refining*. Nor have the courts ultimately adopted *Globe Refining*'s tacit agreement test, though … there are some distressing exceptions. (Garvin, (2012, 259)

Strong stuff. All that impressive authority to the contrary notwithstanding, I still think that Holmes got it right. I will come to that shortly, but first I do want to note that despite all that hostility to the notion of a tacit assumption regarding the remedy, the contracts clerisy is decidedly not hostile to accepting tacit assumptions regarding the interpretation of the contract. Consider both the Restatement and the UCC:

> *Common basis of understanding.* Course of dealing may become part of an agreement either by explicit provision or by tacit recognition, or it may guide the court in supplying an omitted term. Like usage of trade, it may determine the meaning of language or it may annex an agreed but unstated term. There is no requirement that an agreement be ambiguous before evidence of a course of dealing can be shown, nor is it required that the course of dealing be consistent with the meaning the agreement would have apart from the course of dealing. Restatement (Second) § 223.
>
> * * *
>
> Paragraph (a) makes admissible evidence of course of dealing, usage of trade and course of performance to explain or supplement the terms of any writing stating the agreement of the parties in order that the true understanding of the parties as to the agreement may be reached. Such writings are to be read on the assumption that the course of prior dealings between the parties and the usages of trade were taken for granted when the document was phrased. UCC 2-202 Comment (2).

There seems to be no compunction about filling in the (alleged) blanks when interpreting the contractual obligation. We are supposed to recognize that the parties took certain things for granted (that is we recognize the parties' tacit assumptions) when committing some of the terms of their agreement to writing. However, we are not to make tacit assumptions when ascertaining their liability in the event of a breach. On the one hand, fans of such egregious decisions as *Nanakuli* (written contract says posted price at time of delivery, court says that really meant either the posted price or the price at time of contracting, whichever is lower) and *Columbia Nitrogen* (court says fixed price and minimum quantity were only fair estimates) recognize alleged tacit assumptions to trump explicit contract language. On the other, they contemptuously dismiss the tacit assumption regarding consequential damages.

Apparently, not all tacit assumptions are created equal. The distinction, I guess, is the notion that Remedies are Different. The ambivalent treatment of liquidated damages is one manifestation of this. But really, they are not so different. Contract law is generally facilitative. Parties are free to design their relationships as they see fit. If Landa had included a clause in the contract disclaiming consequential damages, that almost certainly would have been enforceable. True, courts are not always hospitable to party-determined remedies, for example, the refusal to enforce penalty clauses and the reluctance to enforce specific performance clauses. Nonetheless, parties do often write remedies into their agreements and courts do often enforce them.

Ironically, a few months before *Hadley v. Baxendale* was decided, the House of Lords invoked the tacit assumption language, albeit for the "custom and usage" purpose, not for dealing with consequential damages.

> The principles on which this case is to be decided are perfectly clear: the difficulty lies in the application of them to the facts. Mercantile contracts are very commonly framed in a language peculiar to merchants: the intention of the parties, though perfectly well known to themselves, would often be defeated if this language were strictly construed according to its ordinary import in the world at large: evidence, therefore, of mercantile custom and usage is admitted in order to expound it and arrive at its true meaning. Again, in all contracts, as to the subject matter of which known usages prevail, parties are found to proceed with the tacit assumption of these usages; they commonly reduce into writing the special particulars of their agreement, but omit to specify these known usages, which are included however, as of course, by mutual understanding: evidence therefore of such incidents is receivable. (*Brown v. Byrne*, 715)

While Holmes's opinion in *Landa* is generally recognized as the fount of the American tacit assumption test, Holmes did not actually use the phrase. The first reported case using the phrase did not appear until World War II. In *Krauss v. Greenbarg*, Judge Goodrich said: "There must have been virtually a tacit agreement to assume the risk of whatever harm was foreseeable. There is some judicial authority for this view in the highest court of this land. [citing *Globe*] … The merits of this subsequent restriction on *Hadley v. Baxendale* have been argued at length. However, as this Court has said many times … our duty is to apply state law as we find it in the state decisions irrespective of what we may regard as its merits. Pennsylvania decisions have clearly held, we think, that knowledge of facts which makes special damages foreseeable imposes liability therefore." (571) Since then, a majority of the states have rejected the tacit assumption approach and, as noted, both the UCC and Restatements have done so as well. Likewise, in England the tacit assumption interpretation had been supplanted until a recent decision by the House of Lords, *The Achilleas* (to be discussed in Chapter 10).

The tacit assumption approach has been derided as indeterminate. How, goes the argument, can people be thought to have made an assumption about something that they had never thought about? This strikes me as a case of the pot calling the kettle black. The alternative has been to invoke foreseeability and some variation on the notion of probability. The Restatement (Second) uses the undefined notion of "probable": "It is enough, however, that the loss was foreseeable as a probable, as distinguished from a necessary, result of his breach." (351, comment a) In *Heron II*, the House of Lords provided a variety of formulations. Lord Reid proposed "not unlikely," which, he said, "denot[ed] a degree of probability considerably less than an even chance, but nevertheless, not very unusual and easily foreseeable." (383) Their Lordships proposed a number of variations including "serious possibility" and "real danger," but unanimously rejected "on the cards" (which had been invoked a generation earlier in *Victoria Laundry*).

In effect the critics of the tacit assumption approach ask: "Would reasonable business people have *contemplated the possibility*?" If they somehow conclude that the contemplation threshold has been met, the plaintiff wins. The tacit assumption approach downplays the possibility question. Even if the threshold had been met, the relevant question is: "How would those same reasonable business people *allocate the risks*?" Thus, both the supporters and critics of *Globe* make a tacit assumption about risk allocation. They just disagree on what that assumption is.

The risks are, to some degree, endogenous. That is, the parties can influence the likelihood of a bad outcome occurring and the magnitude of the damages were it to occur. While the defendant affects the likelihood that things go wrong, the victim can affect the magnitude of the harm both by post-incident (mitigation) and pre-incident behavior. Ronald Coase (1960) won a Nobel Prize by recognizing that both parties can be responsible for the harm. So, for example, in *Hadley v. Baxendale*, the carrier's negligence caused the delay, but the consequences of that delay were in Hadley's hands. It could, as Baron Alderson stated, have had an extra shaft on hand so the delay would not have resulted in an idle mill. There were other things that Hadley could have done. It could have carried a larger inventory of flour (the output); or it could have recouped the lost output by running the mill at a higher level of output after the shaft had arrived. (In effect, that entails carrying a larger inventory of productive capacity – another input.) There is no reason why Hadley had to hold its inventory of inputs or output at this one location – it could have diversified geographically. Any of these actions would have avoided Hadley's loss of profits (or, at least, substantially reduced them). I am not suggesting that a shipper like Hadley would make its inventory decision with regard to this specific transaction; there are a number of potential sources of delay, some due to someone's carelessness others to factors unrelated to anyone's fault (like weather). The inventory decisions would reflect expectations regarding the frequency of delays from all sources.

The tacit assumption concerns the reasonable expectation about the responsibilities of the counterparty. In a typical case one party, A, relies on the successful performance by the other, B, but is disappointed. Perhaps B was negligent (*Hadley*); or perhaps B was not at fault, but for reasons beyond its control B failed to perform (*The Achilleas*). To what extent can A run its business in reliance upon B's successful performance of its contractual obligation? By assigning the responsibility for consequential damages to A, the law would give it the incentive to control the potential damage. The rejection of the tacit assumption in the UCC and Restatement provides A with a weaker incentive (and B with a stronger incentive).

If carriers like Baxendale were held responsible for their customer's lost profits, and if they could not disclaim the liability, they, in effect, would be providing mandatory insurance to all their customers without the tools insurers customarily use (copayments, deductibles, monitoring, etc.) to cope with the inevitable adverse selection and moral hazard. That insurance would be a cost of doing business and the carriers would have to cover that cost by charging higher rates to customers. In at least some instances, the outcome would be that the customers as a group would be worse off than if there had been no liability.

Of course, the carriers could contract out of liability. A modern-day Baxendale would almost certainly contractually limit damages for delay to a modest multiple of the price. Limitations on consequential damages are not restricted to carriers; they are commonly employed in commercial deals. The only real issues of law are setting a default rule and the ease with which parties can contract out of it. Despite the fact that the default rules of the UCC and Restatement (Second) both favor liberal compensation of the consequential damages, the disclaimers are routine.

In a frictionless world it would not matter which default rule applied. However, the default rule can be sticky. First, if judges believe that sellers/carriers should be liable for consequential damages, they can deploy interpretive devices to construe damage limitation clauses narrowly. One of the principles of contract interpretation in English law is that "clear words are necessary before a court will hold that a contract has taken away rights or remedies which one of the parties to it would have had at common law." (*Seadrill Management Services Limited, Seadrill Larissa Limited v OAO Gazprom*, 182) Second, documentation for transactions, even million dollar transactions, can consist of nothing more than the purchase and acknowledgment forms of the parties. Since buyer forms typically allow for the recovery of consequential damages, the "battle of the forms," given the knockout rule adopted by most jurisdictions, would result in consequential damages being recoverable. (Not all courts adopting the knockout rule would allow recovery of consequential damages; *see Dresser Industries, Inc., Waukesha Engine Div. v. Gradall Co.*)

In negotiated contracts, my impression is that the disclaimers are common, consistent with the notion that the buyer is in the best position to protect its reliance. However, I want to note two situations in which the contract might allow for recovery of consequential damages. In Chapter 2, I suggested that when the contract is defining the tradeoff between discretion and reliance, the hostility to the notion that one party to the contract has an option to perform or pay the consequences is misplaced. However, the hostility to the option concept has more bite in cases involving claims for consequential damages. There is a difference between negligently shipping a shaft versus a willful failure to do so.

Although contract law is often characterized as a no-fault regime, courts have found devices for taking fault into account. As McCormick (1935, 517–18) wrote over seventy years ago:

> Would not our courts enhance the realism of the rules and make them easier for juries to accept if they gave formal approval to the tendency, written large upon the actual results of the cases, to discriminate between the liability for consequential damages of the wilful and deliberate contract-breaker on the one hand, and of the party who has failed to carry out his bargain through inability or mischance? Our rules should sanction, as our actual practice probably does, the award of consequential damages against one who deliberately and wantonly breaks faith, regardless of the foreseeability of the loss when the contract was made. We shall then have completed the process, begun piece-meal in *Hadley v. Baxendale*, of borrowing from the French Civil Code its theory of damages in contract.

For more recent arguments recognizing fault and willfulness, see Eisenberg (2009), Cohen (1994), Thel and Siegelman (2009) and Hillman (2014).

There is considerable dispute as to how to distinguish a willful breach from any other. Cancellation of an order is deliberate, but few would find it willful. Corbin was disparaging of the very notion of willfulness: "The word most commonly used is 'wilful'; and it is seldom accompanied by any discussion of its meaning or classification of the cases that should fall within it. Its use indicates a childlike faith in the existence of a plain and obvious line between the good and the bad, between unfortunate virtue and unforgivable sin." Contrast this with his enthusiastic approval of "good faith," which surely suffers from the same flaw. Notwithstanding the difficulties, courts do make that distinction and, more importantly, the parties themselves often do so in their contracts. Even if they disclaim liability for consequential damages, they can include a significant exception – the disclaimer will not apply if the breach were due to gross negligence or willful behavior. They might not have any idea about what they mean by willful; rather than spelling it out, they are content to defer the definition to the ex post determination by courts. The disposition of *Huntsman v. Hexion* (see Chapter 2) provides one illustration. The Chancery Court distinguished Hexion's "knowing and intentional breach of [a] covenant and allowed for liability substantially greater than had the transaction been terminated for an acceptable reason." (715) One of the standard forms of the Federation of Oils, Seeds and Fats Associations (FOSFA) has an interesting variant on the effect of fault on damages: "If the arbitrators consider the circumstances of the default justify it they may, at their absolute discretion, award damages on a different quantity and/or award additional damages." (Cited in *Novasen*, 409) The Grain and Feed Trade Association (GAFTA) default clause also gives the arbitrators absolute discretion to vary the award. (Cited in *Bunge*, 338)

In a *Hadley*-type scenario, a deliberate deviation by a carrier to pick up a more valuable shipment could result in liability for the shipper's consequential damages. Of course, that can be contracted over – the seller could maintain the flexibility to deviate. The shipper might be content to give the carrier that option in exchange for a lower price. Suppliers in many contexts do offer interruptible service at a reduced price. The Terms and Conditions of Ocean World Lines Bill of Lading provides an illustration of that flexibility:

> The Carrier does not undertake that the Goods will be transported from or loaded at the place of receiving or loading or will arrive at the place of discharge, destination or transshipment aboard any particular vessel or other conveyance or at any particular date or time or to meet any particular market or in time for any particular use. Scheduled or advertised departure and arrival

> times are only expected times and may be advanced or delayed if the Carrier or any Connecting Carrier shall find it necessary, prudent or convenient. In no event shall the Carrier be liable for consequential or other damages for delay in the scheduled departures or arrivals of the vessel or other conveyance transporting the Goods or for any other matter.

The willfulness exception can be rationalized in terms of the buyer's reliance. For innocent mistakes by the seller, the onus is on the buyer to protect itself. Buyers can make their decisions relying on the seller's "normal" behavior, even if that behavior results in a seller breach. Behavior by the seller that substantially increased the likelihood of failure, however, would be outside the buyer's reasonable expectations – buyers needn't self-protect against that. However, recognizing a fault-based exception can expose the seller to juridical risk. Given the difficulty in defining willful behavior and the risk that a fact finder would define a garden-variety failure as willful, parties might be reluctant to include a willfulness exception.

The second exception mirrors the second prong of the *Hadley* rule: damages "as may reasonably be supposed to have been in the contemplation of both parties, at the time when they made the contract, as the probable result of the breach." It is not the mere contemplation that matters. The sellers have knowledge of the buyer's vulnerability, they know that the buyer is relying on their performance, and they accept the risk that their failure would result in substantial damages. Contracts between suppliers and automobile manufacturers make clear the buyer's intended use. GM's standard form is typical: "Seller acknowledges that Seller knows of Buyer's intended use and expressly warrants that all goods covered by this order which have been selected, designated, manufactured, or assembled by Seller based upon Buyer's stated use, will be fit and sufficient for the particular purposes intended by Buyer." If there were a breach of warranty (to the consumer) or a product recall, the manufacturers would assess sellers for at least some of the costs. Ford's standard form, for example, said: "At its option, the Buyer may debit the Supplier for up to 50% of the Actual Recall Costs … if the Buyer has made a good faith determination that the Supplier is likely to be liable for some portion of the total costs."

The multi-year supply contract between John Deere and Stanadyne made liability for consequential damages contingent on both knowledge and fault. The wording reversed the usual pattern of saying no liability unless the seller passed some culpability hurdle. Instead the seller would be liable unless it was without fault:

> STANADYNE CORPORATION acknowledges that DEERE requires on-time delivery in order to operate its plants. The parties further acknowledge that the precise amount of damages which DEERE would sustain in the event STANADYNE CORPORATION were to fail to make timely or conforming deliveries of Parts would be difficult to determine. Therefore, the parties agree that STANADYNE CORPORATION shall be responsible for any and all damages resulting from STANADYNE CORPORATION's failure to make timely or conforming deliveries of Parts, including, but not limited to, mutually agreed upon costs DEERE incurs for the correction of Parts with quality problems and mutually agreed upon costs DEERE incurs in connection with DEERE's machining and/or assembly line downtime. … STANADYNE CORPORATION shall not be responsible for the above damages if such out-of-order (late) delivery or non-delivery results from a cause beyond STANADYNE CORPORATION's reasonable control without fault or negligence, provided that STANADYNE CORPORATION has informed DEERE as soon as practical of the problem.

I must reiterate that these remain exceptions to the basic point. When parties design their contracts rarely will they protect the promisee's reliance on the promisor's successful performance. The promisee's ability to control the adverse consequences usually would result in consequential damages being disclaimed.

As the Restatement and UCC note, the tacit assumption approach has been rejected in most U.S. jurisdictions, but not all. One of the few outliers is the biggest elephant in the room – New York. It behooves us, therefore, to examine the leading New York case. *Kenford Co., Inc. v. County of Erie* stands out against the anti-*Globe* trend. The plaintiffs forwarded a variety of claims for damages and after eighteen years of litigation lost on all their claims, except for a fairly minor claim for reliance damages. That case will be discussed in the next chapter.

9. Buffalo's field of dreams: *Kenford Company v. Erie County*

Sometimes you catch a break. My original intent was to include a short discussion of the *Kenford* cases in the previous chapter. To get a copy of the contract at the center of the dispute I emailed one of the County's lawyers, Joseph Finnerty. He gave me a copy of the contract and a whole lot more – briefs and videos of the oral argument, and, in a lovely lunch, great gossip about the case. When he told me that there was testimony that the New York Yankees had contemplated moving the franchise to Buffalo, it was clear that the story merited a chapter of its own. Few litigations have been more pathological. After ten years of discovery and pretrial motions, there was a nine-month, 25,000-page trial. This was followed by two trips to the Court of Appeals. In all, the litigation lasted eighteen years.

Keeping track of all the sources can be complicated since there were four relevant decisions and multiple briefs. I will refer to them as Appellate I, Appellate II, Appeals I, and Appeals II.

It all began in the late 1960s when the movers and shakers of Buffalo were advocating the construction of a domed stadium to house the football Bills and, possibly, to attract a major league baseball team. At the time, the only domed stadium was the Houston Astrodome, referred to at the time as the Eighth Wonder of the World. After a considerable amount of turmoil, the County adopted a plan that would have the dome constructed in the suburb of Lancaster. Kenford, a firm owned by Edward Cottrell, a local wealthy car dealer, would provide the land on which the stadium would be built. Cottrell partnered with Judge Roy Hofheinz, the creator and operator of the Houston Astrodome.

The essence of the deal was that Kenford would donate a parcel of land to the County of Erie for it to build the domed stadium. Kenford had acquired title or options on about seven hundred acres. About a quarter of that land would be used for the stadium; Kenford would develop the remainder. It is not clear from the opinions when it had acquired the property or options, but it appears that most, if not all, were acquired before the stadium was being considered. The County's counsel claimed that the average acquisition price included a premium that took into account the possible future development of the land; its valuation expert claimed that the unimproved land was worth about $1,100 per acre and that the average acquisition price was about $3,100 per acre. (Def. Reply Brief, Appeals II, 63) If correct, that suggests that much of the property was acquired after it became known that a stadium in the Lancaster area was at least a possibility. Finnerty told me that Cottrell's plan had been to sell the property to the County, but after the deal appeared to have died, Judge Hofheinz offered, without informing Cottrell, that the land be a gift.

In May 1968, the County adopted enabling legislation to finance a stadium and a resolution authorizing a $50 million bond issuance for the purpose of financing the construction. Whether that number was realistic was in dispute. The Buffalo News, a strong proponent of the suburban stadium, asserted the estimated cost of $39.7 million. The Courier Express, a proponent of the downtown location, went with an estimate of $63 million. ("How Other Newsmen See Us: Too Many Axes Ground to Fit") Kenford would donate 178 acres of land for the construction of the stadium and in June 1969 the County adopted a resolution accepting the offer. Kenford exercised its options on the remaining parcels and in August, Kenford and the County entered into a contract. The benefits to Kenford were to come in two pieces. First, it anticipated that the stadium would result in appreciation of the value of the peripheral land. While Kenford anticipated substantial appreciation in the value of the adjacent land, the County also anticipated benefits in the form of increased tax revenues both from the new commercial activities on the peripheral land and the increased property taxes. Second, Kenford would get a 40-year lease for the stadium. If, however, the parties failed to negotiate lease terms, it would get a consolation prize – a 20-year management agreement would automatically come into being. In fact, they did fail to negotiate the lease.

The contract was silent on what would happen if the County chose not to build the stadium. Indeed, it was silent on almost everything. It is hard to imagine that so complex a transaction could be handled so carelessly. The dissent in the first significant appellate decision (*Appellate I*) described the contract:

> The County's agreement with Kenford for the construction of the multi-million dollar domed stadium is in a five-page agreement (Exhibit 82–A) consisting of six paragraphs, almost all of which concern the terms of a lease agreement to be agreed upon in the future. The single clause pertaining to the County's undertaking to construct the domed stadium is as follows: "The County shall construct domed facilities comparable to the Houston Astrodome on the stadium site area, and shall construct access roadways as generally depicted on the attached map, Schedule B. Such construction of the domed stadium facilities shall be commenced by the County within twelve (12) months after execution of this Agreement." (fn, 7)

The County solicited bids for construction and, to its surprise, the low bid was $72 million. Efforts to increase the appropriation failed and in January 1971, the County terminated the contract. Kenford sued seeking specific performance or, in the alternative, damages. In the initial complaint, it asked for $90 million, but later amended the complaint to increase the claim to $465 million. The plaintiffs won the liability issue on summary judgment (after ten years of pre-litigation wrangling) and the damage issue went to trial. In the interim, Cottrell tried to find alternative funding for the project. In February 1972, he announced a new stadium with a cost of $55 million and an additional $200–$300 million for developing the peripheral land. (Buffalo Star-News, 2/10/72) However, that deal fell through and the stadium was never built.

At trial, Kenford claimed four forms of damages and introduced months of expert testimony in support. There were two different categories of consequential damages. First, it claimed that had the stadium been built, Kenford would have developed a number of other projects on the peripheral land and that it would have been awarded a major league franchise; the lost profits from all these projects, it argued, were compensable. Most of the trial was devoted to this; the plaintiffs introduced over four months of expert testimony in support of this element of the claim. Second, plaintiffs argued that the value of the peripheral land would have increased had the stadium been built and that the County should be liable for the difference in the value of the land with and without the stadium. Plaintiffs claimed that the management contract would have produced substantial profits and that these too should be compensable. Neither the parties nor the courts distinguished this claim from a consequential damage claim. Since the management contract was the consideration for the promise, it should have been viewed as direct damages. Finally, there was a claim for what was characterized as reliance and mitigation damages. Total damage claims, which exceeded the estimate in the Amended Complaint, were well over $500,000,000. Ultimately, the plaintiffs failed on all the claims except for the reliance and mitigation damages.

ROUND ONE

The plaintiffs produced a parade of witnesses, primarily expert witnesses, for the purpose of demonstrating that had the stadium been built, Kenford would have developed the peripheral lands with a number of projects that would have been profitable. The witnesses did not say that the projects would have been achieved. Rather, they only claimed that had the projects been built, they would have yielded profits and that the experts could measure those expected profits. The court let the evidence in over the defendant's objections, subject to connection. In the end, the judge ruled that connection required satisfaction of multiple conditions. I will focus on two – the "baseball condition" and the "roadway condition." He found that neither condition had been met and struck the testimony, in effect giving a directed verdict for the defense. However, as we shall see, the judge's rationale was quite odd. The result was right; the trial judge's path to that result was not. None of that evidence should have been let in. Had the judge better understood the matter, he would have come to the same result but without having the poor jurors listen to many months of evidence of no value. Before getting to why that was so, I want to first provide some detail on this aspect of the plaintiff's claim.

Had the stadium been constructed, Kenford argued, it had plans to develop the peripheral lands and as a result of the breach, it lost the profits that would otherwise have been earned on those projects. Moreover, it would have received a major league baseball franchise and its damages included the profits it would have received but for the breach. The damages were presented by expert witnesses. In the accompanying table I have included the damage claim for each component and the number of days each witness was on the stand. The projects on the peripheral land, the first five rows of the table, would, according to the experts, have resulted in profits of $385,340,312. Adding the profits from the major league franchise would bring that component to $532,054,569.

Table 9.1 Damage claims by experts

Nature of claim	Amount	Days of testimony
Theme Park	$251 586 742	Wilson 9 days
Three hotels	$99 076 524	McElyea 6 days
Four office buildings	$24 944 286	Bingham 4 days
Golf course	$3 276 866	McElyea 4 days
Specialty retail center	$6 455 894	Cory 4 days
Peripheral lands	$21 186 528	Gray 2 days
Major league baseball franchise	$146 714 257	Gerritson 5 days
Management contract	$58 220 119	Sprouse 7 days
Reliance	$6 763 227	

Source: Def. Brief, Appellate I, pp. 4–XX.

Kenford also presented witnesses who testified that it would have been able to obtain financing for the peripheral development had the County constructed the stadium. One witness, Jerome Steiker, asserted that the lost profits projections were "splendid" and "unusually conservative." (Def. Brief, Appellate I, 21) Of course, that raises an awkward question: if the profits were going to be so substantial, why did Cottrell fail to get financing for the stadium he proposed in 1972? The obvious answer is that lenders had better things to do with their money. The estimates were bogus. I will come back to that.

The expert witnesses, all associated with the same firm, projected costs and revenues associated with each project from 1973, when the stadium would have been completed, to 1992, when, it was assumed, Kenford would have sold everything. The thirteen-year gap between breach and the trial presented two problems. The first was the appropriate treatment of the time value of money. This was of special importance in this period since for much of the period the inflation rate exceeded 7 percent and interest rates were often in double digits, the prime rate on occasion topping 20 percent. For the pre-trial period the experts only used nominal values. If the costs were front-loaded, which they would have been for most of these capital-intensive projects, the lost profits would be overstated, even if pre-judgment interest were applied at the market rate. However, pre-judgment interest was limited by statute for most of the period to 3 percent (Def. Brief, Appellate I,73), exacerbating the difference. To be sure, the statute makes no economic sense. Still, even if one had confidence in all the projections, the use of nominal, rather than real, numbers would have resulted in an overstatement of the damages.

The second problem concerns the use of post-breach information. To what extent should subsequent facts, unknown and unknowable at the time of the breach, be taken into account? So, for example, when Gerritson, the baseball expert, was reckoning the projected costs and benefits of a new franchise in Buffalo, he took into account such facts as the demise of the reserve clause, the advent of free agency in 1975, and the strike of 1981. Indeed, all his projections were based on post-breach data.

When I first read the decisions, I thought that the notion of a major league franchise moving to Buffalo was ludicrous. After more research, I realized that I was wrong. It was at least plausible that with a domed stadium, Buffalo would have attracted a major league franchise. Could it have been the Yankees? Possibly. The Yankees run as a dominant team (the team had won 14 of 16 American League championships and 9 World Series) ended in 1964 and the team had had a series of losing years. The Yankees had been purchased by CBS in 1964, and, by 1970,

CBS was looking to unload them. Michael Burke, who had been installed as president in 1966, testified. "I had been commissioned, if that's the right word, by Mr. Paley [CBS President] to seek out a buyer for the club, and on a discrete basis. … I was seeking out people who might, in my opinion, be interested in buying the team and it was in that context that – that was the context of my discussions with Mr. Cottrell." (Testimony of Michael Burke, 22–23) He had, in fact, had at least three meetings with Cottrell. Moving the Yankees to Buffalo, he testified, could have been possible, contingent upon approval of three-quarters of the owners of the other American League teams. (29–32, 51) He was authorized to sell the club for $12 million. (59) (In fact, he did manage to sell the team to a group headed by George Steinbrenner in 1973 for $10 million.) Burke also testified on how desperate the owner of the Washington Senators was to sell and move his team (which shortly thereafter moved to Arlington, Texas).

The move of either team to Buffalo would have required approval by three-quarters of the American League owners. Burke testified that he believed that approval would have been forthcoming. However, the trial judge disallowed the testimony. He initially ruled that the question of league approval would be left to the jury to determine:

> Ladies and gentlemen of the Jury, the question of those facts that have been enunciated previously and some additional facts that have been enunciated by this witness concerning whether or not the American League, in these cases, would have granted Mr. Cottrell a franchise is a question with facts within your purview and your capacity to comprehend, and it will be for you to determine from these facts and any other facts that may be supplied which you may determine whether or not, in your judgment, a baseball franchise would have been, in one case been approved in terms of a transfer from the Yankees to Buffalo, and in another would have been approved from Washington to Buffalo. This will be facts from which you will determine that situation. (85)

At the end of the trial, the judge reversed himself, holding that there was a "baseball condition" and since it had not been met, all the baseball damages would be disallowed. What was that condition? "[T]he trial judge ruled that plaintiffs would have to provide direct proof of the ultimate fact that if the County had not breached the Contract and had constructed the domed stadium facilities, the required number of votes in either the American League or National League would have been obtained by Kenford for the acquisition of a franchise for operation in that facility … . [T]he jury would not be permitted to consider relevant facts and circumstances from which a determination could be made that

Kenford would have acquired such a franchise." (Pl. Brief, Appellate I, 11) It is not clear what proof would have sufficed, the judge having disallowed Burke's opinion. So, ironically, the expert's flawed projections were rejected, but on irrelevant grounds.

And, to be clear, the expert's methodology was fundamentally flawed. To see why, assume that had Kenford succeeded in buying either the Yankees or Senators, league approval would have been certain, so we can set that uncertainty aside. The relevant question, which the expert (and the counsel and court) failed to ask, was this: What did Kenford lose at the time of the breach? It lost the right to buy a major league franchise at its fair market value (at the time, roughly \$10–\$12 million). Since the market value reflects expectations about the future earnings, the value of that right would be zero. This is a straightforward application of the efficient market approach to asset valuation.

The claimed lost profits from the proposed developments on the peripheral lands were disallowed because of a second condition, the so-called "roadway condition."

> At the virtual end of plaintiffs' case, the trial judge ruled that it would be necessary for plaintiffs to prove some kind of "contractual" obligation on the State to effect the highway improvements or some kind of similar "obligation" on the part of the State to accomplish those improvements if the dome had been built. At that late date, the lower court's ruling was that without direct proof of such a "contractual" obligation on the State, the jury would not be permitted to consider the relevant facts and circumstances from which the determination could be made that if the County had constructed the dome and related access roadways the State would have completed the additional highway improvements it was working on until the breach. (Pl. Brief Appellate I, 10–11)

With no direct proof that the roadways would be built, one could not conclude that the improvements would have been made. The trial judge, therefore, disallowed all the lost profits from the proposed developments. Again, this misses the point. The problem with the lost-profit projections is not the uncertainty that the roadways would be built. Rather, the problem is another variation on the efficient market story told above. To build and operate a theme park would require a stream of expenditures over the twenty years. We have to take into account the opportunity cost of that investment when projecting the future profits. Thus, after the breach, the plaintiff could have taken the same dollars that it would have invested in the theme park and invested them anywhere else. There is no reason to believe that the expected returns on investment in this project would exceed the returns on the next best use of those dollars. So, the expected value of the future stream of profits, taking into account the cost of capital, is zero. Again, there should be no recovery. If this sounds odd, consider a simple illustration. Suppose you have the right to buy 100 shares of IBM at the market price. If you are prevented from buying the shares, you still have the money which you can use to buy shares of another company. The expected returns on the IBM shares are the same as the expected returns of your next best alternative; therefore, you have suffered no loss. The question that should have been asked is not "would a particular investment be profitable?" but rather "would this investment have been more profitable than the next best investment alternative?" The market gave a clear answer. Despite the plaintiff expert's claim that the lost profits projections were "splendid" and "unusually conservative," Cottrell was unable to find funding.

Some claims did survive. The jury gave a positive response to the following question on the Verdict Sheet:

> Did the plaintiff Kenford agree to pay Edward H. Cottrell interest on advances and loans made by Mr. Cottrell at the annual rate of 1% above prime? ...
>
> Was such interest charge reasonably incurred in reliance upon the resolution of the Erie County legislature or the contract with the County or in mitigation of damages resulting from the breach of the contract?

Apparently, Cottrell continued to refinance the peripheral properties at the prime rate plus 1 percent up to the time of the trial. I would think that mitigation would have required selling the property at some point. If the property had been sold, the reliance damages should have been the difference between the acquisition price and the market price of the land without the domed stadium. The defendant's expert witness claimed that the average purchase price was $3,100 per acre and the average value of the unimproved land was $1,100 per acre. (Def. Brief Appeals II, 28–29) If that is correct, the reliance damages as of the time of the breach, or when it became clear that Cottrell could not effectively mitigate by finding alternative financing, would have been less than $400,000. In any event, the jury dutifully filled out the Verdict Sheet with the interest paid by Kenford each year coming to a total of $6,160,030.46. The judge found some minor error in the jury's award for reliance and mitigation and awarded Kenford the amount it had demanded, $6,762,645.63. (Def. Brief, Appellate I, 2)

Of greater significance were two other findings. The judge, a former plaintiff's personal injury lawyer, framed the questions in terms of proximate cause. The jury concluded that the breach was "a direct and proximate cause" of lost profits on the management contract and that there was "a rational basis upon which to compute loss of profits." The jury found that lost profits from the expected management contract were $28,190,749, roughly half of what Kenford had asked for. It also found that the breach was the proximate cause of the lost appreciation on the value of the peripheral lands, an additional $18,915,638. After adjustments for present value and pre-judgment interest, the court awarded $61,923,109.63 plus interest. Both sides appealed.

ROUND TWO

On the first trip to the Appellate Division, the trial court's refusal to send the claims to the jury was affirmed. While invoking the aforementioned conditions, the court put weight on the speculative nature of the claim and the possibility that the projects might not be profitable:

> Application of these rules to the instant case leads to the inescapable conclusion that the trial court properly refused to submit to the jury Kenford's claims pertaining to the peripheral land development and the baseball franchise. Although it was known that Kenford would try to buy a baseball franchise and would try to develop the land surrounding the stadium, it was by no means certain that Kenford would have been successful in doing so or that these enterprises would have thrived. Not all business ventures prove to be profitmaking. Moreover, although Cottrell had ideas for developing the peripheral land, these plans were by no means certain as of August 8, 1969. We know of no precedent for holding a defendant liable for profits lost on collateral matters that are as remote and undeveloped as the plans involved herein. The office buildings, golf course, and theme park for which plaintiff now seeks lost profits were nothing more than visions at the time the parties entered into the contract. No specific plans had been drawn for any of these ventures. The proposed baseball franchise was equally speculative. It was by no means certain that Cottrell would have been able to purchase a baseball franchise since such a purchase would have required approval of a percentage of league owners. Moreover, it is completely speculative to say that the franchise would have been a profitable one. (Appellate I, 136)

The court trimmed the remedy in two respects. The management contract profits were disallowed in entirety and the land appreciation claim was scaled back. I will come to the land appreciation question shortly, but first, let's consider the management contract. Unlike the breached contract, the management contract, which was adopted at the same time, was a detailed document including default and termination clauses.

Because the management contract would have been a new business, the court confronted a hurdle – New York had been characterized as having a per se rule regarding the nonrecoverability of lost profits for a new business. The court concluded that this was not a per se rule, but only that "as an evidentiary matter a new business would almost never be able to establish sufficient proof to recover lost profits." It cited *Perma Research & Devel. Co. v. Singer Co.*, a federal decision purporting to interpret New York law, which converted the recoverability rule into a rule of evidence. The new business would have "to establish some rational basis on which to calculate lost profits." (140) The court concluded "that there is no per se rule precluding a new business from recovering lost profits and we adopt the test employed by the Second Circuit Court of Appeals in *Perma Research & Devel. Co. v. Singer Co.*" (141)

The court then applied the *Perma* rational basis test and concluded that Kenford had "failed to establish a rational basis upon which lost profits may be calculated." (141) To establish its lost profits on the management contract, Kenford's expert:

> prepared a series of projections based on the experience of other domed facilities as well as an analysis of the market in the Buffalo area. The expert opined that the facility would hold 10 professional football games a year, as well as 42 open time events including three consumer shows, six high school football games, five circuses and seven musical or entertainment events. The expert then developed an average ticket price per event, which was multiplied by his estimate of anticipated attendance. The expert also developed an approximation of what each person would spend on parking and concessions. These figures were then computed to arrive at an anticipated revenue stream. The expert also gave his opinion of what the expenses of running the operation would be. He used a flat figure for salaries and then estimated that other expenses, such as advertising and legal fees, would be a percentage of gross revenue. His projected expenses were then subtracted from his projected revenue to arrive at a before-tax net income figure. One sheet summarizing the foregoing information was prepared for each of the 20 years of the management contract. The expert's opinion of net profit for each year ranged from just under $1 million for the first year to over $4 million in the twentieth year. Based upon these projections of net income, the jury found lost profits totalling over $28 million, which the court reduced to $25.6 million after applying a formula to arrive at present value. (141–42)

The court concluded that, as a matter of law, this estimate was too conjectural and denied recovery. The method required guesses as to which events would take place over the twenty years, the attendance, the ticket price, the parking concessions, and the advertising and marketing costs. The court noted: "It is not inconceivable that [Kenford] could have ended up spending more promoting events than it took in as receipts." (143) The Court of Appeals came to the same conclusion in the next round but for a different reason. I will defer discussion of this element of the claimed damages until then.

Regarding the land appreciation, the Appellate Division majority stated: "There is no dispute that Kenford suffered a monetary loss in land appreciation as a result of defendant's breach of contract." (137) However, it rejected the methodology of Kenford's appraiser:

> Plaintiff's appraiser valued the land as of projected completion dates ranging from 1973 to 1979 and based his estimates on the assumption that the property was improved with the specific items that we now find speculative as a matter of law, i.e., theme park, office buildings, and golf course. Plaintiff should have produced appraisal testimony indicating what the land would have been worth as raw acreage immediately following construction of the stadium. Any further appreciation to the land resulting from theme parks and the like makes the evidence of value too speculative to permit recovery. (Appellate I, 138)

The appropriate measure, said the majority, was the difference in price between the value of the land sans dome and its value with the dome, but as raw, undeveloped acreage. It ordered retrial on the sole issue of the lost appreciation of the land value. The dissent would simply have disallowed the claim. The damages were disproportionate and the County would never have agreed to them. It recognized that the tacit agreement test was "now largely out of favor," but it proceeded to apply it:

> One must also assume that if the county officials had been advised in August of 1969 that the county was then considered to be the only potential funding source for the project and that it might in the future be held accountable as such, the county would never have agreed to the contract without a clause excluding claims for loss of profits and consequential damages. (148)

> We must assume that the county, if there had been the slightest hint of the allocation of risks which plaintiffs now seek to impose, would either never have signed the Kenford contract or would, through its attorneys, have insisted on a contract appropriate for a governmental entity with proper clauses excluding claims for consequential damages and loss of profit. (152)

The land value claim should be rejected in its entirety, claimed the dissent, either because the loss would not have been in the County's contemplation or "in the interest of justice 'in order to avoid disproportionate compensation.'" (155, citing Restatement (Second) Contracts § 351 (3) Comment f)

ROUND THREE

While the land valuation issue was remanded to the jury, the rejection of the management contract damages went up for appeal. The Court of Appeals agreed with the result, although it differed in its rationale. It based the rejection on three arguments. First, it reprised *Globe*. Second, it reasserted the per se rule against compensating for lost profits of a new business. Third, despite effusive praise for the efforts of the expert witnesses, it found their conclusions too speculative. After dealing with the first two arguments, I will show why that praise was misplaced.

In reprising *Globe*, the court said that there was no proof that the County had assumed liability for the loss of profits over a twenty-year period. The losses were not within the contemplation of the parties at the time of execution or at the time of the breach. "In the absence of any provision for such an eventuality, the commonsense rule to apply is to consider what the parties would have concluded had they considered the subject. The evidence here fails to demonstrate that liability for loss of profits over the length of the contract would have been in the contemplation of the parties at the relevant times." (262) This would be a powerful argument if the claim were for consequential damages, but the management contract was the County's payment to Kenford for the "donated" land. I will come back to that when considering the court's third argument.

Second, while the Appellate Division had rejected the claim by invoking the "rational basis" test for a new business, the Court of Appeals reached the same conclusion but rejected that test, instead, reasserting the per se rule. "It is our view that the record in this case demonstrates the efficacy of the principles set forth by this court in *Cramer v. Grand Rapids Show Case Co.* principles to which we continue to adhere. In so doing, we specifically reject the 'rational basis' test enunciated in *Perma Research & Dev. Co. v. Singer Co.*, and adopted by the Appellate Division." (263) New York is one of the small minority that holds that a new business that has not yet begun to operate cannot recover projected lost profits. Indeed, the Dunn treatise claims that *Kenford* "may be the only modern authority rejecting the rational basis test." (2005, 429, § 5.6) As Judge Posner asserted in a later case: "The rule doesn't work because it manages to be at once vague and arbitrary. One reason is that the facts that it makes determinative, 'new,' 'business,' and 'profits,' are not facts, but rather are the conclusions of a reasoning process that is based on the rationale for the rule and that as a result turns the rule into an implicit standard." (*MindGames, Inc. v. Western Pub. Co., Inc.* (657))

Posner is surely correct. The relevant question is not the newness of the business. The key point is that the plaintiff was to make an investment (or series of investments) and, as before, the opportunity cost of those dollars would have to be considered. For some new businesses, the efficient market hypothesis means that there would be no lost profits – the dollars saved by not entering into the business would be as productive, in expectation, as the dollars that would have gone into the new business. For some other new businesses, however, that would not be the case. In *Perma*, for example, the claimed damages were for royalty payments that, it was claimed, would have been forthcoming had the defendant utilized the patents. The plaintiff did not have to make any additional expenditures, so there would have been some royalty payments and the losses would have been positive, even if the magnitude was too speculative.

Third, the court found the estimate to be too speculative. It first went out of its way to praise the expert's method:

> We note the procedure for computing damages selected by [Kenford] was in accord with contemporary economic theory and was presented through the testimony of recognized experts … . The quantity of proof is massive and, unquestionably, represents business and industry's most advanced and sophisticated method for predicting the probable results of contemplated projects. (Appeals I, 261–62)

However, this was not enough: "Quite simply, the multitude of assumptions required to establish projections of profitability over the life of this contract require speculation and conjecture, making it beyond the capability of even the most sophisticated procedures to satisfy the legal requirements of proof with reasonable certainty." (Appeals I, 262) Professor Eisenberg questioned the court's result: "It might be thought that massive proof that 'unquestionably … represents … [the] most advanced and sophisticated method for predicting the probable results of' a business project would have sufficed." (Eisenberg, 1998, 155) Professor Eisenberg was misled by the court's praise of the experts' sophistication. Rather than being "advanced and sophisticated," the damage calculations were all smoke and mirrors.

The court was asking the wrong question. The management contract was the consideration for the donated land. To illustrate the problem, suppose that instead, the consideration had been cash. Then, if the County had rejected the transaction, the damages would have been the difference between the cash price at the time of the breach and the value of the donated land. The only difference here is that the consideration was not cash, but a future contract, the value of which had to be determined. The land value was roughly $200,000. How much more than that would someone pay for the right to that management contract if the stadium had been built? The $58 million figure proffered by the expert for the value of the management contract bore no relationship to reality – it was determined by the same methodology that yielded an estimate of more than $140 million for the privilege to buy a baseball franchise at its fair market value. Was the value greater than the value of the 178 acres? Perhaps. Valuation of the contract then would have been difficult and today it is not possible. Rejecting the measure could be justified on the ground that the court did use (too speculative) or on the one it didn't use (the plaintiffs did not ask the right question). For my purposes in this chapter – considering the tacit assumption approach to consequential damages – the proper disposition of this claim does not matter.

ROUND FOUR

Not much happened at the next stage. At the retrial, the plaintiff's expert opined that the lost appreciation on the peripheral lands was about $14 million. The jury awarded $6.5 million. It did not say how it had come to this valuation. The Appellate Division did not have to weigh the merits of the expert's method since the jury's determination suggested that it had not adopted the expert's measure. It therefore approved the finding. The two members of the panel, who had dissented in the previous round, concurred on the grounds that this was the law of the case.

ROUND FIVE

In the final round, the remaining issue was what to do with the lost appreciation of the peripheral lands. There can be little doubt that both parties anticipated (or contemplated, if you prefer) that had the domed stadium been built, the peripheral lands would have increased in value. The appellate court opinions forwarded two different interpretations of foreseeability. Was the loss contemplated (majority) and had the defendant assumed responsibility for the risk (dissent)? The County's position, the tacit assumption, was articulated in its Reply Brief:

> It is *not* the County's argument … that Kenford could recover its claimed damages only if it proved that the County had *in fact* contemplated or foreseen those damages and had *in fact* agreed to be liable for them. Rather … under *Hadley* and subsequent decisions a plaintiff can recover if it can show that the breaching party had knowledge of the particular circumstances which would give rise to the purported lost benefit and, on an *objective* level, can be held to have promised to assume that loss in the event of a breach. This is the meaning of the requirement that special damages must be within the "contemplation" of the parties. (10–11, emphasis in original)

The Court of Appeals agreed:

> In the case before us, it is beyond dispute that at the time the contract was executed, all parties thereto harbored an expectation and anticipation that the proposed domed stadium facility would bring about an economic boom in the County and would result in increased land values and increased property taxes. … We cannot conclude, however, that this hope or expectation of increased property values and taxes necessarily or logically leads to the conclusion that the parties contemplated that the County would assume liability for Kenford's loss of anticipated appreciation in the value of its peripheral lands if the stadium were not built. … Indeed, the provisions in the contract providing remedy for a default do not suggest or provide for such a heavy responsibility on the part of the County. In the absence of any provision for such an eventuality, *the commonsense rule to apply is to consider what the parties would have concluded had they considered the subject.* (Appeals II, 319–20, emphasis in original)

The reference to "provisions in the contract" is a bit odd, I should note, since there were no such provisions. Kenford could not presume, the court continued, that it would receive all of its anticipated gains with or without a stadium:

> Undoubtedly, Kenford purchased the peripheral lands in question with the hope of benefiting from the expected appreciation in the value of those lands once the stadium was completed and became operational. In doing so, Kenford voluntarily and knowingly assumed the risk that, if the stadium were not built, its expectations of financial gain would be unrealized. There is no indication that either Kenford or the County reasonably contemplated at the time of the contract that this risk was assumed, either wholly or partially, by the County. To hold otherwise would lead to the irrational conclusion that the County, in addition to promising to build the domed stadium, provided a guarantee that if for any reason the stadium were not built, Kenford would still receive all the hoped for financial benefits from the peripheral lands it anticipated to receive upon the completion of the stadium. According to Kenford's version of the facts, Kenford was to realize all of its anticipated gains with or without the stadium. Clearly, such a result is illogical and without any basis whatsoever in the record. (Kenford Appeals II, 321)

The peculiar structure of the contract (the site was a "gift") and the incompetent contract design complicate application of the assumption of the risk test. Had the transaction taken a more normal form – purchase or condemnation – the problem would have been more straightforward. There would be no compensation for changes in the value of peripheral property, whether owned by the condemnee or others. Incidentally, the contract did note that if more land for the stadium project was needed, the County would "proceed to acquire by purchase, condemnation, or otherwise." Had the County drafted a proper contract, there would have been no issue. Government contracts often include a termination for convenience clause. At the least, the contract should have included a clause making performance contingent upon the availability of financing. Either clause would have meant that the failure to go forward with the project was just the exercise of its contractual right and not a breach.

How, then, should the court have interpreted the contractual silence? Two very different versions of the completeness of the written contract emerged. The dissent in *Appellate I* emphasized the limited content of the *five-page* agreement, implying that not much thought had gone into the contract. Kenford, on the other hand, emphasized the extensive negotiation that went into producing a *nineteen-page* contract. The difference was the additional fourteen pages of the appended management agreement:

> Where, as here, the Contract is not only explicit and unambiguous, but also the product of intensive arm's length negotiation involving the parties and their attorneys, which result in a non-standard agreement, the prohibition against judicial re-writing of the contract is most vigorously applied. …
>
> The Contract consists of nineteen pages of carefully worded non-form language negotiated during more than seven weeks of intensive bargaining, following weeks of previous negotiations with the Legislature. Being the product of the most searing public scrutiny ever known in Erie County, it fully sets forth the duties and obligations of each of the Contract parties. …
>
> It is against this background of the parties' thorough consideration of every possibility and contingency that the defendants' counsel make their manifestly and inherently preposterous litigation claim that the defendants (but not the plaintiffs) intended, but forgot, to include in the Contract claimed conditions to performance. (Pl. Brief, Appeals I, 34–35)

Would it have been reasonable for the County to guarantee the appreciation of the peripheral lands? The court said it would be both "irrational" and "illogical" to presume that it had done so. While I think that is correct, it does smack of proof by adjective. The remedy for breach was in reality a Band-Aid for a botched deal. As the court noted, "the commonsense rule to apply is to consider what the parties would have concluded had they considered the subject." Had the parties dealt with this contingency in their agreement, as they should have, the County's liability would almost certainly have been a modest amount, perhaps zero. Unfortunately, they failed to do so and left the problem to the court to determine how reasonable parties would have priced the County's termination option.

DENOUEMENT

And so it came to pass that Kenford was awarded an amount labeled reliance damages. After adjusting for post-judgment interest the county paid about $10.2 million. To put that number in perspective, at the time of the breach, had Kenford invested about $1 million in instruments paying at prime rate plus 1 percent (allegedly Cottrell's borrowing rate), by 1989 that would have had a value of about $8 million. Judge Hofheinz borrowed at a floating rate of prime-plus-four (Ray (1979, 509)); at that rate, one million dollars in 1970 would have grown to well over $10 million by 1989. That ended the litigation for the County, but not for Kenford. Cottrell was not happy with the outcome and paid his lawyers only $1 million rather than their contingent fee (which Finnerty believes was one-third). The lawyers sued him and he countersued, claiming that they had committed malpractice by, among other things, not informing him of the new business rule. The suit was settled in 1994. Cottrell faced another claim, this one from Judge Hofheinz's widow (the Judge died in 1982 about one year before the first trial). Mary Frances Hofheinz had paid $350,000 for the team of experts and made additional loans to Cottrell of over $800,000 over the course of the litigation. She filed a suit for $1.4 million in November 1989. (Gryta) The results of both claims are not available. Cottrell died in February 1995, presumably concluding all the Kenford litigation.

CONCLUDING REMARKS

The task of ascertaining damages in Kenford was exacerbated by the long lag between breach and resolution, the high inflation rate and interest rates, and the low statutory pre-judgment interest rates. The long gestation enabled the plaintiff's experts to incorporate post-breach facts when reckoning damages, deflecting attention from the basic question: what was lost at the time of the breach? When we recognize that future projected profits have to take into account the opportunity cost of the invested funds, most of Kenford's claimed consequential damages disappear. There would be no reason to believe that the particular investment of concern would be more attractive than the next best alternative. The claim for the appreciation of the peripheral lands posed the tacit assumption question squarely. The appreciation was obviously contemplated, but the issue was to whom the risk had been allocated. The court concluded, reasonably, that the risk was meant to be borne by the plaintiff.

Whether the tacit agreement approach will remain good law in New York is unclear. In *Bi-Economy Market, Inc. v. Harleysville Ins. Co. of New York*, the Court of Appeals cited *Kenford* with approval but intermixed quotations from it and the Restatement (the loss to be "foreseeable and probable"). It then argued that if an insurer delayed in paying out business interruption insurance, that could be a breach of its duty of good faith and fair dealing and that it could be liable for consequential damages. Specifically, it would be responsible for losses beyond the policy limits if the failure to pay promptly caused the firm to fail. The "claim for consequential damages including the demise of its business, was reasonably foreseeable and contemplated by the parties, and thus cannot be dismissed on summary judgment." (196) The dissent suggested how far this strayed from *Kenford*: "Can anyone seriously believe that the parties in these cases would, if they had 'considered the subject,' have contracted for the results reached here? Imagine the dialogue. Applicant for insurance: 'Suppose you refuse, in bad faith, to pay a claim. Will you agree to be liable for the consequences, including lost business, without regard to the policy limits?' Insurance company: 'Oh, sure. Sorry, we forgot to put that in the policy.'" (198) The majority opinion does not bode well for the future of the tacit assumption in New York.

As an aside, I should note that the per se rule regarding new business seems also to be in jeopardy. Only a few years after the last *Kenford* case had been decided, the Court of Appeals cited *Kenford* approvingly and then proceeded to misapply it. "Whether the claim involves an established business or a new business, however, the test remains the same, i.e., whether future profits can be calculated with reasonable certainty." (*Ashland Management Inc. v. Janien*, 404) It then held that the plaintiff could recover lost profits even though there was a new business. I have no problem with the conclusion that damages could be recovered, but it would have been much cleaner had the court conceded that it was reverting to the rational basis test that it had specifically rejected only a few years earlier.

In his *Globe* opinion, Holmes relied on English precedents, notably *Nettleship*. In England the tacit assumption approach had suffered a fate similar to *Globe*'s; the courts put ever more weight on contemplation, exemplified in the House of Lords discussion in *Heron II* of the various synonyms for "probable." The tacit assumption approach received new life in Lord Hoffmann's decision in *The Achilleas*. That case will be analysed in the next chapter.

10. *The Achilleas*: forsaking foreseeability

The House of Lords opinion in *The Achilleas* has generated a considerable amount of commentary. A Westlaw search yielded five pages worth of citations. Lawyers from various parts of the Commonwealth, and even the author of the opinion, have weighed in. (Hoffmann, 2010) It might perhaps be helpful to add to this burgeoning literature the perspective of an outsider – a Yank and non-lawyer.

The case provided a platform for a reassessment of *Hadley v. Baxendale*. The facts will be developed more fully below in Section V. The bare bones version is this. A charterer breached its contract by redelivering the ship nine days late. The owner had entered into a subsequent charter with Cargill for four months relying on the ship being returned on time. While the market rate when the Cargill fixture was set was substantially greater than the original charter rate, the rates had fallen by the time the ship had been redelivered. Cargill took advantage of the late delivery by rejecting the ship and then renegotiating its charter at the lower rate. The charterer claimed that the damages were the market rate for the nine days (roughly $158,000); the owner claimed that the damages were for the "loss of fixture," the difference between the two rates for the four months (more than $1.3 million). The issue as posed by all parties was whether the loss of fixture was "foreseeable" under the *Hadley v. Baxendale* standard. The majority arbitrators and the courts below the House of Lords said Yes. The Lords said No.

The *Hadley* rule typically has been stated in terms of foreseeability or remoteness. In *The Heron II*, the *Hadley* standard was framed in terms of the "requisite degree of probability of loss." Lord Reid put it in terms of consequences "not unlikely" to arise from the breach. "So the question for decision is whether a plaintiff can recover as damages for breach of contract a loss of a kind which the defendant, when he made the contract, ought to have realised was not unlikely to result from a breach of contract causing delay in delivery. I use the words 'not unlikely' as denoting a degree of probability considerably less than an even chance but nevertheless not very unusual and easily foreseeable." (382–83) As Lord Hoffmann said: "The *Heron II* contains a thesaurus of expressions which can be used to describe the necessary degree of probability, but no one has said that Lord Reid's test was wrong. It is in practice the one most frequently adopted." (Hoffmann (2010, 51)) Lord Hoffmann found this formulation unattractive: "The problem is the intellectual sleight of hand which is needed to arrive at that conclusion with the sole aid of the tools provided by *Hadley v. Baxendale* and *The Heron II.* It seems to me that the time has come to look for a broader principle which can explain not only the, so to speak, run of the mill cases like *Hadley v. Baxendale* but also the more puzzling cases like *The Achilleas.*" (54) In *The Achilleas*, he focused instead on the intentions of the parties – the "tacit assumption" formulation. "It seems to me logical to found liability for damages upon the intention of the parties (objectively ascertained) because all contractual liability is voluntarily undertaken." (*The Achilleas*, 12) While the Lords were unanimous in finding for the owner, there was less agreement on the rationale.

Pre-*The Achilleas*, the courts had been liberalizing the *Hadley* doctrine by expanding the reach of foreseeability. One Commonwealth court went so far as to conclude that the recent formulation "would apparently mean that *Hadley v. Baxendale* was wrongly decided." (*McElroy Milne v. Commercial Elecs., Ltd.*, 42–43) The foreseeability of an event shows up in another corner of contract law – the excuse doctrines of impossibility and frustration. There, ironically, the courts have taken a different tack, finding things unforeseeable that the parties, or similarly situated parties, have in fact contracted about. For example, in *Krell v. Henry*, Vaughan Williams, LJ said "I think it cannot reasonably be supposed to have been in the contemplation of the contracting parties when the contract was made, that the coronation would not be held on the proclaimed days …" (750) The possibility that a 60-year-old overweight smoker might not make it to the coronation was not so far-fetched. Was it foreseeable? In fact, as I show in Chapter 11, it was foreseen by thousands who bought insurance policies and in a number of the contracts for viewing, even some that were subsequently litigated.

The Achilleas decisions are littered with references to remoteness and foreseeability. A count of variations on the two terms yields the following: For Clarke, J in the Commercial Court, there are 17 variations on "foresee" and 16 on "remote." For Rix, J in the Court of Appeal, the numbers were eight and 24, respectively. In the House of Lords the relative frequency reversed with 33 foresees and only 11 remotes. Their frequent invocation does not provide much guidance on how they should be applied. Lord Hoffmann emphasized the indeterminacy of the foreseeability standard. His critics have countered with the same complaint about the tacit assumption formulation. To give the notion some content,

Lord Hoffmann relied on the expectations of the relevant community and common sense. Buttressing this with a bit of theory can further narrow the range of indeterminacy. In particular, I will argue that Lord Reid's formulation of the *Hadley* rule in terms of "degree of probability" is unhelpful. Rather, the appropriate concerns are the ability of the respective parties to control the outcome and the reasonable expectations regarding the responsibilities of the two parties, as was developed in Chapter 8.

Applying the analysis to the problem in *The Achilleas* requires a bit of background. Before considering *The Achilleas* decisions, I will describe the basic features of a time charter, in particular, the last voyage problem. The various solutions to the last voyage problem – by drafters of time charters and arbitrators, as well as the English courts – will then be covered.

I. TIME CHARTERS

In a time charter, a charterer has the right to use a ship for a period of time, say ten months. (For background on time charters, see Eder (2011) or Coghlin (2008).) If the charter simply states the period, the charterer would have reasonable leeway, perhaps an additional ten or fifteen days. If, however, the charter makes the extra time period explicit – for example, ten months plus or minus fifteen days – then there would be no further leeway. If redelivery were to take place even one hour late, the charterer would be in breach. The ship in a time charter remains in the control of the owner. Captain and crew are supplied by the owner. The captain, subject to a few exceptions, must obey the orders of the charterer regarding the employment of the vessel. The charterer proposes voyages and in the normal course of things, the owner acquiesces. (Coghlin, ch. 19) There are a number of standard form time charters from which the parties can choose and they can vary the forms by adding additional language. The various charters have the same basic structure, but they do differ on some significant terms. In particular, as we shall see, there are significant differences in the treatment of the last voyage.

The owner could refuse a proposed voyage on certain grounds, one being that the proposed voyage would be dangerous. More relevant to *The Achilleas* context is "the last voyage" problem. If the proposed voyage were one that was expected to be completed within the time period, it would be *legitimate*. If, for reasons beyond the control of the parties, the vessel were redelivered late, the charterer would be in breach – liability would be no fault. If the owner were to refuse a legitimate voyage, it would be in breach of the agreement and subject to damages – the charterer's expected lost profits from that voyage. If, however, the proposed voyage could not be completed in the charter period, the voyage would be *illegitimate* and the owner could refuse. Lord Mustill described the situation in *The Gregos*:

> Where the charterparty is for a period of time rather than a voyage, and the remuneration is calculated according to the time used rather than the service performed, the risk of delay is primarily on the charterer. For the shipowner, so long as he commits no breach and nothing puts the ship off-hire, his right to remuneration is unaffected by a disturbance of the charterer's plans. It is for the latter to choose between cautious planning, which may leave gaps between employments, and bolder scheduling with the risk of setting aims which cannot be realised in practice.
>
> This distribution of risk holds good during for most of the chartered service. As the time for redelivery approaches things become more complicated. (The word "redelivery" is inaccurate, but it is convenient, and I will use it.) If the market is rising, the charterer wants to have the use of the vessel at the chartered rate for as long as possible. Conversely, the shipowner must think ahead to the next employment, and if as is common he has made a forward fixture he will be in difficulties if the vessel is retained by the charterer longer than had been foreseen. This conflict of interest becomes particularly acute when there is time left for only one more voyage before the expiry of the charter, and disputes may arise if the charterer orders the ship to perform a service which the shipowner believes will extend beyond the date fixed for redelivery. (*The Gregos*, 1468–69)

If the proposed voyage were illegitimate, the owner could refuse to perform. Or, it could choose to perform, perhaps negotiating new terms for the last voyage. If the owner knew whether the proposed voyage would be deemed legitimate, the decision would be easy. However, the line between the legitimate and illegitimate is a fuzzy one. Legitimacy is only determined afterwards by arbitrators. If the owner were to declare the voyage illegitimate and the arbitrators held otherwise, it would be liable for damages.

It is useful to characterize the time charter by focusing on the choices open to the owner when the charterer proposes a new voyage. In effect, the owner has a series of nested options. It could simply treat the voyage as legitimate; the charterer would be allowed to continue under the existing terms and the owner would have no right to reject the voyage or to renegotiate the terms. Alternatively, the owner could claim that the proposed voyage was illegitimate. That would give it an option – the right to refuse to undertake the voyage. The price of that option would be a function of the risk that the arbitrators would disagree and hold it liable for the charterer's loss. That "price" would be high if the owner declared the voyage illegitimate at a very early stage of the charter. The price would be near zero if the proposed voyage would clearly exceed the charter period. While the owner would have the right to refuse an illegitimate voyage, it could instead choose to allow the voyage. Unlike the case of the legitimate voyage, the owner could insist upon bargaining over the terms of the new voyage. The terms could be contingent upon a holding that the voyage was illegitimate, but that need not be necessary. The "without prejudice" agreement in *The Gregos* (see below) is an illustration. At the time the new agreement is negotiated, the terms would reflect the opportunity cost of the last voyage. The owner would know the current market conditions and the price would reflect the availability and price of a new fixture (adjusted for the possibility that the arbitrators would conclude that the voyage was legitimate). The time charter, therefore, establishes a set of terms that apply to all legitimate voyages. The charter rate would reflect information available to the parties at the formation stage. For an illegitimate voyage, the owner can incorporate current information, either by terminating the charter and entering into a new fixture with someone else or by negotiating a new rate for the charterer's last voyage.

The parties might choose to substitute an objective test for a subjective reasonableness standard, thereby avoiding the fact-intensive question of legitimacy. The legitimate/illegitimate distinction can be, and has been, supplanted in some standard forms, but not others. The agreement could approve any voyage that commenced before the termination date – all last voyages would be legitimate and the charter terms would apply. This is how the American arbitrators interpreted the Texacotime 2 form in *The Pacific Sun*. The disputed clause modified the clause (#3) that determined the length of the voyage:

> Notwithstanding the provisions of Clause 3 hereof, should the Vessel be upon a voyage at expiry of the period of this charter, Charterer shall have the use of the Vessel at the same rate and conditions for such extended time as may be necessary for the completion of the round voyage on which she is engaged until her return to a port of redelivery as provided by the Charter. (831)

The arbitrators interpreted this to mean that the charterer could propose a voyage one day before the time charter would expire and the owner would have to perform. The English courts agreed with this interpretation of a similar clause in the Shelltime 3 charter in *The World Symphony*. The *Pacific Sun* arbitrators noted that the Texacotime 2 and Shelltime 3 charters contained similar language, while others did not. Indeed, the

Shelltime 4 charter was reworded and has been interpreted as applying to legitimate voyages only. (*The Ambor*)

Alternatively, the parties could treat all overruns as a breach, setting a liquidated damage formula that applied regardless of the timing of the decision to embark on the last voyage. The charter in *The Paragon* (discussed below) took this approach, although the court ultimately rejected the attempt, invoking the penalty clause doctrine. Thus, at the time of the initial contract, the parties have an incentive to balance the benefits of being able to fine-tune the terms of a last voyage against the costs of assessing legitimacy. However, the ability to balance will be skewed by the judicial treatment of these alternatives.

In charter forms that did recognize the distinction between the legitimate and illegitimate, the treatment of overruns for legitimate voyages differed. The Intertanktime 80 charter used the charter rate for any late redelivery; that is, late redelivery would not be a breach. Other charters, for example, the Baltime charter, on the other hand, set the rate for late redelivery for a legitimate voyage at the market rate if higher than the charter rate. (*The Pacific Sun*, 834–35) So the standard forms give a variety of solutions to the last voyage problem. Given that it is a problem in all time charters, I find it remarkable that the drafters of the standard forms have chosen opaque language to deal with the problem; I will elaborate on this point in the following section.

II. THE LAST VOYAGE REMEDY

The default rule, which was promulgated in *The Peonia*, is to treat the late redelivery as a breach. In *The Peonia*, the parties used a New York Produce Exchange form. The termination date for the charter was about June 11, 1988. The charterer proposed a last voyage that would commence in May and would not be completed until July 19 at the earliest. The owner refused, claiming that this would be an illegitimate voyage. All parties agreed that it would have been illegitimate, unless language in the time charter said otherwise. The charterer claimed that it did and the arbitrators agreed. The decision hinged on interpretation of a clause which read: "The said owners agree to let and the said charterers agree to hire the said vessel from the time of delivery for about minimum ten months' maximum twelve months' time charter, exact duration in charterers' option. Charterers have *further option to complete the last voyage* …" The clause was not on the standard form, a fact the court neglected to mention. The NYPE form made no mention of the last voyage problem. (The same form was used in *The Achilleas*.) The arbitrators interpreted the clause to mean that the charterer would have the right to order a voyage if it *commenced* before the termination date – the expected termination date would be irrelevant. In effect, they treated the language the same as the *Pacific Sun/World Symphony* interpretation of the Shelltime 3 clause.

That strikes me as a plausible interpretation, but the judges disagreed. To give meaning to the notion that the charterer would have a "further option," they reasoned, it was necessary to first determine the default rule – further from what? After a somewhat convoluted tour of the case law, Lord Bingham concluded that the default rule concerned a *legitimate* voyage in which redelivery was late; late delivery would be a breach of contract entitling the owner to damages. For a legitimate voyage absent this clause, payment of hire would be due at the contract price until the time of redelivery and damages for delay would be the difference between the contract and market price, if the market price were greater. The "further option," then, would mean that the parties had contracted out of the default rule for a legitimate last voyage. So, the clause did not, as Saville, J characterized the arbitrator's argument, have "the effect of making that legitimate which would otherwise be illegitimate." (102) Instead, it simply opted out of the default remedy for delayed redelivery following a legitimate last voyage; there would be no breach for late delivery and therefore no damages.

With that interpretation, the question of the legitimacy of the voyage was then on the table. The court concluded that the voyage at question was illegitimate and, since the owner's refusal to perform was proper, it would not be liable to the charterer for the lost profits of the voyage-that-wasn't. The default rule for damages following a legitimate voyage, the starting point in *The Achilleas*, emerged as a byproduct of the owner's refusal to undertake an illegitimate voyage. Ironically, Lord Bingham rejected the remedy proposed by Lord Denning in *The Democritos* precisely because it was proffered in a case that also involved an illegitimate voyage. Denning said: "Now if the vessel was sent on a legitimate voyage and was delayed in getting to her destination, being a delay for which neither party was responsible, the charter continues until the end of the voyage: and freight is only payable at the charter rate." (153) That is, Lord Denning's default rule was that late redelivery following a legitimate voyage was not a breach. But, said Lord Bingham: "It must, however, be doubted whether Lords Justices Lawton and Bridge, giving unreserved judgments in an appeal involving a clearly illegitimate last voyage, intended to lay down any rule of law on a charterer's liability of failing to redeliver by the final terminal date on a legitimate last voyage." (115) No such doubts have followed Lord Bingham's decision, despite its vulnerability to the same objection.

In *The Gregos*, the owner did accede to undertake a voyage it believed illegitimate. However, prior to the last voyage the parties entered into a "without prejudice" agreement. If the ship were redelivered late and if the voyage were found to be illegitimate, then the charterers would pay for the entire last voyage at the current (higher) freight rate plus a notional ballast bonus. Redelivery was eight days late. The charterers claimed that the damages for that brief delay would have been roughly $35,000. The owner's claim was for the amount specified in the without prejudice agreement, roughly $300,000. The House of Lords found for the owners. The Lords did not put it quite this way. In essence they held that at the time the last voyage was being contemplated, the owners had the option to refuse to undertake an illegitimate voyage; the without prejudice agreement enabled the parties to contract for the specific voyage, taking into account the circumstances existing at that time. By finding the voyage to be illegitimate, the Lords found that the charterer had repudiated and that a new contract had been formed. If the voyage was characterized as legitimate, then, I believe, the charterer would not have been found to have repudiated and the without prejudice agreement would not have come into play – damages would have been limited to the $35,000 for the eight-day overrun.

The Gregos dealt with a contractual solution to the illegitimacy problem at the time the last voyage was to begin. Alternatively, the issue could have been dealt with in the initial charterparty, as was the case in *The Paragon*. The parties entered into a charter months after the arbitrators' decision in *The Achilleas* and the decision was rendered months after the House of Lords reversed it. So, at the time they entered into the time charter, it would have been reasonable for the parties to believe that the default rule would have subjected the charterer to loss-of-fixture damages for a late redelivery. Redelivery was late and the owner attempted to enforce a clause that set a formula for damages. Blair, J held that the clause was an unenforceable penalty. The controversial clause provided as follows:

> The Charterers hereby undertake the obligation/responsibility to make thorough investigations and every arrangement in order to ensure that the last voyage of this Charter will in no way exceed the maximum period under this Charter Party. If, however, Charterers fail to comply with this obligation and the last voyage will exceed the maximum period, should the market rise above the Charter Party rate in the meantime, it is hereby agreed that the charter hire will be adjusted to reflect the prevailing market level from the 30th day prior

> to the maximum period [d]ate until actual redelivery of the vessel to the Owners. (468)

That is, the damage remedy set both a price formula and a time period. The price would be for the market-contract differential one month prior to the termination date, and the time period would begin one month before the termination date. Like the Shelltime 3 clause, this clause would render the distinction between legitimate and illegitimate voyages irrelevant. Unlike that clause, however, a late redelivery would constitute a breach and the consequences could be substantial. Given that *The Achilleas* arbitrators had just found damages in excess of $1,000,000 for a brief delay in redelivery following a legitimate voyage, it would not have been unreasonable for the parties to opt for formulaic damages. The parties would avoid litigating the legitimacy question and the owner would be shielded from the risk of having to pay lost profits damages from refusing a last voyage request that arbitrators might determine was legitimate. It is unclear whether the owner would have had the right to refuse to undertake a voyage that it perceived to be illegitimate.

The arbitrators and Blair, J held that the clause should apply only to illegitimate voyages. Since the penalty would have been almost $500,000 even if the redelivery were only one hour late, they regarded this as unconscionable and concluded therefore that the clause was a penalty, not "a genuine pre-estimate of damage." (467) Since the charter was entered into shortly after the arbitrators' decision in *The Achilleas*, the possibility that a very short overrun could give rise to very large damages for a lost fixture should have been a consideration. My concern is not with the merits of the decision. I confess to being surprised and disappointed in learning that the English treatment of penalty clauses is no better than the American. But that can be left for another day. Rather, the case provides another illustration of how parties might cope with the joint perils of the sea and the litigation process. The parties could deal with the consequences of a last voyage either ex ante or ex post. In this instance (and in forms like the Shelltime 3), they could do so at the time of contracting; or, as in *The Gregos*, they could wait until the time of the last voyage to negotiate the consequences of late delivery with current information on the state of the charter market.

The Shelltime 3 form was revised in 1984. The wording of the last voyage clause was modified:

> If at the time this charter would otherwise terminate in accordance with Clause 4 the vessel is on a ballast voyage to a port of redelivery or is upon a laden voyage, Charterers shall continue to have the use of the vessel at the same rate and conditions as stand herein for as long as necessary to complete

> such ballast voyage, or to complete such laden voyage and return to a port of redelivery as provided by this charter, as the case may be. (*The Ambor*, 139)

Did that change the meaning? In *The Ambor*, Peter Gross QC, sitting as a deputy judge of the High Court, held that it did. He cited the conflicting writings of Mr. Bonnick, the principal draftsman of the Shelltime 4 form. In 1988, Bonnick wrote that "[t]his clause has been re-worded but the basic principles remain the same." However, in 1996, he wrote:

> The Final Voyage clause in Shelltime 3 [Clause 18] would permit the charterer to order the vessel on a voyage of a duration that could substantially overrun the charter period (The World Symphony ...). Unlike the clause in Shelltime 3, this Shelltime 4 Clause does not expressly override Clause 4 (Clause 3 in Shelltime 3) and therefore the charterer must not order the vessel to perform a voyage which would not reasonably permit the vessel to be redelivered punctually. If, however, the charterer gives a legitimate last voyage order and without fault on his part the vessel cannot be redelivered punctually, then he will not be in breach and the charter rate and conditions will apply to such extended service. (*The Ambor*, 144)

The difference between the two charter forms came down to the presence in Shelltime 3 of the "crucial words" in cl. 18, "notwithstanding the provisions of clause 3 hereof" and their non-appearance in Shelltime 4. The "crucial words" were invoked over twenty times in the opinion. One might be tempted to conclude that the interpretation of Shelltime 3 was a mistake and the revision simply clarified things. However, the Shelltime 3 form did not disappear from use. It was, for example, the chosen charter form in 2000 in *Kriti Akti*, sixteen years after the Shelltime 4 form had been introduced.

I confess that I remain mystified as to why the meaning of final voyage clauses should require nuanced interpretation of "crucial words" when simple words would do. These standard forms apply to thousands of transactions and the alternative approaches are easy enough to state. Either the last voyage clause applies only to legitimate voyages or it allows the charterer to commence any voyage during the charter period at the rate set in the charter. If it is to be limited to legitimate voyages only, the charter could continue after the redelivery date at the charter rate or it could continue at the market rate (if that is higher). Simple enough. *The Achilleas* added one more wrinkle. If redelivery following a legitimate voyage is late, could the owner get compensation for a lost fixture?

III. THE ACHILLEAS

Lord Hoffmann set out the basic facts clearly in his Edinburgh talk:

> The Achilleas was a 69,000 tonne bulk carrier, fixed under a time charter in January 2003 which had been extended in September 2003 at the rate of $16,750 a day for a further five to seven months at the charterers' option, the last date for redelivery being 2 May 2004. On 20 April 2004 the charterers gave notice of redelivery between 20 April and 2 May. Next day the owners fixed the vessel to another charterer, on a falling market, for four to six months at $39,500 a day. The last date for delivery to the new charterers was 8 May, which gave the owners six days clearance. Unfortunately, through no fault of the charterers, the vessel was delayed in port during her last voyage and was not redelivered until 11 May. That meant that, with the market still on the slide, the new charterers were entitled to cancel. However, as they still wanted the ship, they agreed on 5 May not to cancel in return for a reduction of the hire to $31,500 a day; in other words. 20% less than they had agreed two weeks earlier. (Hoffmann, 47–48)

All parties agreed that the last voyage was legitimate and that the delay was not the fault of either owner or charterer. As per *The Peonia*, the delay constituted a breach by the charterer and the issue was damages. The charterer claimed, again following *The Peonia*, damages would be the market rate for the eight-day overrun ($158,301.17) and the owner claimed damages were the loss of the Cargill fixture (the difference between the daily rates for the four-month period ($1,364.584.17)).

The majority arbitrators agreed with the owner, as did all the judges prior to the case being heard by the House of Lords. The owner's claim was not "too remote." That late delivery might result in the vessel missing the cancellation date for the next fixture was not unusual. It was something within the contemplation of the parties as a not unlikely result of the breach. The charterer emphasized the uncertainty of its exposure to the loss-of-fixture measure. "A charterer guilty only of a short late redelivery is not to be faced in law with uncapped loss of profit claims based on unknown contracts of unknown length made at unknown times." (*The Achilleas* (2007), 82)

What if the owner had entered into a multi-year charter? The minority arbitrator was concerned about that possibility: "The fundamental problem [is that] … it was difficult to see where a line was to be drawn" (*The Achilleas* (2007), 111) Rix, LJ rejected that argument:

> I can see that such a question might raise a problem on particular facts, but such problems of line-drawing are often inevitable in the law. … On our facts, however, I see no difficulty. The previous two periods of charter to the

> charterers … had both been of plus or minus 6 months: and the Cargill fixture was again of around this length, in fact a little shorter at 4 to 6 months. It appears to be within a standard length. Such a fixture was plainly "not unlikely". It may be, but I see no need to decide, that as a rule of thumb a charterer should not, without further knowledge, be held liable in such a situation for the loss of a new fixture of longer length than that which he had himself contracted for. If need be, and the market feels that such a question should be determined by contract, a standard form or even special provision could be agreed. But as a matter of principle, the claimant should not be kept out of any compensation because of an argument about the length of the new fixture: any more than the launderers in *Victoria Laundry* should be prevented from recovering any loss of profits because the particular dyeing contracts which formed one of their heads of loss were too special to form the basis of a calculation. It seems to me that the authoritative phrase "extravagant or unusual" is equal to the situation … . A contract at other than market prices, where the market price is relevant, is liable to be extravagant, and an unusual contract is likely to be outside the "usual course of things" which is the essential focus of the remoteness rule. (*The Achilleas* (2007), 112)

The upshot of the opinion was that charterers should know that owner's might have lined up their next fixture and that a late redelivery might result in cancellation by the next charterer. They also should know that charter market rates are volatile and that late redelivery could result in a loss of fixture. Although he did not mention this, time charter forms all include a cancellation clause – charterers know that if a vessel is not available by the cancellation date they have the right to walk away from the charter. They know this because the right to cancel is in this contract and every time charter they have ever entered into.

The cancellation clause in the NYPE 93 Form is typical:

> 16. **Delivery/Cancelling**
>
> If required by the Charterers, time shall not commence before ……………… ………………… and should the Vessel not be ready for delivery on or before ……………………………… but not later than ……………………… hours, the Charterers shall have the option of cancelling this Charter Party.
>
> *Extension of Cancelling*
>
> If the Owners warrant that, despite the exercise of due diligence by them, the Vessel will not be ready for delivery by the cancelling date, and provided the Owners are able to state with reasonable certainty the date on which the Vessel will be ready, they may, at the earliest seven days before the Vessel is expected to sail for the port or place of delivery, require the Charterers to declare whether or not they will cancel the Charter Party. Should the Charterers elect not to cancel, or should they fail to reply within two days or by the cancelling date, whichever shall first occur, then the seventh day after

> the expected date of readiness for delivery as notified by the Owners shall replace the original cancelling date. Should the Vessel be further delayed, the Owners shall be entitled to require further declarations of the Charterers in accordance with this Clause. (Coghlin (2008), Reproducing NYPE 93)

Rix, LJ concluded his opinion by asserting that denying recovery for loss of fixture would be uncommercial.

> Moreover, it seems to me that the rule for which [charterer] contends, namely that damages for late redelivery should be limited to the overrun period measure unless the owners can show that, at the time of contract, they had given their charterers special information of their follow-on fixture, is both undesirable and uncommercial. It is undesirable, because it puts the owners too much at the mercy of their charterers: who can happily drain the last drop and more of profit at a time of raised market rates, taking the risk of late redelivery, knowing that they will never have to pay their owners more than the current market rate for the overrun period, a rate which will never in truth properly reflect the value to the charterers of being able to fit in another spot voyage at the last moment. It is uncommercial, because, if it is demanded that the charterers need to know more than they already do in the ordinary course of events, when they already know that a new fixture, in all probability fixed at or around the time of redelivery, will follow on their own charter, then the demand is for something that cannot be provided. All that an owner will be able to tell his charterer in most cases is that he plans to fix his vessel anew at the time of redelivery. To which the charterer might well reply: "Well, I know that already! But don't expect that your telling me that is enough to put me on notice for the purpose of claiming loss of fixture damages if I redeliver the vessel late and you turn out to lose your fixture!" Such an answer, however, reflects the uncommerciality and error of the charterers' submission. (*The Achilleas* (2007), 119)

In a unanimous decision the House of Lords reversed. As most observers noted, there was not unanimity on the reason. For Lord Hoffmann, liability depended on the intention of the parties, objectively ascertained – the tacit assumption. "I think it is clear that they would have considered losses arising from the loss of the following fixture a type or kind of loss for which the charterer was not assuming responsibility." (*The Achilleas* 2008, 23) As he put it in his Edinburgh talk: "The question is: what obligation to make compensation for breach of contract would a reasonable observer understand the contracting party to have undertaken?" (55) He was joined by Lord Hope of Craighead, who went on to dispute Rix's contention regarding the commercial considerations:

> In my opinion the commercial considerations point the other way. … [a] party cannot be expected to assume responsibility for something that he cannot control and, because he does not know anything about it, cannot quantify. It is

> not enough for him to know in general and on open-ended terms that there is likely to be a follow-on fixture. … What he needs is some information that will enable him to assess the extent of any liability. The policy of the law is that effect should be given to the presumed intention of the parties. That is why the damages that are recoverable for breach of contract are limited to what happens in ordinary circumstances – in the great multitude of cases. (36)

They were joined by Lord Walker of Gestingthorpe who noted that lawyers and brokers would have assumed that liability for late redelivery would only be for the market rate for the period of overrun (70) and that what mattered was "the common intention of reasonable parties." (84)

Lord Rodger of Earlsferry and Baroness Hale relied on the orthodox approach holding that the extreme volatility in the market was the "unusual occurrence" that made the loss-of-fixture damages too remote. In his Edinburgh lecture, Lord Hoffmann pointed out that in *Jackson v. Royal Bank of Scotland*, the Lords held that the magnitude of the losses did not enter into the finding of liability; that would undermine the extreme volatility rationale. (Hoffmann, 51–53)

Note that the extreme volatility had little to do with the general question of whether loss-of-fixture damages should be allowed. Suppose an alternative scenario in which there was no change in the market price at the time of redelivery. Damages measured by the contract/market differential would be zero. But suppose that the new fixture was for seven months and was one percent below the original. Volatility is trivial; the probability that charter prices would change by that amount in the interim is high. The Rodger-Hale view of remoteness would seem to require a finding of liability. If redelivery were even one hour past the cancellation date on the new fixture, the liability would be for about twice the day rate. (If the day rate were $X, liability would be .01X*210.) If the price fell 20 percent (as it did in *The Achilleas*), then, rather than find damages of forty times the day rate, Rodger/Hale would presumably find no liability. The percentage decline defining the boundary between no liability and substantial damages would lie somewhere in between. Alternatively, they could argue that even though volatility in this particular case was low, volatility in general is high and there would therefore be no liability even in this case. Their opinion does not distinguish between actual volatility and potential volatility. They could, I suppose, argue that liability should be capped at a certain level of price change, but beyond that the damages would be too remote. That would be consistent with the distinction between normal lost profits (recoverable) and the exceptional good deal (not recoverable) in *Victoria Laundry*.

IV. THE *HADLEY* ANALYSIS

The variation in time charter treatment of the last voyage problem indicates that there is not a unique solution from which one could confidently derive a unique "tacit assumption." The range of solutions is, however, not without limit. For a legitimate last voyage, the loss-of-fixture measure falls outside those limits.

It is best to begin the discussion by recognizing an obvious point. Every time charter has a first and a last voyage. All have a cancellation clause that allows the charterer to cancel if the vessel is not timely delivered. Many, but not all, have a clause regarding the last voyage. *The Achilleas* only concerned a default rule when the parties neglected to include a last voyage clause. If the charter did include a last voyage clause, then that would preclude finding damages for a lost fixture. If we characterize foreseeability in terms of "contemplation," then, surely, the parties would be aware of the fact that there would be a potential last voyage problem, that the owner would want to enter into a subsequent charter, and that charter would give the next charterer the option to cancel if delivery were late. That a late redelivery might result in a loss of fixture would not be a surprise. If that variant of foreseeability were the relevant one, then the Lordships were wrong. But it is not.

Consider first the illegitimate last voyage. According to Scrutton, the default remedy is the contract-market differential for the period of the delay. (Eder (2011), 349) Foxton, one of the editors of Scrutton, argues that legitimacy should be irrelevant in determining damages:

> The last voyage in *The Achilleas* was legitimate. Would the conclusion have been different if the order to proceed to Quingdao had been illegitimate? The issue is not considered in the case, but the reasoning suggests that the answer is no: the lack of precedent, the difficulty of calculating the consequences of such a breach when the contract is made, the volatility of market conditions and the relevance of the dealings between the shipowner and the new charterer would not be changed by the illegitimacy of the last voyage. … It might also be thought unusual for the charterer to have assumed responsibility for a particular kind of loss following one type of breach leading to late redelivery, but not another which had exactly the same consequences. (Foxton (2008), 478)

The reasoning is dubious since it ignores the most salient difference between the legitimate and illegitimate voyages – whether the owner has a veto right. Whether Foxton is technically correct on the default rule for an illegitimate voyage is irrelevant since there is no reason for parties to ever have to fall back on the default rule. By declaring a voyage illegitimate the owner has, in effect, declared that future performance would require that the parties form a new contract. The owner could refuse the last voyage order or it could negotiate new terms that take into account the current market conditions. If it had a potentially lucrative fixture lined up, the negotiations would reflect the value of that fixture and the importance of the timing of the redelivery. The significant point is that for an illegitimate last voyage the owner has the opportunity to bargain, to set a new price and, if it so chose, to coordinate the terms of the last voyage with the next fixture.

For a legitimate last voyage, the charter rate is fixed for the duration when the parties enter into the charter agreement. Market conditions change over the course of the agreement and, as is often the case, there can be a substantial gap between the charter price and current market price. Recall that in *The Achilleas*, the charter rate was $16,750 a day and the market rate had risen to $39,500 by the time the last voyage began. Neither party has the right to terminate or to force a renegotiation. At the formation stage, the charterer has little knowledge about the future course of prices and no knowledge of the terms of any follow-on fixture. The charterer's ability to control the possibility of late redelivery is limited. By definition, the expected overrun for a legitimate last voyage is zero. However, at the time it is proposing a last voyage, the charterer does have choices. It could designate a voyage that, for example, had an expected arrival one day early or one expected to arrive ten days early; it could choose locations that are less prone to delays due to weather, labor problems, hostilities, or other factors. That is, not all legitimate voyages are created equal. Even though the timely redelivery of a specific voyage is beyond the control of the charterer, the charterer does have some control of timeliness by its choice between alternative legitimate voyages. The charter gives it the incentive to choose a legitimate last voyage that maximizes its expected profits.

The issue comes down to this. Should the charterer be free to determine which legitimate voyage to undertake unencumbered by concerns for the owner's decision regarding the follow-on fixture? The owner has no duty to reveal whether it has already entered into the fixture and, if so, on what terms. If, as in *The Achilleas*, the new fixture was secured after the last voyage had been set, the owner would not have any obligation to reveal the terms or clear the terms with the charterer. Nor would there be an opportunity for the charterer to reset the price to take into account the terms of the new fixture. In *The Achilleas* litigation, the charterer did not contest the reasonableness of the length of the new fixture, the rate, or the gap between the redelivery date and the cancelling date. (*Achilleas* 2007, 19) But if the loss of fixture remedy were to be the rule, the reasonableness of all would be a fact question.

The owner has one powerful tool to constrain the charterer's decisions when negotiating a follow-on fixture. It could deem the proposed voyage illegitimate. If it did so, there are a number of possible outcomes. The charterer could substitute an alternative voyage which the owner would accept as legitimate. The parties could negotiate a "without prejudice" clause which would allow the voyage to proceed, but would leave the legitimacy issue to arbitrators (as in *The Gregos*). The terms of that new agreement would take account of the possibility of a new fixture and the further possibility of that fixture being subject to cancellation. Or, the charterer could forgo the voyage, redeliver early, and sue for the difference between the contract and market price for the duration of the charter period. Both parties stand to suffer a considerable loss if the arbitrators were to find against them.

If the parties agreed that the voyage would be legitimate, it puts the onus of adapting on the owner. The owner then would take the last voyage as given when negotiating a follow-on fixture. It would then have to determine how close to the redelivery date it should set the next fixture, the length of the next charterer's cancellation option, and the consequences of that charterer exercising that option. All those are beyond the first charterer's control. While many of the standard time charter forms do not vary the cancellation time period, the parties are free to set the period. For example, a three-year time charter between Senatore Shipping Company and BP Shipping Ltd. had a cancellation period of thirty days. (The charter was on a BPTime3 form.) Rather than having the charterer adapt its decision on the last voyage to the unknown future decision of the owner, the owner can adapt its new fixture decision to the known decision of the charterer, so long as that decision was legitimate.

Does it matter if the default rule sets the rate for the late redelivery at the contract rate or the market rate? Probably not, which is why the standard forms can differ with little consequence. Once a voyage has been deemed legitimate, the no-fault redelivery date is beyond the control of both owner and charterer; the choice of remedy should have no effect. A large market/contract differential might induce the charterer to choose a riskier voyage; but it also might induce the owner to be more aggressive in declaring a proposed voyage illegitimate. If there is an impact on the nature of the last voyage, it is likely to be small. There is one advantage to choosing the charter rate – ease of administration. Determining the market rate presents some measurement problems that can be avoided by sticking with the charter rate. (Coghlin (2008), 37.24)

V. CONCLUDING REMARKS

For understanding liability for consequential damages, neither "foreseeability" nor "remoteness" is particularly useful. They are, however, too firmly rooted in the literature and case law to be abandoned. I am suggesting that they be understood not in terms of probability, but in terms of the effects both parties have on the outcome. That is implicit in Lord Hoffmann's tacit assumption approach.

The concern with the tacit assumption approach is that the court might not be able to determine what the parties have tacitly assumed. That is, it might turn out to be indeterminate. I have argued that theory can be useful in narrowing the zone of indeterminacy. For carriers like Baxendale, the narrowing is nearly complete. Responsibility for the shipper's losses would be the shipper's unless the carrier specifically agreed (*Hadley*'s second limb) or the delay was deliberate. Responsibility for loss of fixture, the issue in *The Achilleas*, is even easier. Common standard time charter forms differed on whether the charterer would have to pay charter or market rates for late redelivery. None, however, go so far as to give the owner loss-of-fixture damages for a legitimate last voyage.

There is good reason for that. In cases like *Hadley*, the promisor controlled the probability of harm. Here, however, the probability of late delivery in a legitimate voyage is beyond the control of both parties. The only factor to be set is the gap between the end of the first charter and the beginning of the second, which is completely in the control of the owner. The charterer is free to choose a legitimate last voyage that maximizes its expected value. The owner takes this decision as given when negotiating the follow-on charter and it can set the start date and cancellation date accordingly. It adapts to information available at the time of its decision. Contrast this to the case in which the charterer orders an illegitimate voyage. If the owner permitted the voyage and said nothing, then the default rule, apparently, would be the contract/market differential for the period of the overrun. But, there is no reason to fall back on the default rule. The owner's right to declare the last voyage illegitimate gives it a veto right and it can insist upon negotiating terms for the next voyage. In effect, it is in a position to write a single voyage agreement in which both parties can take into account conditions at the time the last voyage is proposed, and decide how, if at all, they want to treat the loss of fixture. The terms should, as in *The Gregos*, reflect the value of any subsequent fixture.

The real puzzle in *The Achilleas* is why smart people dealing with a recurring problem have not managed to produce clear and simple language to deal with the problem. Every time charter has a first and last voyage; every time charter form has a cancellation clause; only some forms explicitly deal with the last voyage and those clauses are not written in the clearest prose. Why not simply have a check-the-box approach? For late redelivery of a legitimate last voyage, the charterer pays: (a) the charter rate or (b) the market rate (if it is higher than the contract rate). If the parties want to avoid the question of legitimacy, then they should say so. The charterer could have the right to commence a last voyage any time during the term – there would be no specified end date for the last voyage. Or, they could set a formula for determining liquidated damages for any late redelivery, regardless of the reason – if they could avoid the penalty clause trap. Why the drafters of the forms choose to rely on "crucial words" or convoluted language remains a mystery to me.

PART III

Excuse and changed circumstances

11. Excuse doctrine: the Eisenberg uncertainty principle

The world following the economic collapse of 2008 was in a bit of a mess. Oil prices which had soared to over $140 per barrel plummeted to below $40. The pound sterling fell from $2 to less than $1.40. Housing and stock prices crashed. Foreclosures, bankruptcies, and bailouts became newspaper staples. When things go awry like this, inevitably there will be many people and firms that regret having entered into contracts under more favorable circumstances. Many of them will be looking for ways to limit or, better yet, avoid the consequences. In a recent paper, a pre-eminent contracts scholar, Professor Melvin Eisenberg (2009), has provided them with considerable ammunition, arguing for expanding the domain of the excuse doctrines. His arguments for giving the disappointed contracting party a "get out of jail (almost) free" card, however, are seriously flawed.

The core of his argument is the inability of private actors to anticipate remote risks. Contracting parties, he argues, have bounded rationality; they can't think of everything. If the parties shared an incorrect tacit assumption about some low probability event, then performance would be excused (the shared-assumption test). He breaks out a subcategory for special treatment: when a change in prices would be sufficiently large to leave the promisor with a loss significantly greater than would have reasonably been expected (the bounded-risk test). He argues that courts should have a broader set of responses than excuse or don't excuse. Rather than an on-off switch, he suggests the more appropriate analogy is to a dimmer. Relief need not mean that the contract is terminated with no remedy for the promisee. He proposes remedies that fall short of full expectation damages.

At first glance, Professor Eisenberg's emphasis on the parties' awareness of the risk of low-probability events seems plausible. Nonetheless, it is an unsatisfactory default rule, relying as it does on difficult to verify facts. To answer the question of whether the parties contemplated the occurrence of a particular event when entering into their agreement, a number of fact issues would have to be determined. Was the event part of a larger class of events that the parties did contemplate or should have contemplated? What if other similarly situated parties explicitly dealt with the problem; what inference should be drawn from silence? What if the risk was impounded in the market price? How could one tell? To illustrate the problematic nature of the test, in Section I, I will re-examine the case he uses as his primary illustration, *Krell v. Henry*. I will follow that up with a brief discussion of the granddaddy of the impossibility cases, *Taylor v. Caldwell*.

Application of the shared-assumption test, especially after the qualifications proposed by Professor Eisenberg, would be difficult, at best. But that does a lot better than the bounded-risk test, which is simply, and fundamentally, wrong. By focusing on market-wide changes, rather than promisor-specific events, he recognizes the wrong set of instances in which parties would likely choose to limit their exposure to large cost changes. The bounded-risk test will be analysed in Section II.

Parties can, of course, design their contracts to take changed circumstances into account. Professor Eisenberg implicitly assumes that courts will do this better ex post than the parties could do it either in their original agreement or in a voluntary post-agreement modification. While we cannot rule out the possibility that a wise court could do better, we can conclude with confidence that a court following Professor Eisenberg's advice would do worse. It is important to bear in mind that what is at stake is "only" a set of default rules. If the law were too liberal in granting excuses, sophisticated parties would draft around the rule and vice versa. Courts do, however, impose barriers to contracting around defaults; and the unwary might well be trapped, so it would be helpful if the rule would conform with what reasonable parties would have chosen had they thought of it.

I. WHO COULDA THUNK IT?

The first Eisenberg principle is: "Judicial relief normally should be granted if the parties shared a tacit incorrect assumption that the non-occurrence of some circumstance during the life of the contract was certain rather than problematic, and the incorrectness of that assumption would have provided a basis for judicial relief if the assumption had been explicit rather than tacit." (209) This standard raises three immediate issues: how certain must we be; how can we tell if we meet that threshold; and how would we deal with the problem if the assumption were made explicit? His answer to the first two questions is a reasonable person standard, combined, perhaps, with observation of what other parties actually do. "[T]he tacit assumptions of contracting parties … are normally best determined by considering what similarly situated parties would likely have assumed." (209) "As a practical matter that question will usually be resolved on the basis of the fact-finder's common sense intuition." (216)

Professor Eisenberg recognizes some exceptions to the shared-assumption test. If the assumption were merely problematic, or the circumstance foreseeable, then there would be no excuse. So, if we were to observe a number of similarly situated contracts which dealt with precisely this circumstance, then presumably, we should conclude that the circumstance would not be an excusable ground. Likewise, if the circumstance were so well foreshadowed that the probability of its occurrence was impounded in the market price, he would not excuse.

He argues that unexpected circumstances are *really* unexpected, and therefore it would have been unreasonable for parties to have planned for their occurrence:

> Most unexpected-circumstances cases arise because the parties tacitly assume that a given kind of circumstance will not occur during the contract time. In such cases the parties do not consider or even foresee, let alone appraise, the risk that the unexpected circumstance will occur. Indeed, if the parties do foresee the relevant risk, judicial relief normally should not be granted. Accordingly, it is more or less irrelevant for present purposes which party can better appraise the probability or magnitude of an unexpected circumstance, because most unexpected-circumstances cases arise precisely because neither party has thought about engaging in such an appraisal. (251)

His primary illustration of the application of the shared-assumption test is one of the "coronation cases," *Krell v. Henry.* A closer look highlights the weakness of the test and calls into question Professor Eisenberg's presumptions about the ability of actors to anticipate remote events. *Taylor v. Caldwell* provided the basis for the coronation cases; the notion that parties would fail to foresee the possible risks in this type of situation is even less plausible.

A. *Krell v. Henry* and the Coronation of Edward VII

I will begin with a bare bones version of the story and with Professor Eisenberg's analysis. Queen Victoria reigned from 1837 to 1901. The Coronation of her son Edward VII, was to take place on June 26, 1902 and two great processions were planned in London – the Coronation Procession on June 26 and the Royal Progress on the following day. On June 20, Henry entered into a written agreement with Krell in which Henry would have access to Krell's rooms overlooking the procession routes for two days (but not the nights). The purpose, obviously, was to view the processions, but that was not stated explicitly. Henry agreed to pay £75 for the two days and immediately paid £25. On June 24, the king came down with appendicitis and the processions were postponed. Krell sued for the remaining £50 and Henry counterclaimed for the return of the £25. The counterclaim was subsequently dropped and the House of Lords found that the basic purpose of the contract had been frustrated. "I think it cannot reasonably be supposed to have been in the contemplation of the contracting parties when the contract was made, that the coronation would not be held on the proclaimed days … or along the proclaimed route." (740)

For Professor Eisenberg, the postponement was clearly an unanticipated shock:

> So in *Krell v. Henry* we can be pretty confident that: (i) actors in the positions of the contracting parties would have shared the tacit assumption that the coronation would take place in six days scheduled; (ii) the contract was made on the basis of that assumption; (iii) Henry was not assuming the risk that the assumption was incorrect – was not gambling, and was not being paid to gamble, on whether the coronation would take place. (214)

He is hardly alone in this characterization. Judge Posner, for example, makes a similar statement in *Northern Indiana Public Service Company v. Carbon County Coal Company*: "The question was, to which party did the contract (implicitly) allocate the risk? Surely Henry had not intended to insure Krell against the possibility of the coronation's being postponed, since Krell could always relet the room, at the premium rental, for the coronation's new date. So Henry was excused." (277) Professor Eisenberg used Krell's ability to relet the room as a ground for denying him any compensation. While it is true that the rescheduled procession passed by Krell's flat, that was not true for all the coronation cases. Many of the dignitaries chose not to return to London for the subsequent processions and the value of viewing sites apparently fell; see Treitel (2004, 316) and 'Crowning' (1902).

Eisenberg then asserted that "many or most unexpected-circumstances cases involve either events that are too special to be covered by normal market insurance, such as the illness of a king on a given day." (250) Notice the subtle switch. The "tacit assumption" was that the coronation would take place as scheduled. But here he appears to narrow the focus to a single cause – the illness of the king. Even with that more restrictive definition of the intervening event, his argument fails.

The risk of postponement looks less remote if we tell the story differently. While this particular contract was entered into only six days before the event, the planning horizon for the event was roughly six months, the date and route being announced in December 1901. (Treitel (2004, 315)) The likelihood that a 60-year-old, grossly overweight, heavy smoker, who had been the target of at least one assassination attempt, might be unavailable was not trivial. Moreover, the procession was to be in a city renowned for its miserable weather. That someone might have thought about a possible postponement or cancellation no longer seems so far-fetched.

And, in fact, they did. Less than a week before the coronation, Lloyds was quoting odds of 300 to 1 against cancellation. "Many thousands of pounds sterling were underwritten on this basis. This shows to what extent public nervousness has grown in certain circles." (*New York Times*, June 22, 1902) In an article the day after the postponement was announced, the *New York Times* provided an indication of the extensive insurance coverage:

> The loss of the British insurance companies, particularly those of London, which accepted risks on the coronation, will, it is estimated, run into the millions. … [T]housands of insurance policies have been issued during the past year to tradesmen and others who depended for their livelihood for some time to come upon the ability of the King to pass through the coronation ceremonies. The business took a great boom when active preparations were begun for the coronation, and nearly all classes of tradesmen who were directly or indirectly dependent upon the successful termination of the great event bought policies.
>
> * * *
>
> The companies at first promised large sums if the coronation should not take place. The rate was 10 guineas for each £100. This rate was due to the fact that Lloyds, with whom much of the insurance was taken, unlike regular insurance companies, had no means of arriving at the state of health of the person insured. It was therefore age merely – the general allowance that would be placed on the average man at the age of the King – which was considered. Thus the premium for insurance of the late Queen Victoria at the time of the diamond jubilee was £14 per £100 for a year.
>
> * * *
>
> Hotel proprietors, restaurant men, costumers, owners of grand stands, managers of places of amusement have all insured themselves against loss in the event of the failure of the coronation to take place.
>
> Many thousands of pounds sterling against the coronation were underwritten at Lloyds at long odds and the large amount of business done was taken as an indication of the extent of the public nervousness. (*New York Times*, June 25, 1902)

For those too young to remember, there were twelve pence in a shilling, twenty shillings in a pound, and twenty-one shillings in a guinea. The next day, the *New York Times* noted that, "Few of the caterers of hotels availed themselves of insurance, the recently offered Lloyd's rate of 10 per cent, being considered too high. Many proprietors of reviewing stands were protected by insurance."

The opinion in *Krell* tells us nothing about Henry's identity. Was he just a very rich guy who wanted to watch the procession? Since per capita annual income in England at the time was only around £45, this would have been a very expensive impulse purchase. Perhaps he was an entrepreneur who intended to charge admission to spectators and for reasons unknown waited till the last minute. This seems plausible given some of the prices mentioned in other coronation cases. However, Justice Darling, who decided the initial decision in Krell, stated in a subsequent decision "there was no evidence in [*Krell*] that the letter of the room had gone to any expense in providing a stand or seats." (*Lumden v. Barton and Co.* 54) The lack of evidence does not, of course, mean that it didn't happen. In both *Blakeley v. Muller & Co.* and *Hobson v. Pattenden & Co.* the plaintiff was a customer who had already paid for seats; in the former case, he paid £15 for three seats, in the latter £14 for two. In *Lumsden v. Barton and Co.*, the plaintiff had paid £42 for eight seats for the first day. In *Chandler v. Webster*, the price was £141 for the first day with the intention of building a stand and letting seats. We aren't even certain as to whether Krell or Henry had insured against the postponement. We do know that their contract did not explicitly deal with a possible postponement or cancellation. In some of the other litigated coronation cases, the possibility of postponement was explicitly taken into account. For example, *Victoria Seats Agency v. Paget* dealt with two contracts for spectators to watch the Royal Progress (the June 27 event). One provided for the room on the date "or such other day as the said processions should pass the premises. Should the procession not pass the premises, I agree to refund the money." The second said that in the event that the procession did not take place, the renter would get back his money less 10 percent. According to the *New York Times* (June 26, 1902), an "important question remains as to whether the money paid for seats will necessarily be refunded. Only a few seats out of nearly half a million were sold with any specific proviso on this point."

So, if Professor Eisenberg wants to place his reliance upon an event that no one could have foreseen, *Krell* turns out to be a poor vehicle. The postponement of the coronation was clearly foreseen by others – lots of others. The fact that Lloyds had offered insurance on Queen Victoria's diamond jubilee (1897) suggests that the English were quite prepared to deal with such unfortunate matters well before Edward's appendicitis. If an event that seemed to him (and others) so obviously beyond the imagination of the contracting parties was, in fact, anticipated by many, then that suggests that courts and commentators should be more cautious about their ability to recognize tacit assumptions. In this, Professor Eisenberg is not alone. Numerous commentators and the Restatement (Second) emphasize the role of the unexpected or remote risks. Indeed, despite the wealth of information about the public's awareness of the coronation risks available to the Law Lords, they too invoked the unexpected to justify excuse – "it cannot reasonably be supposed to have been in the contemplation of the contracting parties."

B. *Taylor v. Caldwell*

Krell and other coronation decisions relied on *Taylor v. Caldwell*, generally considered to be the first case to recognize the impossibility defense. On May 27, 1861 the parties entered into a contract for the use of the Surrey Gardens and Music Hall in which Taylor, the promoter, was to put on four grand concerts in the summer, paying the owners £100 for each concert. On June 11, before any of the concerts had been held, the Music Hall was destroyed by a fire caused by a careless plumber. The concerts were cancelled and Taylor sued for £58, the costs incurred in preparation for the concerts. Holding that "in contracts in which the performance depends on the continued existence of a given person or thing, a condition is implied that the impossibility of performance arising from the perishing of the person or thing shall excuse performance." (309) Impossibility would relieve both parties of their contractual obligations. The expenses incurred by Taylor in preparation could not be recovered.

Professor Eisenberg gives the case much less attention, simply asserting that it was an "unexpected circumstance" case (225) and focusing instead on whether Taylor should have been compensated for his reliance expenditures. (231) He argues that even though the defendant was not at fault and should be excused, Taylor should still have been compensated for his reliance (the £58). His argument is based on the notion that the owners were "in control" of the premises, even if they were not at fault. "Liability in such cases can be based on the ground that responsibility follows from control, because control implies some ability to take steps to prevent the loss from occurring." (230) He continues:

> The facts (although not the decision) in *Taylor v. Caldwell* illustrate how the control principle should be applied. … The court said, "we must take it on the

> evidence [that the destruction of the hall] was without the fault of either party," and held that the owners were excused. That result was correct as far as expectation damages but seems doubtful as far as reliance damages. The owners were in control of the hall and, therefore, had at least some ability to prevent a fire; the lessee did not. Although the owners were not *proven* to be at fault, given their control over the premises they bore some responsibility to ensure its safety, and it would have been appropriate to make the owners responsible for the lessee's costs on that basis. (231, emphasis in original)

I think that is wrong, but that is beside the point. When Michael Jackson died suddenly less than a month before the start of his fifty-show English tour, the company running the tour had spent over $20 million in reliance. Jackson was "in control," but I don't believe anyone (even Professor Eisenberg) would have had the Jackson estate compensate the reliance costs. The more significant point is that this was hardly an unexpected event. That a structure might be destroyed by fire should not come as a shock to contracting parties. Fire insurance had been available in England since shortly after the Great Fire of London of 1666; the owners of the Surrey Gardens had fire insurance. The notion of a shared tacit assumption works even worse in this context. The possibility that a venue or artist would be unavailable without fault is a predictable risk and parties can contract to determine how the risks should be allocated. *Taylor v. Caldwell* merely establishes a default rule if the parties neglected to provide for the possibility in their agreement.

While we do not know how parties dealt with these contingencies in the nineteenth century, nowadays, parties routinely allocate the risks through insurance and specific contract language. News accounts following Michael Jackson's death discussed the efforts of the tour packager, AEG, to obtain insurance. Because of questions regarding Jackson's health and his history of concert cancellations, those efforts were only partially successful. If the artists are popular (and therefore have a high opportunity cost) and have substantial pre-concert expenses, they are likely to require that the venue give them substantial compensation if the venue were to become unavailable. Indeed, they might even require that the venue pay some of their fee, even if the artist is unable to perform. For example, a Paula Abdul contract included this: "In the event that ARTIST is unable to perform during the period of time specified in the Contract due to no fault of her own, ARTIST shall be paid the full compensation agreed upon without the necessity of ARTIST'S performing." A Rod Stewart contract distinguished between the artist's health problems and other excusing events:

> If any party's obligations contained in this Agreement are rendered impossible by any act, requirement or regulation of any public authority or bureau, strike or labor dispute (except for claims by the musicians' or other performers' unions, which are expressly excluded from this paragraph), flood, fire, riot, Acts of God, absence of power or other essential services, failure of technical facilities, or failure or delay of transportation facilities, or any other cause beyond such party's reasonable control (excepting causes of which [Rod Stewart] or Rio had knowledge, or in the exercise of due diligence should have had knowledge), then there shall be no claim for damages by either party to this Agreement, and the performance shall be rescheduled to a mutually agreeable time.
>
> In the event Stewart is ill or incapacitated for any reason, and as a result incapable of performing as determined by Stewart in his absolute discretion, the show(s) will be canceled, and Rio shall have no obligation to pay any further sums in connection with the canceled show and Stewart … shall refund the payment made by the Rio to [him]. (*Rio Properties, Inc. v. Stewart Annoyances, Ltd.* 2005 WL 3767233 (D.Nev.) Rio's Trial Brief, pp. 2–3)

Notwithstanding that language, his failure to perform and refusal to repay the $2 million fee precipitated a nasty, costly litigation that went on for about a decade.

I do not mean to argue that the default rule should never be to excuse performance, nor do I undertake to specify the content of that default rule. My aim is more modest – to undercut the notion that "unexpected circumstances" should be the basis for excusing performance. Professor Eisenberg's standard – "if the parties do foresee the relevant risk, judicial relief normally should not be granted" (251) – should lead him to refuse to excuse in both *Krell* and *Taylor* (and, certainly, in post-*Taylor* entertainment contracts). One of the Restatement (Second) illustrations regarding excuse is the claim by a contractor working on a building that is destroyed. (§ 377 illustration 4). I will consider the problem in the following chapter. Here, I just want to note that some of the cases that excuse on this ground involve claims by companies installing sprinkler systems and other fire safety equipment. (Goldberg (2011b, fn. 105)) It would be hard to argue with a straight face that parties to such a contract did not contemplate the possibility of a fire. I have no problem with a default rule that would excuse those contracts. However, you can't get there with Eisenberg's shared-assumption test. If he is to excuse these, as well as *Krell* and *Taylor*, some other doctrinal hook will be necessary.

II. MAGNITUDE DOES MATTER, BUT …

Whatever the problems with the shared-assumption test, they pale in comparison with Professor Eisenberg's bounded-risk test. While the shared-assumption test was concerned with the unforeseeability of an event, the bounded-risk test concerns the magnitude:

> Under this test, which I will call the *bounded-risk test*, a promisor should be entitled to judicial relief if as a result of a dramatic and unexpected rise in costs, performance would result in a financial loss significantly greater than the risk of loss that the parties would reasonably have expected the promisor to have undertaken. … [F]or purposes of unexpected circumstances cases a circumstance can be defined not only by its characteristics but also by its magnitude, that is, its dollar cost. (234)

If the event causing the rise in the seller's costs were specific to that seller, this test would be plausible. It is consistent with excuses routinely incorporated into force majeure clauses. But, that is not what Professor Eisenberg has in mind. He is concerned primarily with market-wide cost (and demand) changes. "Cases in which the seller's cost of performance unexpectedly rises above the contract price often, perhaps usually, involve a cost increase that is market-wide. In such cases, the increase normally will raise not only the seller's costs but also the buyer's value for, and the market value of, the contracted-for commodity." (238) "[T]he bounded-risk test should apply *only when a cost increase is market-wide*." (246, emphasis added) However, all four of his illustrations, *Vernon v. Los Angeles*, *Mishara v. Transit-Mixed Concrete Corp.*, *Mineral Park v. Howard*, and *Moyer v. Little Falls*, were completely unrelated to overall market conditions. How he reconciles the principle and these cases remains a mystery.

Assuming for the moment that he really means that his concern is with market-wide cost increases, then it raises an obvious question of symmetry. Why should the test only apply when costs and prices rise; why doesn't it apply when costs and prices decline in tandem? I will return to that question below.

To understand why Professor Eisenberg's bounded-risk test is flawed, consider his illustration:

> For example, suppose that Packer agrees to sell 10,000 pounds of N nuts, a delicacy, to Distributor at a price of $1.00/pound. Packer expects to purchase the nuts from farmers at 50¢/pound. Distributor operates at a 100 percent gross margin and expects to resell the nuts to retailers at $2.00/pound, for a total profit of $10,000. Because of a blight, the quantity of N nuts available

> on the market falls dramatically, and the price of N nuts to Packers rockets to \$6.00/pound. The demand for N nuts is relatively inelastic. The price charged by Packers to distributors rises to \$7.00/pound, and the price charged by distributors to retailers rises to \$14.00/pound. If Packer does not perform and is not entitled to judicial relief, she will incur damages of \$60,000 (based on the difference between the \$1.00/pound contract price and the \$7.00/pound market price to distributors). Distributor, in turn, will reap a windfall profit of \$130,000 (based on damages of \$60,000 plus the \$70,000 difference between the \$7.00/pound market price to distributors and the \$14.00/pound charged by distributors), compared with its ex ante expected profit of \$10,000. (239)

What's wrong with this picture? Lots. To begin, there is no good economic reason for the notion that the percentage markup is fixed. The margin is payment for the Distributor's services and there is no reason to believe that these have become relatively scarcer. But, that is merely a quibble when compared to the other problems. The example depends on the timing of the contracting of both parties. If the Distributor entered into her distribution contract at the same time as her contract with the Packer, upon breach she suffers a serious loss – she has sold at \$2, but now has to cover at \$7. Not only does she not get a windfall, but she might even be able to cry "excuse me" under the Eisenberg principles. In all his chain-of-transactions examples, Professor Eisenberg assumes a specific time structure. The Distributor's hypothesized windfall comes because he bought early/low and, in a separate contract, apparently sold late/high. The nut Packer, on the other hand, is hypothesized to have sold early/low and bought late/high. Timing itself is an economic decision. If the Packer deliberately took a short position, that reflected his judgment, which happened in this instance to be wrong. The Distributor, on the other hand, happened to be right. The Packer's liability should not be conditional on whether the Distributor entered into a forward contract and when it did so.

Professor Eisenberg's linking of the two contracts is a common error that shows up in another area of contract law – the measurement of damages in the "middleman" cases in which the middleman contracts for a fixed fee (or percentage fee), for example, *Tongish v. Thomas* and *Allied Canners v. Victor*. Following a substantial increase in the market price, the seller breaches, the contract-market price difference being substantially greater than the middleman's fee. The seller argues that awarding anything more than the middleman's expected profit (its fee) would amount to a windfall. If the middleman were acting as a broker, the ultimate buyer would be able to sue for the entire market-contract price difference and the middleman would indeed be entitled to only its fee. However, when the middleman contracts separately with both buyer and seller, then it assumes the counterparty risk in both contracts. It would potentially be liable to the buyer for the market-contract price difference. In cases like *Tongish* and *Allied*, the middleman succeeded in limiting its liability in its contract with the buyer – hence the appearance of a windfall gain. That parallels Eisenberg's distributor who bought early in one contract and sold late in another. I should note that Professor Eisenberg (2013, 399–403) is consistent in this regard since in a subsequent article he again conflated the two contracts arguing that the middleman would receive an unwarranted windfall. For more detail on the middleman cases, see Goldberg (2006, ch. 11).

The most significant problem with his analysis, however, is that he directs attention to precisely the wrong set of circumstances – where the change was market-wide. I will come back to this point, but first I want to underscore some further problems, even if we were to assume that the market-wide cost increase is the relevant concern.

His argument hinges on the correlation between the supply and demand side. How tight does that correlation need to be? Does the change have to affect all suppliers equally? Does the increase have to pass through completely to the final price? Mere pass-through is not enough. His illustration is pass-through on steroids – a 100 percent increase in the seller's cost ballooned to a 700 percent increase in the distributor's price. There is no reason to think that the correlation would be very high, unless the root cause of the price increase was not specific to the particular market but was due to a very high rate of inflation. A good example of an instance in which the correlation was negative comes from a casebook standard – *Columbia Nitrogen v. Royster*. The price of the primary input – sulphur – soared while demand for (and the price of) the final product – fertilizer – fell. One anecdote by itself does not prove anything, but the broader point is that if the bounded-risk test would be triggered only if the correlation was high enough, then we would have to figure out how much is enough and whether that is to vary between contexts. Whether the high correlation scenario is a common one is an empirical question. I doubt that it is. But, and this is the important point, it doesn't matter.

It is hard to determine the domain of the bounded-risk test. There is a hint of a Goldilocks test – the time frame should be neither too long nor too short:

> In some cases, it can be inferred from the circumstances that the seller was taking the risk of a very large loss due to market-wide cost increases. The most obvious case is that in which one or both parties are speculators. Within limits, the acceptance of such a risk may also be inferred from the fact that a

> contract is for a period of many years, because the longer the term of a contract, the more it becomes reasonably foreseeable that a very large increase in costs may occur during that term. Price-escalation provisions in a long-term contract may also suggest that the seller made an evaluative choice among various types of such provisions and was taking the risk that her choice would turn out badly. (241–42)

Professor Eisenberg adds another wrinkle. Courts should not confine their attention to the contract in dispute; rather, they should look at how the event affected the rest of the promisor's business as well. He illustrates this with *Missouri Public Service Company v. Peabody Coal Company*. Peabody had entered into a ten-year contract to deliver coal in 1967. The parties negotiated over a proper escalator, finally agreeing on the Industrial Commodities Index of the Wholesale Price Index (the WPI-IC). Following the 1973 oil shock, the price of coal increased much more than the WPI-IC and Peabody tried to renegotiate the price. It failed, and informed the power company that it would not deliver more coal. Missouri sued for specific performance and in its defense, Peabody invoked commercial impracticability. The defense was rejected and the court granted specific performance. The court noted that "Public Service, over objection, was permitted to show that since performance of the contract began, Peabody had experienced an approximate three-fold increase in the value of its coal reserves, presumably brought about by the same inflationary trend and other causes to which it ascribes its loss under the contract." (723) For that reason, Professor Eisenberg would have denied Peabody's defense. Implicit in his analysis is the notion that but for the profitability in the remainder of the business, he would have acceded to Peabody's demand to renegotiate the price. That presents a problem for him because the claim is problematic on three of his criteria. First, the buyer did not get a windfall – it was a regulated public utility. Second, the contract was for ten years, a time horizon plausibly long enough so that "it becomes reasonably foreseeable that a very large increase in costs may occur during that term." (241) Third, the parties negotiated extensively over the index, with Peabody initially proposing indexing with the CPI, finally agreeing to the WPI-IC.

Many of the major excuse cases were like *Peabody*, in that they involved long-term energy-related contracts, large changes in the energy markets, and negotiated price indexes that didn't work properly. In neither *In Re Westinghouse* nor *Eastern Airlines v. Gulf* was there any correlation between the price of the input (fuel) and the output (electric power and airplane tickets). *Alcoa v. Essex* even shared the same flawed price index; it differs from the others only because the price of the final product – aluminum – had risen. That price increase was not linked to the rise in Alcoa's fuel costs, however, as in Professor Eisenberg's example; it resulted from general inflation and an increase in the demand for aluminum. Are all these casebook favorites to be excluded from the bounded-risk test? I should make clear that I would not have excused in any of these. The question is whether Professor Eisenberg would have ruled them out.

Professor Eisenberg suggests one other limit on the test. "In the normal case, however, a seller would not be willing to accept an extremely large risk, or perhaps more accurately, would charge the buyer a steep premium to accept such a risk, because if the loss materialized it would significantly decrease the seller's wealth." (242) Most contracts, even with the huge cost increases that concern Professor Eisenberg, are not bet-the-company affairs. Westinghouse's many uranium contracts taken together would fall into this category. But, by and large, companies have a large portfolio of contracts and will rarely suffer a significant decrease in wealth because of extreme losses in one. When we put all these criteria together, it is possible that no cases would pass the bounded-risk test. I don't believe that is what Professor Eisenberg had in mind.

The "cotton cases" might possibly have fit his criteria. Bad weather in 1973 resulted in a huge increase in the price of cotton. "The present actions are the result of an unprecedented rise in the price of domestic cotton from approximately $.30 per pound to $.80 or $.90 per pound between the spring and the fall of 1973. This has been the fastest rise and to the highest price known in more than a century. Suits for specific performance of cotton contracts have been brought throughout the southeastern part of the United States." (*Carolinas Cotton Growers Association, Inc. v. Arnette*, 66) Cotton producers tried every trick in the book to avoid their contracts. Not only did they fail to get excused, the courts in many of the litigated cases ordered specific performance despite the fact that the cotton was fungible. Courts came to a similar conclusion in cases involving Campbell Soup's contracts with growers when market prices were large multiples of the contract price. In *Campbell Soup v. Wentz* the court denied specific performance because it found the force majeure clause unconscionable. However, with that clause removed, specific performance was upheld in subsequent Campbell Soup-grower cases; see Goldberg (2006, ch. 9). The one factor distinguishing these cases from Professor Eisenberg's hypothetical is that there is no reason to believe that the costs of the parties asking to be excused had changed – they just wanted the windfall for themselves.

If parties excuse performance, they typically do so for events that are specific to a particular contract. Indeed, the expected low correlation with market conditions is at the core of force majeure clauses. The asymmetry implied by Professor Eisenberg – only excuse for a cost increase – makes some sense if the event were specific to the promisor. Performance can be excused if some act of God causes the costs of this particular seller to increase; the expected effect on the market price would be zero. That sort of shock is common – a local fire, burst water pipe, etc. In expectation, the buyer does not lose a good deal since there is no reason to believe that the local problem would be associated with a market-wide price increase. The buyer would expect that on average it could cover at the original contract price. The converse, an act of God that lowers the seller's costs without also lowering the costs of other suppliers, is less likely. Not surprisingly, parties are unlikely to excuse performance when circumstances result in a reduction of the seller's costs unrelated to market conditions. Thus, if crops are destroyed, a farmer would be excused if the contract referred to crops grown on the seller's land (or if that could be inferred). (UCC 2-615 comment 9) A generic contract to deliver crops, however, would not be excused, regardless of the magnitude of the price change – the promisor could buy the goods on the market. The Campbell contracts illustrate one way parties deal with extreme conditions that might cause a crop failure. Campbell would agree to take all the output (subject to a maximum) from a particular grower. If the crop failed completely, the seller would have no liability – no excuse necessary. If the crop failure were less than complete, the grower would be responsible only for delivery of the surviving crop.

As a general rule, contracts do not excuse performance because of changes in the market price. That does not mean that they simply set a price that is unvarying with conditions. Magnitude does matter. But, that should not give courts a license to revise. The parties are perfectly capable of doing it themselves. They can, and often do, impose boundaries on the price. They have available a rich variety of price adjustment mechanisms. These include indexing, but they also include floors and ceilings, meeting competition clauses, renegotiation mechanisms, and third-party determination (for example, gross inequity clauses). Some of these mechanisms will include the possibility of termination. A contract might, for example, say that if the indexed price exceeds a maximum, the parties should renegotiate in good faith and if that fails, the contract would terminate after a certain period. For examples, see Goldberg and Erickson (1987, 387–96) Instead of relying on the parties' determination of the boundaries on their price risk, Professor Eisenberg proposes that the courts impose the boundaries ex post. Actually, because of the asymmetry in his argument, there would be only one boundary – a cap.

He proposes a modified expectation damage measure: If the price increase is too extreme, the court should substitute a new price:

> The remedy under that test should follow from the underlying theory of relief. This theory is that if the parties had addressed the issue, the seller would have accepted the risk of cost increases up to a certain point but not beyond. Accordingly, the buyer should be entitled to expectation damages measured by the difference between the contract price and a hypothetical price based on the increased costs the seller could reasonably have been expected to bear. (244)

And how is that hypothetical price to be determined?

> [T]he buyer should be entitled to the expectation damages that would have been awarded if there had been a reasonably foreseeable increase in the seller's cost of performance and a corresponding increase in the market value of the commodity. What constitutes a reasonably foreseeable increase in the seller's cost of performance should be historically based; more specifically, it should be the maximum percentage increase in the cost of the relevant inputs over a comparable stretch of time during a reasonable past period. In most cases, consideration of price movements during the prior ten to twenty years probably would suffice. (245)

This remedy seems inextricably linked to his assumption that the triggering event is a market-wide increase in costs. He continues:

> [T]he remedy should be the difference between the contract price, and a hypothetical price based on maximum historical percentage price increases for the relevant inputs. It might be objected that this remedy would saddle the buyer with an opportunity cost, on the theory that if the buyer had made a contract with another supplier, he would have been able to acquire the contracted-for commodity at the contract price. However, the bounded-risk test *should apply only when a cost increase is market-wide.* As a result, the costs of all sellers of the relevant commodity would have increased in the same way, and all sellers would have the same defense, so that the buyer would have done no better if he had contracted with another seller. (246, emphasis added)

Historical data over the previous ten to twenty years would determine the seller's maximum exposure. The constraint would not be input cost per se but rather the maximum rate of change of cost in that period. I guess that means if this were a two-year contract we would search for the greatest two-year price increase in the preceding decades. That is, we would match the length of the comparison period with the length of the contract. Again, in the context of his market-wide paradigm, Professor Eisenberg provides a simple version: "The easiest kind of situation in which to apply the bounded-risk test consists of cases, like the nut … [hypothetical], in which the buyer is purchasing for resale. In such cases the buyer's only expectation is to make a profit, and if the buyer is awarded the maximum profit that he would have reasonably expected ex ante, this expectation will be fulfilled." (245)

This last version of the remedy bears a familial resemblance to the one imposed by the court, and later rejected by the parties, in *Alcoa v. Essex.* He caps the buyer's profits; the *Alcoa* judge put a floor under the seller's profits. *Alcoa* is, in a sense, the dog that didn't bark. It is one of the rare American cases that arguably took a bounded-risk argument seriously; yet, it is nowhere mentioned in Professor Eisenberg's paper. Perhaps, he avoided it because he feared that his analysis would be tainted if it were associated with such a bad decision.

It is possible, as I have suggested, that hardly any cases would be affected by the bounded-risk test. The correlation would be too low, the length of the contract too long or too short, etc. However, almost certainly, that is not Professor Eisenberg's intent. His use of non-market-wide cases as illustrations suggests that he does not feel at all bound by his assumptions. He, in effect, is proposing that all (many? some?) contracts would include an implied gross inequity clause. The relative rarity of explicit gross inequity clauses suggests that parties would not welcome such a clause. Parties do contract over the possibility of large cost changes all the time, and they will sometimes include caps, floors, and instructions as to what should happen if either were hit. If parties choose not to include caps or floors, that is pretty good evidence that they didn't want them. If Professor Eisenberg's rule were to become the default rule, then we should expect anti-court-modification clauses in response. Any judicial presumption in favor of his default rule would give the disappointed party one more handful of sand to throw into the machinery of justice. I should emphasize that this does not mean that parties would never adjust the contract price. Price concessions in the face of changed market conditions are commonplace. But the grantor of the concession often expects a quid pro quo, either express (e.g., an increase in the term of the contract) or implied (e.g., enhanced good will). The grantor, that is, maintains the right to make (or not make) price concessions.

III. CONCLUDING REMARKS

Oliver Wendell Holmes (1897, 462) observed that "the duty to keep a contract at common law means a prediction that you must pay damages if you do not keep it, and nothing else. … If you commit a contract, you are liable to pay a compensatory sum unless the promised event comes to pass." That aphorism has to be qualified by recognizing that in the face of changed circumstances, the performance might be modified or excused and that parties often do include such qualifications in their agreements. Contract law adds some default rules to these qualifications for impossibility, impracticability, and frustration. Professor Eisenberg presumes that parties would not be very good at designing responses to changed conditions and proposes a beefed-up excuse doctrine. He proffers two tests and associated remedies. His first test – the shared-assumption test – is based on the notion that some events are so unlikely that no one would actually have thought of them. When such an event comes to pass, the promisor should be excused. Case law often invokes the unforeseeability of such events, but a quick review of the core cases – the coronation cases and *Taylor v. Caldwell* – suggests that parties are better at this than Professor Eisenberg gives them credit for. His emphasis on the remoteness of the event is not, unfortunately, out of line with the Restatement (Second). The boldness of Professor Eisenberg's argument illuminates the more subtle flaws of the Restatement, which uses softer, vaguer language.

His bigger errors concern his bounded-risk test. He asserts that large changes in costs are typically associated with large changes in final market demand and this dubious proposition drives his analysis (even as he abandons it for his application to actual cases). If the magnitude of a cost (or price) change is large enough, he argues, the courts should insert a ceiling that would provide some protection for the seller. There are some serious logical errors in his analysis, as noted above. But the biggest problem is that it identifies the wrong set of instances in which parties would be most likely to excuse, ex ante, for an unanticipated change in costs.

12. After frustration: three cheers for *Chandler v. Webster*

When Edward VII's appendicitis caused the postponement of his coronation processions, the postponement was only temporary, but its impact on contract doctrine was enduring. A number of disputes involving contracts for viewing the processions reached the House of Lords, which held that the purpose of those contracts had been frustrated and that any obligations due following the postponement were excused. What of obligations that arose before the frustrating event? Following *Taylor v. Caldwell*, the Law Lords let the losses lie where they fell. Absent any language to the contrary, no expenses incurred in reliance prior to the frustrating event would be shifted to the other party. The additional wrinkle added by the coronation cases, notably *Chandler v. Webster*, was that there would be no restitution for any payments made prior to the frustrating event. If something had been done (or was owing) prior to the frustrating event, it would not be undone by the occurrence of that event. That stood as law in England for forty years despite frequent criticism. The critics finally won when *Chandler v. Webster* was overturned by *Fibrosa Spolka Akcyjna v. Fairbairn Lawson Combe Barbour*.

The demise of *Chandler v. Webster* has met with widespread approval, see Treitel (2004). In their article on the coronation cases, R.G. McElroy and Glanville Williams (1941a,b) reflect the negative perceptions of *Chandler v. Webster* on the eve of its overruling: The decision "established a rule of English law which is generally acknowledged to be unjust." Nor has *Chandler v. Webster* been treated kindly in American casebooks. Multiple editions of the Dawson & Harvey casebook say that "the absurdity of this solution is at once apparent." See, for example, Dawson, et al. (2013, 578). Likewise Ayres and Speidel (2008, 901) refer to the "dubious result." For one of the rare papers sympathetic to *Chandler v. Webster*, see Kull (1991).

I will argue that this was a mistake. *Chandler* provided a nice, clean default rule – award neither restitution nor reliance. It is administratively simple and, I believe, it corresponds reasonably well with what sophisticated parties actually do. Or, at least, try to do, since courts will on occasion read the parties' resolution out of the contract and substitute some alternative remedy. In *Fibrosa*, the Lords recognized the restitution claim but explicitly refused to recognize any reliance interest. The Lords encouraged Parliament to rectify this. It did so with the Law Reform (Frustrated Contracts) Act, which would recognize some claims in reliance. American courts have generally favored awarding restitution and on occasion have recognized reliance expenses as well.

Consider a simple example to which we will return a number of times. Smith promises to paint Brown's factory for $100,000. A fire destroys the factory after Smith has incurred cost of $30,000 and received progress payments of $20,000. Should Brown get back any of his $20,000? Should Smith be compensated for any of the costs that he has incurred? Leave aside for the moment that their contract would normally deal with such a contingency. My default rule (*Chandler*) would be to leave things alone. No restitution for Brown and no reliance for Smith. The American and post-*Fibrosa* English default rule would return Brown's $20,000, and, *maybe*, require that Brown compensate Smith for at least some of his costs incurred in reliance.

The case law and commentary have generally approved the demise of *Chandler*, invoking loss-sharing, fairness, and justice. This, I suggest, misses the point. If loss-sharing were indeed important to the parties, they are capable of saying so in their initial agreement. The focus should not be on ex post justice but on ex ante planning. To be sure, parties, even very sophisticated parties advised by top-notch legal counsel, are not omniscient. Circumstances could arise which, had they thought of it, the parties would have dealt with differently. Nonetheless, the starting point for post-excuse remedies should be the ex ante concerns of the parties.

In particular, we should recognize that in the face of changed circumstances, parties would like to be able to adjust their obligations. Termination of the agreement should be viewed as one form of adjustment. The parties could, for example, include force majeure and material adverse change clauses. Or, they could rely on the excuse doctrines of impossibility, impracticability, and frustration. The agreement could determine what transfers, if any, would have to be made following the termination. The response, particularly with regard to the questions of reliance and restitution, need not be one size fits all. That is, even within a single contract, the parties might choose, for example, to give restitution for some events but not others.

Case law and commentary on the excuse doctrines often emphasize the unlikely nature of the particular event. This is taken as license to impose a remedy because the parties had not (could not have?) considered the possibility of such an occurrence. As I noted in the previous chapter, I think this is wrong on two counts. First, parties do often contemplate events that outsiders would not expect them to. Second, if the excuse clauses are broad enough, they can include many low-probability, unanticipated events. But, that is not the primary concern in this chapter. My concern here is not with *why* performance might be excused, but with what should happen *when* it is excused.

I focus on English and American law. I should note that a casual survey of other legal systems suggests that they have many similarities with the English/American solutions. This presents an interesting puzzle. Why do formal legal regimes approach the problem in a similar manner, emphasizing "justice" and "unfairness," while the economic actors designing their relationships within those regimes contract around those defaults?

In Section I, I will discuss the English cases, starting with *Taylor v. Caldwell*. At present, the English law is defined by two decisions interpreting the application of the Frustrated Contracts Act. Both decisions, I will argue, are contrary to what the parties would have wanted. While most American contract scholars are aware of *Fibrosa* and the Frustrated Contracts Act, they know little or nothing about the details. The consensus view is that whatever the facts, the decision and statute together were an improvement. To appreciate the virtues of *Chandler v. Webster*, it is necessary that we understand what has replaced it. I confess that there might be more detail here than most American contract scholars would find necessary. The short version, for those who lack the time or interest, is that in the name of "justice," the English managed to produce a loose standard that contracting parties would almost certainly have rejected. In Section II, I turn to the American law, with emphasis on the Restatement (Second) of Contracts. I focus on the class of cases described above in which a construction contract is excused because a structure has been destroyed, paying special attention to the disconnect between the Restatement and actual practice.

I. THE ENGLISH CASES

A. *Taylor v. Caldwell*

On May 27, 1861, Taylor, a promoter, entered into a contract for the use of the Surrey Gardens and Music Hall in which he would put on four grand concerts during the summer. He would pay £100 for each concert and pocket 100 per cent of the revenues. On June 11, before any of the concerts had been held, the Music Hall was destroyed by a fire caused by a careless plumber. The concerts were cancelled and Taylor sued. Taylor did not sue for expectation damages; he sued only for his reliance damages, £58, the costs incurred in preparation for the concerts. I should note that that was not a trivial amount, since per capita annual income in England at the time was around £40. Blackburn, J held that "in contracts in which the performance depends on the continued existence of a given person or thing, a condition is implied that the impossibility of performance arising from the perishing of the person or thing shall excuse performance." (839) Impossibility would relieve both parties of their contractual obligations. The reliance expenses incurred by Taylor in preparation could not be recovered. Taylor had not, apparently, paid any of the £100 installments, so restitution was not an issue. Shortly after deciding *Taylor*, Blackburn, J clarified the post-excuse picture: "We think that where… the premises are destroyed without fault on either side, it is a misfortune equally affecting both parties; excusing both from further performance of the contract, but giving a cause of action to neither." (*Appleby v. Meyers*, 659) *Appleby* was cited for the "English rule" in a number of nineteenth-century American cases.

Blackburn, J held that the fire was not covered in the contract: "The parties when framing their agreement evidently had not present to their minds the possibility of such a disaster, and have made no express stipulation with reference to it." (832) Defense counsel pointed to the term "God's will permitting," which I take to be a variation on "act of God," but the Lords appeared to give it no weight. It is not clear why the contract would be silent regarding the possibility that a fire might destroy the premises. The possible unavailability without fault of the venue or artist is a predictable risk. The parties could excuse each other (the *Taylor* solution), insure against it, or require pre-payment or restitution of some or all of any pre-payment. Fires, after all, were not so rare that people could not anticipate the possibility. Fire insurance had been available in England since the Great Fire of London, roughly two centuries earlier. Indeed, the Surrey Music Hall was covered by fire insurance. Taylor most likely did not have insurance to cover either his expected gains or his reliance losses, although nowadays such insurance would not be unusual.

It would also be common for parties today to include in their agreements what should happen if some intervening event meant that either the artist or the venue were unavailable. If the artists are popular (and therefore have a high opportunity cost) and have substantial pre-concert expenses, they are likely to require that the venue give them substantial compensation if the venue were to become unavailable. The amount of the compensation would likely depend on whether the artists had adequate time to find a satisfactory replacement gig. Indeed, they might even require that the venue pay some, or all, of their fee, regardless of the timing. Likewise, a major venue might insist that the artist pay liquidated damages if it has to cancel. The magnitude of the damages could depend on both the timing of the cancellation and the reasons for it. As noted in Chapter 11, not all excuses, whether for the artist or the venue, need be treated equally.

B. The Coronation Cases

In Chapter 11, I considered the arguments for excusing performance. My concern here is not whether performance should have been excused, but with what happened next. In *Krell*, Henry had agreed to pay £75 for the rooms and had already paid £25 before the postponement was announced. Krell sued for the additional £50 and Henry counterclaimed for his prepayment. The trial judge held that both claims were covered by *Taylor v. Caldwell* and denied recovery for both. While it is not germane to the restitution/reliance question, I think it is at least amusing to note one of the hypotheticals posed by Mr. Justice Darling: "When people used to take to the Magpie and Stump, opposite the Old Bailey, for the purpose of seeing a hanging, would the landlord be held to guarantee that there would be no reprieve?" Krell's counsel responded by claiming that his opponent "would have to say if there was a reprieve the defendant got no fun for his money and need not pay." (Krell, 1902, 5) Henry dropped his counterclaim, so the Lords did not have to deal with the restitution issue. Since there was no evidence that either party had made any expenditures in reliance upon the procession, they did not have to deal with the reliance issue either.

The restitution question was resolved in *Chandler v. Webster*. Chandler rented a room for £141 15s for the first day with the intention of erecting a stand and selling tickets. The money was all due prior to the postponement and £100 had been paid. Chandler sued for return of his £100 and Webster counterclaimed for the remainder. The House of Lords held that the parties should be left where they were at the time of the frustrating event. That is, the buyer would be responsible for any prepayments or money due prior to the event – there would be no restitution. Webster, therefore, could keep the £100 and also was entitled to the £41 and 15 shillings that had not yet been paid.

In neither *Krell* nor *Chandler* did the contract give a hint as to the function of the prepayment. Nor did the courts ask. There was no evidence that either Krell or Webster had made any investments in reliance upon the contract. Indeed, in addition to promising to pay the entire amount up front, Chandler was going to erect a viewing stand and let seats. There is no evidence on whether Chandler had succeeded in letting seats, whether he had received any payment for them, and, if so, whether he had any obligation to return money. Most likely, the owners' primary concern was that the counterparty would walk away on the eve of the coronation, leaving them with a vacant room and the need to initiate a suit for payment. I suspect, although there is no direct evidence, that in the six months leading up to the coronation, entrepreneurs, in effect, took options, making modest down payments on one viewing site while searching for a more attractive one. As the date drew near, the option price increased. This is, I concede, speculation. There are a lot of reasons for prepayments. As we shall see, in overturning *Chandler v. Webster*, the House of Lords (Lord Porter) put the burden of explaining the purpose on the party that had received the payment. For my purposes, the relevant point is that the coronation cases established a clear rule, a rule that survived for forty years.

C. *Fibrosa* and the Frustrated Contracts Act

Chandler v. Webster generated considerable criticism and it was finally overturned in *Fibrosa Spolka Akcyjna v. Fairbairn Lawson Combe Barbour, Ltd.* In July 1939, a Polish company ordered flax-hackling machines from an English company, at a price of £4,800, with delivery to be in three to four months. One-third was supposed to be paid when the order was placed, although only £1,000 had actually been paid. In September, Germany invaded Poland and Great Britain declared war on Germany. The purchaser sued for the return of its £1,000. "Counsel added that he was not counterclaiming for £600, the balance of the £1600, payment of which was a term of the contract, first, because he thought there might not be much chance of getting it, and, secondly, because it might have been used against him on the question of security for costs of the appeal." (*Fibrosa*, 1942, 12)

The force majeure clause included a war contingency: "Should the despatch be hindered or delayed by your instructions, or lack of instructions, or by any cause whatsoever beyond our reasonable control, including strikes, lock-outs, war, fire, accidents, defective material or approval of drawings, a reasonable extension of time shall be granted." (*Fibrosa* 1941, 98) The Law Lords held that this clause did not cover the prolonged and indefinite delay of World War II (the decision came down in mid-1942) and they therefore had to fall back on the default rules of the common law. I cannot understand how a war clause in 1939 would not include the possibility that a war would go on for years; had they already forgotten the "War to End All Wars"? I would think that the sensible interpretation of the clause would be that it included this war and that after a "reasonable time," the contract would terminate. The defense argued that the force majeure clause did not apply and that the contract was frustrated. I suspect that it did so because it believed that frustration would put them under *Chandler*, but it was less certain what would happen under force majeure. (*Fibrosa*, 1943, 39) The plaintiffs argued that the clause did operate and that performance would be suspended, perhaps indefinitely. (*Fibrosa*, 1942, 22)

Indefinite suspension, in fact, is what German courts did following the war. Dawson (1983, 1083–88) describes the case in which purchasers of Volkswagens ("VWs") in 1938–39 prepaid a part of the price; the war intervened before delivery. Following the war, some purchasers sued and the court ruled in 1951 that they could receive a Volkswagen at a price to be fixed by the court. The trial court was directed to find the other 330,000 people who had ordered the pre-war VW to see if they had survived the war and still desired a VW.

The notion that force majeure and frustration are not related strikes me as peculiar. However, the defense made just that argument emphatically: "Frustration operates independently of the intention of the parties. The fact that an express term in the contract appears to provide for the actual occurrence leading to the frustration in no way prevents there being read into the contract the implied term the existence of which is the basis of the doctrine of frustration. … That frustration does not depend on the intention, opinion, or even knowledge of the parties is established. … Even where the contract seems to have provided expressly for what has happened in wide terms, it does not prevent frustration by the operation of law." (*Fibrosa*, 1942, 23–24) This theme, we will see, is repeated in *B.P. Exploration Co. (Libya) Ltd. v. Hunt (No. 2)*.

Regardless, the Lords treated the force majeure clause as irrelevant and then held that the contract had been frustrated. They then overturned *Chandler v. Webster*, holding that the £1000 should be returned. What of the reliance expenditures of the seller in the weeks before the deal was frustrated? There was considerable confusion as to the extent of the manufacturer's reliance. Counsel for the sellers argued that the "machines were of an unusual type." (38) That suggests that these were customized machines and that their value to others, therefore, would be reduced. The decisions suggest that this was probably not the case, but they are a bit murky on this point. Near the beginning of his judgment in the Court of Appeal, Mackinnon, LJ suggests that there was not really a reliance problem.

> On Dec. 1 the solicitors for the defendants wrote to the solicitors for the plaintiffs that two of the machines had been completed before the war. They go on to say that the defendants can sell all the machinery, "which will leave them with no loss on these particular machines arising from the non-performance of this contract," and ask the plaintiffs to concur in this disposal. (32)

Near the end of his judgment, however, he disclaims any knowledge:

> We know nothing of the work done by the defendants on these machines, or how they disposed of them, or to what extent the £1000 has been a pure windfall to them. If the House of Lords should find themselves able to overrule *Chandler v. Webster*, and substitute a rule like the more civilised rule of Roman and Scottish law, presumably some inquiry will be necessary to determine how much. (34)

The Law Lords added some thoughts on the extent of the manufacturer's reliance, although it is not clear that there was any evidence on the point. Lord Roche concluded (apparently with no evidence) that in this instance, there was no reliance issue:

> My Lords, I only desire to add that I am conscious that a conclusion relegating parties in cases of frustration to their contracts may not work out a completely just solution in the pecuniary sense. It happens that in this case it will do so, for the appellants, who did not get the goods or the documents, will get their money back, and the respondents have had the machines, which, so far as completed, were said by the respondents themselves to be realizable without loss. (76)

Lord Porter suggested a default rule – if the reason for the prepayment was unstated, it is returnable. "It is possible to say that the seller in such a case who has been prudent enough to stipulate for a payment in advance should reap the advantage of his foresight, but to do so is to speculate as to the object for which the advance was obtained, not to ascertain what his legal remedies are upon the facts as known." (78) If, therefore, the seller had included in the contract an acceptable rationale for the down payment being nonrefundable were the contract excused, then the law would honor its intent.

As Lord Porter suggested, there are many reasons why a buyer might prepay some, or all, of the price. Here are a few of them. (1) If a dispute arises, it determines who has to sue to change the status quo. (2) The prepayment can give the buyer an option. If I book a hotel, for example, I typically have a free option until 24 hours before the date, after which they will then charge my credit card for one night; in certain high demand contexts (graduation day in a college town) the cancellation date might be earlier and the commitment greater. (3) The prepayment might establish the credibility of the buyer. Prepayment, or payment to a reliable third party (escrow), can ameliorate the credibility problem. (4) Opportunity cost; for example, Krell might have been concerned that Henry might walk away from the deal prior to the procession, leaving Krell with an unrented room. (5) Progress payments provide a seller with working capital. (6) They also provide some protection from opportunistic rebargaining. (7) The seller might have to make some relation-specific expenditures (e.g., customizing goods or advertising for a specific event). It is not clear to me why a plethora of reasons would lead to the conclusion that, absent specific language, we should ignore all of them.

Ultimately, the Lords didn't care about reliance. It might be unfortunate, said Lord Chancellor Simon, if the seller had relied, but, absent specific language, the reliance would not be protected.

> While this result obviates the harshness with which the previous view in some instances treated the party who had made a prepayment, it cannot be regarded as dealing fairly between the parties in all cases, and must sometimes have the result of leaving the recipient who has to return the money at a grave disadvantage. He may have incurred expenses in connexion with the partial carrying out of the contract which are equivalent, or more than equivalent, to the money which he prudently stipulated should be prepaid, but which he now has to return for reasons which are no fault of his. He may have to repay the money, though he has executed almost the whole of the contractual work, which will be left on his hands. (1943, 49)

New legislation, he said, would be required. Parliament responded shortly thereafter by passing the Law Reform (Frustrated Contracts) Act 1943, which allowed for compensation for reasonable reliance.

Section 1(2) provides for restitution of money paid before the discharging event subject to a key proviso. The repayment could be offset, in whole or in part, if that party had incurred reliance expenditures if the court "considers it just to do so having regard to all the circumstances of the case." Section 1(3) adds to this recovery of expenses incurred in reliance so long as they do not exceed any valuable benefits received by the counterparty prior to discharge. Two immediate problems arise. First, what, if anything, constrains the judge's notion of what is "just"? Second, what constitutes a benefit? Returning to the example in the Introduction to this chapter, if Smith contracts to paint Brown's factory and the factory burns down after half has been painted, did Brown receive a "benefit"? Would the results be different if the painter had been paid progress payments along the way? That problem was addressed, in part, in sections 2(3) and 2(4). The former would allow the parties to contract out of the Act. The latter applies if the frustrated part of the contract could be treated as severable from the rest; severability would mean that payments for work performed prior to the frustrating event would not be recoverable; severability would be sufficient, but it would not be necessary. That is, even if the contract was not severable, a court might find that Brown could not recover.

The dearth of case law following passage of the Act suggests that parties have contracted out of it – parties did not want to be at the mercy of the whims of judges pursuing their view of a just resolution. In the sixty-plus years since its enactment, only two cases have litigated the meaning of the Act: *B.P. Exploration Co. (Libya) Ltd. v. Hunt (No. 2)* and *Gamerco v. I.C.M.* Neither makes much sense.

D. *B.P. Exploration Co. (Libya) Ltd. v. Hunt (No. 2)*

The deal, a so-called farm-out agreement, was rather complicated, but all we need is a somewhat simplified version. Nelson Bunker Hunt received a 50-year concession from the Libyan government to explore for oil in 1957. One condition of the concession was that he would have to start drilling within three years and so he teamed up with British Petroleum. British Petroleum would do all the exploration and development on its own account. BP made an upfront payment of $2 million in cash and four million barrels of oil (which, I presume, Hunt could resell immediately and convert into cash). Hunt would put up no cash. If oil in commercial quantities were discovered, the oil would be split 50:50. In addition, British Petroleum would recover its exploration and development expenses out of Hunt's 50 percent share. So, until BP had recouped 125 percent of its expenses, three-eighths of Hunt's share would go to BP. Oil was discovered and production commenced in 1967. The contract was amended at that time so that instead of the 125 percent rule, BP's compensation would come from the first 50 million barrels. However, in 1969, the Libyan king was overthrown and Gadaffi (this was the spelling used in the decision) came to power. Subsequently, Gadaffi was in a dispute with the British government; instead of breaking off relations with Britain, Libya expropriated BP's share. A few years later, Hunt's share was also expropriated, but that is essentially irrelevant. BP sued Hunt, arguing that the purpose of their agreement had been frustrated, and, invoking the Act, asked for compensation. After years of fighting over whether the dispute should be resolved in England or Texas, the case was heard in England. The trial lasted 57 days and in a very lengthy judgment (over forty thousand words), Mr. Justice Robert Goff found for BP.

The agreement was spread over two documents, the letter agreement and the operating agreement. Before proceeding I will reproduce some of the relevant terms.

> *Clause 6 of the letter agreement.* It is specifically understood and agreed that Mr. *Hunt* shall have no personal liability to repay the sums required in the operating agreement and this letter agreement to be advanced by B.P. for Mr. Hunt's account or paid to Mr. Hunt, but B.P.'s right to recover any such sums which B.P. is required to pay or advance for Mr. Hunt's account shall be limited to recovery solely out of three-eighths of Mr. Hunt's half of the production, and in the manner specified under section 9 of the operating agreement, if, as and when produced, saved and delivered at the Libyan sea terminal. (828)
>
> *Clause 9 (e) of the operating agreement. Reimbursement of Payments.* B.P. shall be entitled to take and receive as reimbursement three-eighths of Mr. Hunt's share of the oil production from the concession delivered f.o.b. Libyan seaboard until B.P. has received a quantity of crude oil equal to the sum of the following: (1) A quantity equal in value to 125 per cent of all costs and expenses advanced by B.P. for Mr. Hunt's account on exploration, development or any other work performed in or in connection with the concession, then (2) a quantity equal in value to U.S. $2,500,000, and then (3) 5,000,000 barrels. (829)
>
> *Clause 27 of the operating agreement.* If any party is rendered unable wholly or in part by Force Majeure to carry out its obligations under this Agreement other than the obligation to make money payments, that party shall give to all other parties prompt written notice of the Force Majeure with reasonably full particulars concerning it. Thereupon the obligations of the party giving the notice, so far as they are affected by the Force Majeure, *shall be suspended* during, but no longer than, the continuance of the Force Majeure. The affected party shall use all possible diligence to remove the Force Majeure as quickly as possible. The requirement that any Force Majeure should be remedied with all reasonable despatch shall not require the settlement of strikes, lock-outs, or other labour difficulty by the party involved contrary to its wishes. How all such difficulties shall be handled shall be entirely within the discretion of the party concerned. The terms "Force Majeure" as here employed shall mean an act of God, strike, lock-out or other industrial disturbance, act of a public enemy, war, blockade, public riot, lightning, fire, storm and flood, explosion, *governmental restraint*, unavailability of equipment and any other cause whether of a kind specifically enumerated above or otherwise, which is not reasonably within the control of the party claiming suspension. (*BP v. Hunt* (1976, 474 emphasis added)

Expropriation would, I should think, be covered in the force majeure clause under the rubric of "governmental restraint." Not so. Goff, J, in dismissing the clause, found it so irrelevant that he didn't even bother to reproduce the clause in his judgment: "[S]ection 27 is the force majeure clause, but again that only applies during the subsistence of the contract – its effect is only to suspend a party's obligations during the continuance of the force majeure, and it makes no provision for what is to occur in the event of frustration." (830) As in *Fibrosa*, the clause is interpreted as applying only during temporary suspensions. There, because the defendant believed that a finding of frustration would favor it, the defendant argued against finding the force majeure clause governing. Here, the positions were reversed. Farm-out agreements in the United States continue to refer only to "suspension," with no explicit acknowledgment of the possibility of a permanent termination. (Lowe (1987)) My understanding is that had Texas law been binding, the force majeure clause would have terminated the agreement. Surprisingly, the contracts included neither a choice of law nor choice of forum clause, and so the litigation ended up in the English courts using English law. Perhaps, this was a result of the parties adopting a Texas form document without taking into account the possibility that a dispute would end up in England.

Even without the force majeure clause, Hunt would seem to have a strong argument on the basis of clause 6. All expenses are to be paid by BP and BP's only compensation is to come from the produced oil. No oil, no money. That seems about as clear as possible. And that, like the force majeure clause, would have yielded the same outcome as *Chandler v. Webster*, leaving the losses where they fell. However, Mr. Justice Goff found (and the Law Lords unanimously agreed) that once the contract was deemed frustrated, clause 6 no longer applied. "Generally speaking, when a contract is determined by frustration, the whole contract goes. … *It must never be forgotten that the policy of the Act is to prevent the unjust enrichment of the defendant at the expense of the plaintiff.*" (829)

Having freed himself from the contractual language, Goff, J then set about interpreting and applying the Act. In *Fibrosa*, the buyer sought restitution for a prepayment and the seller incurred some expenses, arguably, in reliance. That situation, covered by section 1(2) of the Act, was quite different from this one. Before turning to the actual case, consider a simpler one. Suppose that BP had made a one-time cash payment of $50 million to Hunt and would receive 100 percent of the revenues. If BP was then expropriated, could it get restitution of any part of the $50 million? Unlike in *Fibrosa*, the reliance expenditures would have been made by BP, not Hunt. Rather than being an offset to the initial payment, they would be additional costs. Since Hunt would have no further stake in the operation, this might as well be an outright sale. If indeed there had been a sale and subsequently Libya expropriated the field, there would be no rationale for BP getting any of its $50 million back from Hunt, regardless of how much (or little) oil BP had produced prior to the expropriation. But, if it remained only a contract, even though there would be no substantive difference from the outright sale, the Frustrated Contracts Act might allow BP to recover some of the $50 million. Recovery would depend on how much oil it had produced (and the costs it had incurred) and would be contingent upon whether a judge found it to be "just."

The facts here were more complicated, but the merits of BP's claim were no better. BP made a relatively small down payment, incurred substantial costs, and divided the revenue stream so that Hunt had received 5/16 of the oil revenue when the expropriation occurred. Goff, J interpreted the statute as requiring Hunt to make restitution, with the amount capped by the benefits Hunt had received. Since the bulk of Hunt's benefits were in services, not cash, the first question was whether to evaluate them as the cost of the input or the value of the output. The gap between the two was large since the field had turned out to be a productive one. The judge opted for the value of the output. The value of the output exceeded the cost of the input in this instance, but that need not always be the case. In the class of excuse cases mentioned in the Introduction (the factory that was destroyed before completion of the paint job), Goff, J argued that the value of the output would be zero. The second question was how to value BP's reliance. Third, how should any costs incurred by BP be apportioned between BP and Hunt and what credit, if any, should Hunt get for producing the benefits?

Since the contract was terminated eleven years after formation and the costs were heavily front-loaded, a fourth question concerned the treatment of the time value of money. Goff, J concluded, reluctantly, that the statute required that he ignore it. So, a dollar in 1960 was treated the same as a dollar in 1970.

The benefit received by Hunt included the prepayment, the oil received both before and after BP's expropriation, and the modest compensation Hunt received from Libya following its expropriation. The court held that since the output was due to the effort of both BP and Hunt, it would attribute half of Hunt's benefit to BP's efforts. Hunt's "effort" apparently was the initial acquisition of the concession. (816) No justification was given for this arbitrary allocation. Goff, J then found that Hunt's net benefit was about $85 million. This, then, provided a ceiling for BP's compensation.

To determine BP's reliance costs, the court began with BP's prepayment; it then took the costs BP had incurred on Hunt's behalf (presumably, half of the actual costs being for BP and half for Hunt) and subtracted the market value of the reimbursement oil that it had received – about 33 million barrels. What of the half of the costs incurred on BP's account and the roughly 88 million barrels of oil it received on its own account? Those were ignored. The costs plus the prepayments were approximately $98 million and the value of the reimbursement oil was about $63 million, resulting in an award of roughly $35 million. (838) Since this was less than Hunt's benefit ($85 million), Hunt would have to return the entire $35 million to BP. To this was added interest from the time the cause of action arose.

On appeal, Mr. Justice Goff's conclusion that neither the force majeure clause nor clause 6 survived frustration was upheld. Lord Justice Lawton in the Court of Appeals said:

> The legal effect of frustration is to bring a contract to an end forthwith, without more and automatically: … . It follows that clause 6 ceased to operate after December 7, 1971, unless, on its true construction, it was intended to have effect whether there was frustration or not. We can find no words in it to that effect. … In order to sustain the defendant's submission the clause would have to be read as meaning that the defendant should have no personal liability under the contract or otherwise, including under the Act of 1943, to repay. In our judgment there is no reason why the clause should be read in these terms; and, if it is not so read, it ceased to have effect when the frustrating events occurred. What the defendant has been ordered to pay under the judgment is not what was due under the contract but what was recoverable from him as a just sum under the Act. (241)

In the House of Lords, Lord Brandon added:

> [T]here is nothing in the terms of the contract between the parties, or in the circumstances surrounding the making of it as found by Robert Goff J., to indicate, either expressly or by necessary implication, that the parties, when they made the contract in 1960, had in contemplation political risks, such as expropriation of the concession in whole or in part by the Libyan government, which would operate to frustrate the contract; or that, having had such risks in contemplation, they included in the contract any provision which, expressly or by necessary implication, was to take effect in the event of such risks materialising. (372)

Having satisfied themselves that Section 2(3) was inapposite, both the Court of Appeal and the House of Lords upheld Mr. Justice Goff's findings with little analysis. The law, said Lawton, J, grants the trial court considerable discretion: "What is just is what the trial judge thinks is just. That being so, an appellate court is not entitled to interfere with his decision unless it is so plainly wrong that it cannot be just" (238)

Hunt had one final shot, the European Commission of Human Rights. In rejecting his plea, the Commission noted that the fact that the Frustrated Contracts Law had never been litigated did not matter:

> In the present case the proceedings in the United Kingdom were based upon a statute which preexisted the Farm-In Agreement and of which the parties to that agreement may therefore be assumed to have been aware. However the applicant points out that the statute had never previously been interpreted by the Courts and that it could not have been foreseen to have applied to the Farm-In Agreement. Nevertheless the Commission cannot equate this position with that where the applicable law has been substantially changed by legislation which has affected the established rights of one party, because it is clear from the very fact that BP instituted proceedings against the applicant that it was arguable that the 1943 Act might be found to apply to the Farm-In Agreement. (540)

So, to recapitulate, Hunt brought one thing to the deal – a fifty-year concession to develop an oil field. We know not how he procured it, but we do know that once he had entered into the BP agreement, he had no further responsibilities. BP, on the other hand, agreed to incur the heavy expenses of searching for oil and, if successful, building the infrastructure that would get it to market. If the oil field were successfully developed, the parties would split the revenues evenly. Hunt would pay nothing out of pocket. He would contribute to the costs only out of his share of the produced oil – 3/8 of his share going to BP until a particular hurdle was crossed (125 percent of BP's costs or, after amendment, 50 million barrels of oil). Libya expropriated the property and BP argued successfully that the contract had been frustrated, notwithstanding that the contracts had allocated some of the risks of government restraints in a force majeure clause. The court held that the force majeure clause applied only to temporary suspensions, not to a permanent expropriation. It further held that the Frustrated Contract Act rendered irrelevant any contractual risk allocation that might otherwise have guided the court in fashioning a remedy.

Thus unmoored, Mr. Justice Goff fashioned a remedy that made no sense. By interpreting the statute as precluding consideration of the time value of money, he assured that both Hunt's benefits and BP's reliance would be mismeasured. The artificial split of BP's costs between its account and Hunt's bore no relationship to anything. The apparent disregard of the net revenue from BP's 50 percent share likewise made no sense. All this in the name of "justice." After years of international jockeying, 57 days of trial, and two levels of appeal (three if we count the Commission on Human Rights), the net result was a mishmash that no one could have opted for ex ante. Nonetheless, Treitel speaks of it approvingly: "The machinery of the Act worked satisfactorily in *BP Exploration (Libya) Ltd. v. Hunt* because the value of the benefit, even when reduced in the light of the frustrating event, exceeded the just sum." (604) Virgo criticizes the judgment on totally different grounds from mine: "The judge should have considered *all of the circumstances* of the case, not just the value of services provided." (368, emphasis added) The open-ended invitation of whatever the judge thinks is just apparently was not enough for him.

It is ironic that the first case to interpret the Frustrated Contracts Act fits the pattern so poorly. The paradigm case involves restitution of a prepayment with partial offset for expenses incurred prior to the frustrating event. The time frame is short and the time value of money irrelevant. The only other case did fit that pattern, but the result was not any better.

E. From *Taylor v. Caldwell* to Guns N' Roses

The next case litigated under the Frustrated Contracts Act (*Gamerco*) was a variation on *Taylor v. Caldwell*. For its European tour in 1992, Guns N' Roses was to perform in twenty open air concerts in twelve countries in less than two months. The last concert, scheduled for July 4, was to take place at the Vicente Calderon Stadium in Madrid. The contract with a Spanish promoter for the Madrid performance was for 90 percent of the net door receipts with a guaranteed minimum of $1.1 million. The promoter had arranged for the concert to take place and had prepaid the group $412,500. The promoter was "responsible for erecting the stage … the roof and generally preparing the venue." An engineering report on June 30 found the stadium unsafe and on July 2, the government banned the use of the stadium. Other Madrid venues were unavailable on such short notice and the concert had to be cancelled, disappointing the 44,500 fans who had already purchased tickets. (There do not appear to have been any other problems with venues on the tour. However, during the tour, health problems caused the postponement of one of the concerts and cancellation of another.) The judgment is silent on whether ticket holders were reimbursed and, if so, who bore that burden. The contract between the Spanish promoter and Guns N' Roses did not include a force majeure clause. I find the lack of any clause puzzling. The answer might be in the piecemeal way the contract was put together. There was a short document with a number of riders. For various reasons, the court chose not to recognize one of the riders. It is plausible that that rider would have contained a force majeure clause, but of that we can't be certain. While the parties did not, apparently, allocate the risk contractually between them, they both anticipated the possibility that the event would be cancelled without the fault of either. As Garland, J noted: "Both parties had insured against cancellation and had made recoveries under their respective policies." (1235)

In any event, the promoter sued for the return of the $412,500. The defense argued that it had been ready, willing, and able to perform and that the contract had not been frustrated – the plaintiff had breached by not providing the stadium. That failed. In applying the Act, Garland, J held that the money must be returned, subject to a possible offset for costs incurred by the defendant as required by justice. He did note that the costs of a modern touring rock group could be substantial:

> [They] took with them on tour specialist contractors for sound, video, lighting, catering and transport together with members of their own staff. Apart from the six members of the group there were 20 "band touring personnel" and 76 "crew touring personnel," of whom approximately 30 were either staff or self-employed under a corporate identity. The transport required was a Boeing 727 chartered from M.G.M. Grand Air for 53 days, ten articulated trucks, two generator trucks, four 12-berth sleeper coaches and one 14-berth, all hired with drivers for 53 days. (1229)

The band's reliance expenditures directly attributable to the Madrid engagement were no doubt modest – perhaps they had to pay cancellation fees for some hotels. Their primary reliance costs were a share of the 53-day tour's expenses. How should the costs be apportioned between the various engagements on a tour? Should they be prorated across the twenty engagements? Should an accountant break out the costs specific to the Madrid show? Garland, J took evidence on the band's reliance expenditures but was not persuaded. The band claimed about $180,000; the court figured that it was closer to $50,000, although he provided no rationale for so finding. At the same time, he concluded that the plaintiffs had incurred reliance expenditures, including payments to third parties, for work done in preparation of the stadium. The court found those costs to be about $450,000.

Garland, J's interpretation of the Act was that he should "do justice in a situation which the parties had neither contemplated nor provided for, and to mitigate the possible harshness of allowing all loss to lie where it has fallen." (1238) Since both parties had insured against the contingency, the conclusion that neither party had contemplated the situation is not tenable. But, that is just an aside. The grounds for excusing performance should not depend on the contemplation of the parties or the remoteness of the supervening event. Granted that performance should be excused, Garland, J still had to deal with the plaintiff's claim for restitution. He concluded: "In all the circumstances, and having particular regard to the plaintiffs' loss, I consider that justice is done by making no deduction under the proviso." (1238) That is, the band must repay the entire prepayment.

Lost in this exercise is any concern for why the prepayment in the first place. This interpretation of the statute presumes that the only legitimate ground for making an offset against restitution is the band's out-of-pocket reliance. The band's primary concern, almost certainly, was not the pro rata share of the tour costs, but the fact that they were stuck in Spain earning nothing and not being paid the guaranteed $1.1 million (plus a share of the merchandising income). We cannot be sure about why the parties structured the contract as they did – counsel did not help on this score. The most plausible explanation is, I think, that when negotiating with promoters for the tour, the band could take advantage of the competition amongst promoters and get assurance that it would receive a reasonable fraction of its expected earnings if a show had to be cancelled even if neither party were at fault. The more attractive the act, the greater the nonrefundable fee. And, with per show fees in excess of $1 million, Guns N' Roses was a very attractive act.

II. COMING TO AMERICA

While the English statute displaced the contract entirely, the American approach implied a term. "Since it is the rationale of … [the Restatement (Second)] that, in a case of impracticability or frustration, the contract does not cover the case that has arisen, the court's function can be viewed generally as… supplying a term to deal with that omitted case." (§ 272, comment c.) The majority rule in the United States is spelled out in the Restatement (Second) §§ 272, 371, and 377. The rules purport to soften the impact of the termination of the contract. "Because the rules … might otherwise appear to have the harsh effect of denying either party any recovery following the discharge of one party's duty based on impracticability or frustration, this Section makes it clear that several mitigating doctrines may be used to allow at least some recovery in a proper case." (§ 272, comment a) The recurring theme is that the law should "avoid injustice."

It is useful to focus attention on a particular problem. A contractor is working on an existing structure but before completion of the job, the structure is destroyed by fire and the contractor is excused. That problem is prominently featured in the Restatement. The owner might have made some payments to the contractor prior to the fire. The nineteenth-century common law rule was that neither party would have an action against the other. As the Restatement makes clear, that is no longer the case.

Before turning to the various American responses, I want to return to Mr. Justice Goff's interpretation of the Frustrated Contracts Act's treatment of this problem:

> Suppose that a contract for work on a building is frustrated by a fire which destroys the building and which, therefore, also destroys a substantial amount of work already done by the plaintiff. Although it might be thought just to award the plaintiff a sum assessed on a quantum meruit basis, probably a rateable part of the contract price, in respect of the work he has done, the effect of section 1 (3) (b) will be to reduce the award to nil, because of the effect, in relation to the defendant's benefit, of the circumstances giving rise to the frustration of the contract. … [T]he subsection therefore contemplates that, in such a case, the benefit is the end product of the plaintiff's services, not the services themselves. (801–2)

The owner's benefit could be determined by either the value of the services that had been provided before the fire or the value to the owner after the fire (when everything provided by the contractor had been destroyed). So, if the English courts followed Goff's reading of the Act, there would be no benefit and the contractors would get nothing. The approach in many American jurisdictions is, in effect, to consider the owner's benefit a nanosecond before the fire. The owner at that instant has been "unjustly enriched" and the contractor could be entitled to restitution. The Williston Treatise puts it this way:

> Generally, where full performance has been prevented by impracticability, the right of recovery does not depend on whether the defendant has received and still retains a benefit when further performance becomes impossible. Neither does recovery depend on whether, at any prior time, the performance which the defendant received was personally advantageous. It is enough that the defendant has actually received, in exchange for partial performance of the contract, something for which, when completed, it had agreed to pay. (Lord, ch. 77)

The Restatement (Third) of Restitution & Unjust Enrichment differs from the Restatement (Second) of Contracts in that it avoids the fiction of the owner receiving a benefit: "The necessary analysis does not require the court to determine the extent (if any) to which Owner was 'enriched' by Builder's interrupted performance." (§ 34 illustration 15)

The relation between the owner's benefit, so defined, and the contractor's costs is not perfect and that has resulted in divergent treatments of the owner's obligation to the contractor. While in some jurisdictions courts have stuck with the leave-the-losses-where-they-lie rule, the majority position is that restitution should be made for work performed and money paid before the intervening event. The majority position can be further broken down. The Restatement Illustration is a good place to begin:

> A contracts with B to shingle the roof of B's house for $5,000, payable as the work progresses. After A has spent $2,000 doing part of the work and has been paid $1,800, much of the house including the roof is destroyed by fire without his fault, and the duties of performance of both A and B are discharged … . The work done before the fire increased the market price and the insurable value of the house by $1,500. A is entitled to restitution of $1,500 from B and B is entitled to restitution of $1,800 from A. (§ 377 illustration 4)

Notice that there is no questioning why B might have paid the $1,800 in the first place. The gap between the $1,800 and the $2,000 is unexplained. Nor is there an explanation for why A's costs exceed B's value. It is hard to imagine an appraiser sifting through the ashes to ascertain the value of the partially completed job. Is A being compensated for its reliance or B for its loss? If A's costs were all set-up costs so that at the time of the fire, nothing had been installed, would A get nothing? In the next illustration, the answer appears to be: Yes. "[T]he fire also destroyed shingles that had cost A $500 and that were piled near the house for the rest of the work. A is not entitled to restitution of this loss from B." (§ 377 illustration 5)

The basis for this illustration is two early twentieth-century decisions: *Young v. City of Chicopee* and *Carroll v. Bowersock*. In the former, the contract was for the repair of a wooden bridge with the contractor to be paid for lumber wrought into the bridge. The court noted that "the contract provided that no work should be begun until material for at least one-half of the repairs contemplated should be 'upon the job.'" The fire destroyed both the bridge and the lumber that had been stacked on the job site but had not yet been incorporated into the bridge. The contractor sued. The defendant did not dispute liability for the material "wrought into" the bridge but denied liability for the remaining lumber. The court agreed. Note that the decision does not provide support for the Restatement position regarding restitution. Instead, it followed *Chandler v. Webster*. Even though the contract required that material be stored on site, the contractor was to be paid only if and when lumber actually was wrought into the bridge; there would be no payment for the unincorporated lumber even though the contract required that it be present. So, under *Chandler*, Chicopee had to pay the contractually determined amount. Neither the costs to Young nor the benefits to Chicopee had to be determined.

Building on its misinterpretation of *Young*, the *Carroll* court held that the "wrought-in" test rested on the owner's benefit, however ephemeral:

> A contractor may have purchased special material to be used in repairing a house, and may have had much millwork done upon it. If the material remain in the mill, and the house burn, there can be no recovery. If the milled material be delivered at the house ready for use, and the house burn, there can be no recovery. It takes something more to make the owner liable for what the contractor has done toward performance. The owner must be benefited. He should not be enriched at the expense of the contractor. That would be unjust, and to the extent that the owner has been benefited, the law may properly consider him as resting under a duty to pay. The benefit which the owner has received may or may not be equivalent to the detriment which the contractor has suffered. The only basis on which the law can raise an obligation on the part of the owner is the consideration he has received by way of benefit, advantage, or value to him. (144)

In *Carroll*, the contract payments were phased, a point the court ignores. This is a recurring theme to which I shall return.

The wrought-in standard is a clever answer to a not-so-clever question. In effect, it treats the contract as conveying some property. The risk of destruction of the property conveyed is borne by the owner; the risk to the property not yet conveyed is borne by the contractor. That still left the question of whether ownership had transferred. So, for example, when a building was destroyed after an elevator had been installed, but before completion, the contractor's claim was denied because the contract required that the work be accepted by an architect and that condition had not been met. (*Louisville Foundry & Mach. Co. v. Patterson*) But that is an aside. The main point is that if the purpose is to protect the contractor's reliance, the wrought-in standard is irrelevant. The contractor's costs need bear no relation to whatever had been wrought in at the time of the fire. Reliance expenditures for planning, promotion, or off-site fabrication would all be disallowed. Returning to the English cases, there would be no recovery in *Taylor*, *Gamerco*, or *Fibrosa*.

Not all American jurisdictions accepted the wrought-in rule. *F. M. Gabler, Inc. v. Evans Laboratories, Inc.* allowed for partial recovery. The contract was for installation of fire safety devices. Before installation was complete, the building burnt down. The contractor's costs at the time of the fire were roughly 40 percent for materials installed, 30 percent for materials brought to the site but not yet installed, and 30 percent for materials ready to be supplied but not yet delivered to the job site. The court went beyond the wrought-in standard but fell short of reliance. It awarded compensation for the first two categories, but not the third.

The litigated contracts in the repair cases often include some form of phased compensation which is duly noted by the courts and then ignored. An early case, *Butterfield v. Byron*, noted that if each installment was separate consideration, then no compensation was necessary. But if the payments were merely advances toward a single sum, then actions for both the return of the payments and for the work done prior to the fire would be allowed. The court concluded (why, it is not clear) that:

> the defendant was to receive an entire sum for the performance of the contract, and that the payments made were merely advances on account of it, and that, on his failure to perform the contract, there was a failure of consideration which gave the plaintiff a right to sue for money had and received, and that the like failure of consideration on the other side gave the defendant a right to sue on an implied assumpsit for work done and materials found. (524)

Some cases did, however, recognize the contractual risk allocation. *Hipskind* specifically rejected *Butterfield* despite noting that *Butterfield* was the rule in most other American jurisdictions. In passing, it noted that the standard form of agreement between contractor and owner called for progress payments of 90 percent of the value based on the contractor's prices of labor and materials incorporated in the work, and of materials stored on site. An earlier decision, *H. G. Vogel Co. v. Reinhardt*, concerned the installation of fire extinguishers. There, the contract specifically stated that in the event of fire or other excusing event, the owner was to pay for all materials and labor furnished as of the date of destruction. Despite the fact that nothing had yet been attached to the building, the plaintiff was able to recover all its expenses. The parties specifically contracted around the wrought-in rule in two respects. First, the focus was on the contractor's costs incurred; the owner's "benefit," however reckoned, was irrelevant. Second, the contractor's compensation would not be determined by a court's ex post decision but ex ante by the parties themselves. In both cases, the court honored the parties' risk allocation.

Case law in the last half century is sparse, the reason being that parties typically contract around the clunky Restatement rule. Before turning to the evidence of practice, I want to note a relatively recent case that follows the *Chandler* approach when the contract can reasonably be interpreted as assigning the risks in that manner.

In *One World Trade Center v. Cantor Fitzgerald Securities*, a tenant signed a long-term lease renewal at the World Trade Center less than one year before 9/11. There was no dispute that the tragedy terminated the lease. In response to a claim that they owed rent for the August 1–September 10 period, the tenants argued for relief on the grounds of unjust enrichment. The rent payments, they argued, were front-loaded; the rent in the initial period was high, a payment for "future benefits including a fixed rental rate, restricted rights to terminate the lease," (654) and so forth. The court rejected that argument: "The defendants are sophisticated commercial tenants and there is no reason to excuse them from the operation of the *force majeure* clause which they freely negotiated. Defendants bargained away their right to hold the lessor liable for non-performance in the face of the tragic, unanticipated events which destroyed the Building." (655) The court cited a century-old precedent: "[i]f by the terms of [the] lease rent is to be paid in advance, the tenant comes under an absolute engagement to pay it on the day fixed, and he is not relieved from that engagement by the fact that the property is destroyed… and [tenant] is liable to pay the rent due in advance even though the destruction takes place on the very day it falls due." (*Werner v. Padula*, 138)

The smattering of cases that mentioned, or at least hinted at, a contractual resolution to the post-excuse problem suggested that the contracting parties were by and large content to let the losses lie where they fell. That made me quite confident that contemporary standard construction contracts would embody similar terms. However, when I examined those documents, I was surprised to see no reference at all to the problem, let alone a solution to it. A bit shaken, I met with construction law experts with decades of experience. They had never seen the problem arise, which I found even more puzzling. They patiently explained to me the reason why. The problem is handled in the *insurance clause*. The following excerpt from the AIA Standard contract spells this out:

> **§ 11.3.1** Unless otherwise provided, the Owner shall purchase and maintain, in a company or companies lawfully authorized to do business in the jurisdiction in which the Project is located, property insurance written on a builder's risk "all-risk" or equivalent policy form in the amount of the initial Contract Sum, plus value of subsequent Contract Modifications and cost of materials supplied or installed by others, comprising total value for the entire Project at the site on a replacement cost basis without optional deductibles. Such property insurance shall be maintained, unless otherwise provided in the Contract Documents or otherwise agreed in writing by all persons and entities who are beneficiaries of such insurance, until final payment has been made as provided in Section 9.10 or until no person or entity other than the Owner has an insurable interest in the property required by this Section 11.3 to be

> covered, whichever is later. This insurance shall include interests of the Owner, the Contractor, Subcontractors and Sub-subcontractors in the Project.
>
> **§ 11.3.1.1** Property insurance shall be on an "all-risk" or equivalent policy form and shall include, without limitation, insurance against the perils of fire (with extended coverage) and physical loss or damage including, without duplication of coverage, theft, vandalism, malicious mischief, collapse, earthquake, flood, windstorm, falsework, testing and startup, temporary buildings and debris removal including demolition occasioned by enforcement of any applicable legal requirements, and shall cover reasonable compensation for Architect's and Contractor's services and expenses required as a result of such insured loss.
>
> * * *
>
> **§ 11.3.1.4** This property insurance shall cover portions of the Work stored off the site, and also portions of the Work in transit.

That last clause is a disavowal of the wrought-in rule. And so, it turns out, the *default rule* in the United States might be as stated in the Restatement (Second), but the *default clause* is written by the AIA. *Chandler v. Webster* lives. Contracts scholars have just been looking in the wrong place.

Contracting out of the default rule is hardly new. The standard form contract in the well-known case *Jacob & Youngs v. Kent* included this language: "ART. XI. The Owner shall during the progress of the work maintain insurance on the same against loss or damage by fire, the policies to cover all work incorporated in the building, and all materials for the same in or about the premises, and to be made payable to the parties hereto, as their interest may appear." (*J&Y*)

III. CONCLUDING REMARKS

In a response to my chapter (Chapter 11), Professor Melvin Eisenberg (2010) wrote:

> Most of [the coronation] cases held that the adversely affected party can't get back what he paid before the unexpected circumstance occurred. Professor Goldberg also takes that position, but there is no way that position can be justified in light of the principles of unjust enrichment. Think what this position would mean. A, located in New York, is a manufacturer of machinery. A agrees to manufacture a custom-made machine for B, located in Iran, for a price of $100,000. Because the machine is custom-made, A insists on payment of $50,000 up front. After B pays the $50,000, but before A has done

> any work on the machine, the United States places an embargo on sales of machinery to Iran. Under Professor Goldberg's rule, A can keep the $50,000 and walk away. … Not surprisingly, both the English courts and Parliament later completely repudiated this rule … and American courts never adopted it. (387)

I am guilty as charged. But, I would argue that it is the "principles of unjust enrichment" that are out of step, not me. I do note that I am not alone – the *Cantor Fitzgerald* decision and the century-old precedent it invokes suggests that the New York court (the closest thing we have to a commercial court) would honor the contract language and let A keep the $50,000. Professor Eisenberg presumes that the responsibility for dealing with such a ban is the courts' ex post, not the parties' ex ante. It is his hypothetical and he can do with it as he sees fit. Still, it might be worth asking whether competent businessmen would enter into such a deal in the first place and, if they did, why it might have been a reasonable business decision.

The cry of those in England bent on reversing *Chandler v. Webster* was the obvious injustice of it all. Professor Eisenberg's invocation of unjust enrichment parallels the Restatement (Second)'s mantra that the law should "avoid injustice." Lip service is paid to the notion that the rules are only default rules, but no attention is paid to whether and why sophisticated parties contract around the commentators' notion of what would constitute a just resolution. If default rules derived from notions of justice are out of step with what informed parties actually do, then, I would argue, it is time to rethink the rules.

13. A precedent built on sand: *NorCon v. Niagara Mohawk*

Suppose that A has entered into a contract with B, but B comes to believe that A will not perform. What can B do? It could perform its obligation, and, if A did indeed fail to perform, it could pursue its legal remedies. This might not be a very attractive option if the costs of going to court were high and there was a reasonable likelihood that B would not be able to collect part, or all, of the judgment. It could treat A as a breacher and withhold its performance; it would, however, run the risk that a court might find that B, not A, had breached. It could demand assurance from A that it would perform. The common law did not give B that right, with one exception. If A were insolvent, B could suspend performance or insist upon a cash payment. Otherwise, absent language in the contract allowing B to demand assurance or A's acknowledging its unwillingness to perform (an anticipatory repudiation), B was faced with this awkward choice.

The UCC § 2-609 expanded the insecure B's options by allowing it to demand "adequate assurance" if it had reasonable grounds for believing that A would not perform. But what if the contract were not governed by the UCC? The Restatement (Second) extrapolated from the UCC and recognized a right to demand adequate assurance in contract disputes not involving goods. (It was really sort of a [P]Restatement since the drafters had no precedent outside the UCC):

> (1) Where reasonable grounds arise to believe that the obligor will commit a breach by non-performance that would of itself give the obligee a claim for damages for total breach, … the obligee may demand adequate assurance of due performance and may, if reasonable, suspend any performance for which he has not already received the agreed exchange until he receives such assurance.
>
> (2) The obligee may treat as a repudiation the obligor's failure to provide within a reasonable time such assurance of due performance as is adequate in the circumstances of the particular case.

The issue arose in a federal case applying New York law – *NorCon Power Partners, L.P. v. Niagara Mohawk Power Corp.* The Second Circuit sent the following certified question to the New York Court of Appeals: "Does a party have the right to demand adequate assurance of future performance when reasonable grounds arise to believe that the other party will commit a breach by non-performance of a contract governed by New York law, where the other party is solvent and the contract is not governed by the U.C.C.?" The court could simply have said that we adopt the enlightened reasoning of the Restatement. That might not have been the wisest policy, but the decision would have been unassailable. However, after a lengthy exegesis on the merits of that position, the court chose a more nuanced position. It narrowed the question, making much of the incremental, interstitial method of common law adjudication:

> We conclude, therefore, that it is unnecessary, while fulfilling the important and useful certification role, to promulgate so sweeping a change and proposition in contract law, as has been sought, in one dramatic promulgation. That approach might clash with our customary incremental common-law developmental process, rooted in particular fact patterns and keener wisdom acquired through observations of empirical application of a proportioned, less than absolute, rule in future cases.
>
> * * *
>
> Experience and patience thus offer a more secure and realistic path to a better and fairer rule, in theory and in practical application. Therefore, this Court chooses to take the traditionally subtler approach, consistent with the proven benefits of the maturation process of the common law, including in the very area of anticipatory repudiation which spawns this relatively newer demand for assurance corollary. (662)

The nuanced approach would be guided by the facts of the specific case with future cases fleshing out the contours of the right. That sounds great. We don't have to rely on the example of the UCC or the authority of the Restatement and its distinguished chief reporter, Allan Farnsworth. Following this strategy (or, more precisely, claiming to follow this strategy), the court extended the right to demand assurance but only for a subset of disputes. It was "now persuaded that the policies underlying the UCC 2-609 counterpart should apply with similar cogency for the resolution of *this kind of controversy*." (662, emphasis added) The type of controversy is spelled out later in the opinion: "It should apply to the type of long-term commercial contract between corporate entities … which is complex and not reasonably susceptible of all security features being anticipated, bargained for and incorporated in the original contract." (662)

There is one big problem with this conclusion. There is nothing in the opinion that would suggest why this kind of controversy should be singled out. What, in particular, does the court mean when it says that security features could not be anticipated in the original contract? Perhaps, I thought, the district court's opinion might shed some light on the question. It did, but not in the way I had anticipated. Judge Sprizzo noted that the contract did deal with the security issue. If NorCon failed to perform, Niagara Mohawk would have a lien on its plant. "To secure this risk, the parties negotiated and agreed to a provision in the Encogen Agreement granting Niagara Mohawk a security interest in the Encogen Facility to secure Encogen's performance and any balance in the adjustment account remaining at the end of the third period." (*Encogen Four Partners, L.P. v. Niagara Mohawk Power Corp.*, p. 59) (The Encogen and NorCon contracts were both being litigated; the initial suit was in Encogen's name.) Perhaps Sprizzo mischaracterized the assurance embodied in the contract. Wrong. Indeed, if anything, he understated the contractual assurance afforded Niagara Mohawk.

This struck me as odd. Why would a court go out of its way to find a right to demand assurance when the contracting parties appear to have negotiated a term to deal with this problem? The disconnect, I surmised, must have arisen from the certification process – the question was acontextual and, I thought, perhaps the court had no knowledge of the context. Wrong again. In fact, the briefs included detailed specifics about the contract and its context, including some of the negotiating history regarding the assurance.

There is no way to get from the particular facts of this case to the broad question certified to the New York court or to the narrower question the court answered. The court could, as I noted, have answered the certified question without regard to the NorCon–Niagara Mohawk dispute; the judges were only being asked for a statement of the law. But it didn't. It presented some of the facts and then leapt to a conclusion implying that the conclusion bore some relationship to the stated facts (*this* kind of controversy). If the *NorCon* facts are irrelevant, then the court provides no basis for its conclusion. And if they are relevant, the court provides no basis for its characterization of this kind of controversy.

Well, so what? Why worry that the precedent happens to be built on sand? There are two responses. First, *NorCon* is the leading case in the leading commercial law jurisdiction. If the decision is fundamentally flawed, can future parties rely on its continued vitality? Second, and perhaps more important, *NorCon* provides a good illustration of the "winner's history" problem I spoke of in the book's Introduction. The result is an inaccurate picture and an unsupportable conclusion.

What does one do with such an unfounded precedent? In this instance, a rethinking of the doctrine is in order. If anything, the court got it backwards. The camel's nose is coming under the wrong end of the tent. If the adequate assurance doctrine is to develop incrementally, the appropriate end of the contract spectrum is not complex, heavily negotiated contracts in which the issue of adequate assurance can be (and, arguably, has been) bargained over ex ante. Rather, if the doctrine is to be extended beyond the sale of goods, it should be for contracts in which the parties are not likely to have put much thought into the matter: "They-would-have-included-it-had-they-bothered-to think-about-it" type of case. I am not arguing that the doctrine should be extended, only that this would have been a more appropriate incremental extension.

Now, the court only said that New York would recognize the adequate assurance doctrine in this type of transaction. It does not follow that a court, upon rehearing, would have required that NorCon provide such assurance. That would depend upon the facts. The case did eventually go to trial, but the parties settled before a decision was rendered. As we shall see (Section VI), NorCon did well in the settlement, but the uncertainty of the application of the law might have impacted the settlement negotiations. If the decision were to remain good law, the right to demand assurance, even if the demand were likely to fail, could be a valuable asset in renegotiation of a contract or bargaining over settlement terms.

The case itself was merely one skirmish in a bigger battle, the origins of which precede this particular agreement by over a decade. The story begins with federal legislation that was supposed to reduce American dependence on foreign oil. Public utility electric companies, like Niagara Mohawk, were required to buy power from non-utility generators (or NUGs), like NorCon. The utilities entered into contracts with the NUGs, not because they wanted to, but because they had to. The shape of these agreements was determined in part by years of litigation and by proceedings in state public utility commissions. Niagara Mohawk, like many other utilities, had long-term agreements with a large number of NUGs in the early 1990s – its general counsel claimed that there were more than 150 such contracts in 1996. (Kaleta, 1996, 8) When changed circumstances made these contracts appear very bad from the utilities' perspective, they responded by trying to get the contracts revised, terminated, or bought out. The demand for adequate assurance was only one of the strategies deployed.

The larger context is crucial to understanding why the contract took the form that it did. As will be described in Section I, the *NorCon* decision was only one of many involving disputes between public utilities and independent power producers operating under long-term contracts. The NorCon contract will be described in Section II. Section III presents the problem that triggered Niagara's demand for assurance. The litigation will be summarized in Section IV. The parties' awareness of the risks associated with contracts of this sort and the buyer's need for some form of assurance will be considered in Section V. Niagara settled most of its disputes with the NUGs, including the NorCon dispute; the terms of the settlements will be presented in Section VI.

I. THE CONTEXT

Congress enacted the Public Utility Regulatory Policies Act (PURPA) in 1978. The avowed purpose was to reduce dependence on foreign oil by encouraging the development of alternative power sources. Regulated electric power companies were required to purchase power in long-term Power Purchase Agreements (PPAs) from alternative power producers, like NorCon. PURPA directed the Federal Regulatory Energy Commission (FERC) to issue rules to be implemented by the states to buy electricity from alternative qualifying suppliers (QFs). To complete the alphabet soup, the QFs were also labeled non-utility generators (NUGs) or independent power producers (IPPs). There was not quite a 100 percent overlap between the three categories, but it is close enough so that I will use the terms interchangeably.

To encourage the QFs, much of the price risk was shifted from the QFs to utilities and ratepayers. Almost a decade after passage of the Act, FERC noted:

> A major purpose of PURPA is to encourage cogeneration and small power production. The uncertainty of future revenues from purchases by utilities can make it difficult for the QF developer to obtain project financing. The principal reason for the existence of fixed-price contracts between utilities and QFs is to reduce this uncertainty by shifting risks from the QF to the purchasing utility or its ratepayers. The regulations implementing section 210 of PURPA recognize this and provide specific authority for utilities and QFs to enter into long-term, fixed-price contracts designed to give developers the financial security they need to make these projects viable. (Administrative Determination, 1988, 32,457)

Prices were to be based on long-run avoided costs (LRAC). The LRAC are costs that the utility would have to bear, but for the agreement with this supplier. Significantly, the LRAC could either be reckoned at the time of contracting or at the time of delivery. That difference turns out to be crucial to understanding why the NorCon deal, and others, fell apart so quickly.

In one of the many pieces of litigation generated by this law, the Second Circuit Court of Appeals summarized what happened next in New York:

> In 1980, the New York legislature enacted New York Public Service Law § 66-c, which provided that the PSC [Public Service Commission] would require state-regulated electric utilities to enter into agreements for the purchase of electricity from QFs. The PSC was charged with overseeing the contracting process, including approval of the contracts and setting power purchase rates. New York initially did not adopt PURPA's "avoided cost" ceiling for electricity purchases. In 1981, section 66-c was amended to require the PSC to establish a minimum sales price of at least six cents per kilowatt hour for power purchased from state qualifying QFs. This amendment is commonly referred to as the "Six-Cent Law." The New York legislature amended section 66-c again in 1992, partially repealing the Six-Cent Law. The 1992 amendment, however, preserved the six-cent minimum rate with respect to certain contracts executed and filed with the PSC on or before June 26, 1992. (*Niagara Mohawk Power Corp. v. Federal Energy Regulatory Com'n*, 1266–67)

The six-cent rate was above LRAC when implemented in the early 1980s. After years of litigation and regulatory hearings, FERC ruled that the states could no longer set a minimum price above LRAC. However, the ruling was only prospective so that earlier contracts were grandfathered. (*Orange & Rockland Utils., Inc. ("O & R I")*, 61,185) Niagara Mohawk had eighteen long-term contracts with the six-cent rate. Seven were settled in the Master Restructuring Agreement (to be discussed below). It continued to litigate the others without success, in suits against the PSC and FERC. A second set of contracts were long-term, front-loaded contracts. In some, the contract price was fixed for the life of the agreement (typically fifteen years) at a discount from the projected LRAC. In others, which included the NorCon agreement, it was anticipated that the utility would overpay in the early years and make up the difference with a "tracking account" in the later years. Niagara Mohawk's general counsel noted that most of these were "held by large gas-fired cogeneration projects and represent the most onerous IPP contracts in Niagara Mohawk's generation mix." (Kaleta, 1996, 11)

The higher the expected prices paid to the QFs, the more encouragement there would be for alternative power sources. There is a potential tradeoff between encouraging the alternative sources and consumer prices, although courts and regulators initially denied it. The hoped for results from PURPA were oft-cited. For example: "As noted by PSC, if this project is successful, ratepayers will benefit in the future from cheaper electricity that will more than offset the above avoided-costs rates paid during the first half of the contract, in addition to having a new and innovative garbage-to-energy domestic power supply technology." (*Matter of Niagara Mohawk Power Corp. v. Public Serv. Comm'n. of State of N.Y.*, 629) The Supreme Court held early on that in promulgating its regulations, FERC should err on the side of encouraging the non-traditional producers. As time passed, the adverse impact on future electricity consumers became more likely and the future benefits from encouraging the non-petroleum sources became less likely; the PSC (and some regulators from other states), as we will see, came to put more weight on the high prices to be borne by the utility's customers.

The system worked; indeed, it worked too well. Within a decade, Niagara Mohawk had been required to enter into contracts for IPP output greater than the power demand in its service territory. Years later it summarized the situation:

> Since PURPA and the Six-Cent Law were passed, the Company was obligated to purchase electricity offered from IPPs in quantities in excess of its own demand and at prices in excess of those available to the Company by internal generation or for purchase in the wholesale market. In fact, by 1991, the Company was facing a potential obligation to purchase power from IPPs substantially in excess of its peak demand of 6,093 MW. As a result, the Company's competitive position and financial performance deteriorated and the price of electricity paid per KWh by its customers rose significantly above the national average. Accordingly, in 1991 the Company initiated a parallel strategy of negotiating individual PPA buyouts, cancellations and renegotiations, and of pursuing regulatory and legislative support and litigation to mitigate the Company's obligation under the PPAs. By mid-1996, this strategy resulted in reducing the Company's obligations to purchase power under its PPA portfolio to approximately 2,700 MW. (Niagara Mohawk Power Corp. 1999 Annual Report)

When the regulated electric utilities' actual avoidable costs fell below the contract prices (the six cent rate or the projected avoidable costs), they scrambled to revise or terminate their obligations. The *NorCon* litigation was only one of many involving Niagara that ended up in court or regulatory commission proceedings. Niagara was not the only New York utility enmeshed in such litigation. Nor were the battles limited to New

York utilities. In some states, the regulators were sympathetic to the utilities and their ratepayers, but their efforts to alter the contracts were opposed by the QFs, which argued successfully that modification was preempted by PURPA.

II. THE CONTRACT

NorCon was a limited partnership with the sole purpose of building, owning, and operating this QF. The general partner was Northern Consolidated Power, Inc.. NorCon was a special purpose entity with no other assets. These special purpose entities were often referred to as "PURPA machines." The lender's sole source of repayment would be the future stream of revenue. In April 1989, the NorCon–Niagara PPA was submitted to the PSC, which had to approve all contracts with QFs. The PSC rejected the initial agreement in part because the security was inadequate. An amended agreement dated January 3, 1991 was also rejected. After a second amendment, the agreement was finalized July 22, 1991. NorCon would construct a power plant and Niagara would take all the output for 25 years. NorCon was financed by a 15-year, $120 million loan from GE Capital. Construction was completed in late 1972 and on December 12, 1992, NorCon began delivering electricity to Niagara.

The relevant terms of the agreement for our purposes are the pricing formula and the security arrangements. According to PURPA, the avoidable cost standard could either refer to prices when electricity was actually delivered or estimated LRAC at the time the contract was entered into. The NorCon–Niagara PPA combined the two. It incorporated the 1988 LRAC projections for 15 years, which had been determined by the PSC. LRAC projections for both peak and off-peak sales for the life of the contract were included as an attachment to the contract. Table 13.1 gives a weighted average for the years 1996–2007. The pricing rule covered three periods. It is somewhat confusing because the agreement includes two adjustment accounts. The former divides the first period from the second; the latter accumulates in the second period and is supposed to be eliminated in the course of the third period.

Table 13.1 Niagara Mohawk LRACs 1988 and 1993

Year	1988	1993
1996	80.58	28.70
1997	84.13	30.90
1998	87.73	32.40
1999	91.63	36.70
2000	95.63	41.30
2001	99.73	46.20
2002	104.14	51.00
2003	108.73	56.10
2004	113.43	61.60
2005	118.43	67.30
2006	123.63	72.00
2007	129.04	79.00

Source: Attachment to Demand Letter.

In the first period, the price would be six cents per kilowatt hour (kwh). Since the projected LRAC was below six cents in the early years, the contract deliberately front-loaded the payments. After a few years the projected LRAC would exceed six cents. When the LRAC was less than six cents, the difference would go into a "cumulative avoided cost account." When the LRAC exceeded six cents, that account would be reduced accordingly. When the account reached zero, the first period would be at an end. Because there were two LRAC schedules – peak and off-peak – and because the quantity would vary, the date at which the account reached zero would depend on the mix and interest rates The period was expected to last about four years.

In the second period, the price would be 95 percent of Niagara's "tariff avoided cost," subject to a ceiling and a floor, both of which were based on the 1988 LRAC. The tariff avoided cost is the current avoided cost. So, if the projected LRAC proved to be accurate, this would be a five percent discount. If, however, the two diverge, the ceiling and floor might come into play, as, in fact, happened. The ceiling and floor were both based on the 1988 LRAC schedule. The ceiling was 110 percent and the floor 90 percent. If either were binding, the difference would go into an "adjustment account." The second period ended fifteen years after the initial delivery of electricity. For the remaining ten years, the price would be 90 percent of the tariff avoided cost, adjusted for any amount remaining in the adjustment account. If things worked out, the back-end discounts would more than make up for the front-loaded payments. This mechanism, adopted in many contracts between electric utilities and QFs, is referred to as a "tracking mechanism" or a "true-up." The details of the true-up are not important. Suffice it to say that if, as Niagara projected, NorCon ended up with a considerable surplus, the price it would be paid in the later years would be substantially reduced. Indeed, as we shall see, if Niagara's projections were accurate, they would have resulted in a *negative price* in the last decade.

The litigation concerned Niagara's demand for assurance that NorCon would perform. The initial proposed agreement did, in fact, provide some security:

> In order to secure the operation of the PLANT by the SELLER during the term of this AGREEMENT and to secure the balance of the Adjustment Account, SELLER hereby pledges a security interest in the amount of any positive balance in the Cumulative Avoided Cost Account, or the Adjustment Account, as the case may be, in the PLANT to NIAGARA. The lien created shall be upon all the works, plant, properties, and real and personal, constituting the PLANT in NIAGARA's favor. (Clause 9(5))

The PSC rejected the agreement, deeming this insufficient, and asked for increased assurance. The first amendment to the agreement required that NorCon provide a letter of credit in the thirteenth year if at that time Niagara projected a positive balance at the end of the third period. (This mechanism was included in another litigated case, *Kamine/Besicorp Allegany L.P. v. Rochester Gas & Electric Corp.*) However, the PSC rejected that as well. The second amendment eliminated that letter of credit and instead required that NorCon enter into a long-term fuel supply contract at fixed prices. Since the largest component of LRAC is the cost of fuel, NorCon's fuel costs were expected to be closely correlated with the projected LRAC. Of course, that only provided security if fuel prices rose more than had been anticipated. It did not provide security if, as actually happened, prices or other costs fell.

It is important to bear in mind that Niagara did not want to enter into the contract. In its brief, Niagara stated: "The contract at issue is not an ordinary contract that reflects the voluntary assumption of obligations and risks by contracting parties. Instead, Niagara Mohawk was required to enter into the contract with NorCon by … [PURPA and NY PSL § 66-c]. The terms of the contract were dictated by the New York Public Service Commission." (Def. Brief, 2) In its reply brief, Niagara emphasized the non-voluntary nature of its acquiescence: "The PSC required

Niagara Mohawk to agree to front loaded pricing (i.e., pricing that resulted in overpayments during the initial years of the contract) and security terms that Niagara Mohawk deemed inadequate … . Niagara Mohawk brought an Article 78 challenge against one of the PSC's rulings, but without success … . Even though Niagara Mohawk did not thereafter challenge every additional contract that incorporated similar front loaded pricing and inadequate security terms, Niagara Mohawk's entry into these contracts was hardly voluntary." (Def. Reply Brief, 2–3)
The PSC chimed in. Although the PSC initially had approved the contract, by 1997 it had come to regret that decision. It could neither revise the contract nor order the parties to do so. It did, however, file an amicus brief on Niagara's side, stressing the non-voluntary nature of the agreement:

> In traditional contract law, it is assumed that parties are able to negotiate reasonable agreements and, when necessary, protect themselves against non-performance through agreed-upon damages. This assumption loses force when parties are coerced into agreements by, in this case, federal law. [This agreement] stands for the proposition that *contracts of adhesion* are an exception to the rule that "courts see no harm in express agreements limiting the damages to be recovered for breach of contract." … Here … the contracts were imposed upon Niagara Mohawk. (Brief for PSC as Amicus Curiae, 6 emphasis added)

This is quite a remarkable statement. Despite the fact that it had monitored the negotiations, forced two amendments, and ultimately approved the agreement, the PSC labels this a "*contract of adhesion*." It is not clear whether the PSC's position represents a change of heart when the potential adverse effects on ratepayers became apparent, or whether it was the result of a change in administration. (In the interim, George Pataki had replaced Mario Cuomo as governor, and John O'Mara had replaced Peter Bradford as chairman of the PSC.) Regardless, the not-quite-voluntary nature of the contract was apparent, a fact ignored by the court in its characterization of "this kind of controversy." In the hearing on *NorCon*'s summary judgment after remand, Judge Sprizzo emphasized the non-voluntary nature of the contract: "It wasn't as if they assumed this risk. The state said, you will do this. The state justification for saying, you will do this, was that we don't think your downside is so great and you have the security under the second subordinated lien. Now it turns out the risk is much greater than the state assumed at the time that they forced the contract upon them, and there is a serious question as to whether the state would have forced the contract on them with knowledge of how large a risk this was going to be." (Summary Judgment Hearing, 16)

III. THE PROBLEM

It became apparent almost immediately that the 1988 LRAC was much too high. If the discrepancy continued, the floor price would kick in and the adjustment account would grow rapidly. The tracking mechanism would in principle equalize the payments over the life of the agreement. However, if the adjustment account were substantial, the temptation for NorCon to simply walk away in the final ten years would be great. Niagara (and other electric utilities) wanted out. Many strategies were deployed. So, for example, one utility's complaint alleged "commercial impracticability/impossibility, mutual mistake, frustration of purpose, and anticipatory breach/prospective inability to perform. The action sought a declaration of the rights and obligations of the parties to the PPA, its rescission or, in the alternative, an Order directing the debtor to provide adequate assurances that it would perform the PPA." (*In re Kamine/Besicorp Allegany, L.P.*, 958)

As a result of this contract and others with IPPs, Niagara was overpaying for electricity. In its 1994 annual report, it estimated that "it paid a premium of $206 million in 1993 and expects to overpay by $352 million in 1994 and $421 million in 1995." To extricate itself, Niagara Mohawk utilized buyouts and demands for assurance. Early on, Niagara proposed buyouts: "In 1992 and 1993, Niagara Mohawk had contacted various other developers about the possibility of either delaying the start of construction or canceling projects. Niagara Mohawk makes no secret of the fact that it considers the above-market price terms the PSC imposes on contracts like the Agreement with O'Shanter to be economically unreasonable. As explained in the September 20, 1993 letter to O'Shanter, Niagara Mohawk's buy-out policy was 'to pay up to one and one half (1.5) times of actual project expenditures.'" (*O'Shanter Res., Inc. v. Niagara Mohawk Power Corp.*, 563) As we shall see in Section VI, it did finally succeed in buying out many of the contracts, including NorCon's. Additionally, Niagara sent letters demanding assurance of performance in the out-years to NorCon and eight other IPPs. (FORM 10-Q – for the Quarter Ended June 30, 1994) The extent to which the buy-out offers and demand letters overlapped is unclear.

The utilities also engaged in flyspecking the contracts. A nice example was Niagara's negotiation with O'Shanter. In the early negotiations, the buy-out price was in the $2–3 million range. But in a ruling on another contract, the PSC held that the PPA was "site-specific." (*Consolidated Edison Company of New York, Inc. and Indeck Energy Services of Yonkers, Inc.*) That is, if the contract was for a plant to be built at a specific site, and if the site of the plant changed after the contract had been approved, then the contract would no longer apply. Since the planned location of O'Shanter's plant had been moved after the PSC had approved the agreement, the validity of the contract was now an issue. Niagara thereupon reduced its buy-out offer to $50,000. Ironically, in the course of their dispute, O'Shanter demanded assurance that Niagara would perform and Niagara denied that it had to do so. (*O'Shanter*, 566)

The Niagara–NorCon contract established a floor and ceiling in the second period based on the 1988 LRAC. Within months of NorCon's completing the plant and beginning production, the PSC produced a new schedule of LRAC, substantially below the 1988 numbers. Both schedules are shown in Table 13.1. A puzzle, which none of the briefs addressed, is how Niagara (and the other electric utilities and the PSC) failed to anticipate the sharp decline in LRAC projections, given that the new projections were produced so close to the contract date. I will return to that question in Section V.

In October 1992, before NorCon had delivered any power, Niagara filed a petition with the PSC asking that it require NorCon and other IPPs "to provide additional assurance to secure their future performance." (Plaintiff Brief, 10) Subsequently, Niagara asked that the PSC suspend action; the PSC refused and in June 1993, deemed the petition withdrawn. On February 4, 1994, two and a half years after the contract was signed and a little over a year after NorCon's first delivery, Niagara sent NorCon a letter demanding that it provide assurance that it would meet its obligations in the third period.

> Niagara Mohawk believes that due to changes in economic conditions since the agreement was entered, NorCon cannot and will not perform its repayment obligations in the later years of the Agreement. Niagara Mohawk, therefore, is demanding that within 30 days from receipt of this letter, NorCon provide adequate assurance to Niagara Mohawk that NorCon will duly perform all of its future repayment obligations, including the obligation to deliver electricity in the later years of the Agreement at prices less than Niagara Mohawk's avoided costs and the obligations to repay in full any balance on the advance extended by Niagara Mohawk's customers which remains at the end of the Agreement's twenty-five year term. (Demand Letter, 1)

If NorCon failed to give such assurance within 30 days, Niagara claimed that it would treat the failure as a repudiation and it would have the right to terminate the agreement.

Niagara commissioned a study by an economic consulting firm to support its claim:

> [b]ased on reasonable assumptions for NorCon's fuel costs and operating and maintenance expenses – determined by Niagara Mohawk's independent consultants [NERA] based on their many years of experience in the power production business – NorCon would have negative operating income ranging from approximately $23.2 million to $108.9 million in every year of the third period. Because it seems unlikely that NorCon would continue to operate the plant in the face of such substantial operating losses, but rather would more likely abandon the plant, Niagara Mohawk's customers appear unlikely to receive any repayment during the third period of the excess payment accrued in the Cumulative Avoided Cost Account during the second period. In effect, Niagara Mohawk's customers would be advancing over $610 million to NorCon during the second period with no prospect of repayment. (Demand Letter, 6)

In its brief, Niagara restated the argument more forcefully:

> Due to a dramatic drop in the price of electricity from other sources of supply, which the PSC did not foresee at the time that it dictated the terms of the contract, the estimated amount that NorCon will have to repay under the contract has skyrocketed from about $21 million to over $610 million, a nearly 30-fold increase. To repay the latter amount, NorCon would have to supply electricity for free and pay Niagara Mohawk between $25 million and $125 million each year during the last ten years of the contract. (Def. Brief, 2–3)

Moreover, it claimed that the value of the plant, the contractual security, would fall well short of the cumulative account. By the end of the second period (15 years) the shortfall was projected to be $412 million. (Demand Letter, 7)

What could NorCon do that would satisfy Niagara? The letter provided a number of suggestions:

> The adequate assurances of NorCon's future performance requested by this letter conceivably could take many forms. Without attempting to be exhaustive, Niagara Mohawk would be willing to accept any step that reasonably ensures the performance of NorCon's future repayment options, including the posting of a letter of credit or the creation of an escrow account to reserve the amounts necessary to meet the repayment obligations as they mature. Niagara Mohawk, however, invites any other proposal that assures performance of

> NorCon's repayment obligations in a commercially reasonable manner in light of the particular nature of the insecurity described above. (Demand Letter, 8)

NorCon disputed both the numbers and the notion that it should provide any assurance beyond that already in the contract. To determine the annual prices, the consultants simply plugged in the best current estimate of future prices, namely the 1993 projected LRAC. NorCon objected on the ground that there were large fluctuations in the components making up the LRAC and that the projected LRAC did not necessarily correspond to actual prices. It noted that the PSC's amicus brief, while supporting Niagara, used 1997 LRAC and concluded that the shortfall would be $330 million, not $610 million. (Plaintiff Brief, 31) NorCon was certainly correct in arguing that the fifteen-year projection of LRAC in 1993 would diverge from realized avoided costs in the same period, and, given the volatility of fuel prices, the deviation could be large. It suggested that Niagara should have foreseen the price decline. With regard to the adequate assurance claim, NorCon made three points. First, it argued that the agreement already did take the assurance issue into account. Second, Niagara (and the PSC) knew the risks. Third, it would not have been able to provide such assurance and Niagara knew it. NorCon pointed out that increased assurance would be at the expense of its lender who relied entirely on the cash flow. The lender would most likely refuse to allow a change. "As is common in the independent power production industry … NorCon financed the construction of its power plant under a project financing commitment. Niagara is fully aware that a project financed facility cannot provide additional security, in cash or other assets, after the plant has been financed." (Verified Complaint, 30) Moreover, if the Niagara projections were at all plausible, no third party would be willing to guarantee NorCon's third period obligation.

IV. THE LITIGATION

Shortly after receiving the Demand Letter, NorCon filed suit asking for a Declaratory Judgment that it need not provide additional assurance. Niagara counterclaimed, seeking a counter declaration that it had properly invoked a right to demand adequate assurance. A second IPP, Encogen, which had entered into a similar three-period, 25-year contract, also sued and the two cases were considered together. (*Encogen Four Partners, L.P. v. Niagara Mohawk Power Corp.*) Niagara sent Encogen a demand letter the same day that it sent NorCon's, claiming projected losses of $330 million. The Encogen agreement also included a lien upon the plant as assurance. The court emphasized that the lien was Niagara's exclusive remedy – the contract language was stronger than in the NorCon agreement. "The Encogen Agreement provides that 'Niagara's exclusive remedy for [Encogen's] failure to pay the balance of the Adjustment Account is to foreclose its lien upon the [Encogen] plant.'" (62 n. 5)

Niagara argued that the right to demand adequate assurance was implicit in the regulatory framework, but the court would have none of that:

> Niagara Mohawk further contends that the right to demand adequate assurances is a corollary to the prohibition under New York regulatory law against electricity rates set by the PSC that "would result in a substantial overcharge to [the utility's] rate payers." … Notwithstanding that comprehensive regulatory scheme, neither Congress nor the New York legislature created a right to demand adequate assurances where an otherwise approved rate might, in the distant future, prove economically disadvantageous to the utility purchaser. (62)

Holding that New York law does not provide for a right to demand adequate assurance, the court granted Encogen's motion to dismiss Niagara's counterclaim. The Court of Appeals certified the question to the New York Court of Appeals, which, as noted in the Introduction, gave an affirmative answer to a narrower question.

The court noted with approval some of the commentary favoring the recognition of the right to demand assurance and was "now persuaded that the policies underlying the UCC 2-609 counterpart should apply with similar cogency for the resolution of this kind of controversy." It continued with language that failed to distinguish this kind of controversy from any other: "A useful analogy can be drawn between the contract at issue and a contract for the sale of goods. If the contract here was in all respects the same, except that it was for the sale of oil or some other tangible commodity instead of the sale of electricity, the parties would unquestionably be governed by the demand for adequate assurance of performance factors in UCC 2-609." (160) The court does not hint at what might distinguish electricity from other non-goods transactions. Nor, for that matter, does it distinguish between long-term electricity contracts and shorter term, or spot, electricity contracts. And, of course, it says nothing about whether the regulatory framework or contractual language dealing with assurance had any bearing on the right to demand assurance.

The Second Circuit then vacated the district court opinion and remanded for further proceedings consistent with the opinion. A bench trial was held in the summer of 1999, but on November 23, 1999, before a verdict was handed down, the case settled. The terms of the settlement will be presented in Section VI.

V. THE CONTRACT ASSIGNED THE RISKS

Had the contract worked as planned, there would have been a modest overpayment in the first few years (the six-cent rate exceeded the projected LRAC). This would have been made up in the later years so that the present value of the payment stream would have been about five per cent less than if Niagara Mohawk had paid current LRAC for the entire 25-year period. The 15-year loan would have been paid off by the revenue stream from the first two periods. Things do not always go as they are planned however, especially when the planning horizon is as long as 25 years and the underlying data are volatile. When, as happened, things did go awry, Niagara responded with its demand for assurance. NorCon's grounds for refusing to provide that assurance were (A) Niagara should have known that the 1988 LRACs were too high; (B) fuel prices were volatile and so, therefore, were Niagara's tariff rates; and (C) Niagara was keenly aware of the need for security and bargained for it. There was ample evidence in the materials available to the courts to support the last two propositions; although the first would appear to be obvious, it turns out to be problematic.

A. The 1988 LRACs Were Too High

Shortly after the agreement was approved, the PSC issued new LRACs that were, as noted, about 50 percent below the 1988 LRACs which had been incorporated into the contract. NorCon emphasized Niagara's role in the determination of LRAC schedules in the past and the new LRAC schedule. "Niagara was aware at the time of the execution of the Second Amendment of the possibility that LRACs would be dropping significantly. Niagara was aware of this from, among other sources, its participation commencing in March 1991 in the LRAC adjustment proceeding, the PSC's suspension of the 1990 LRACs in 1991, the PSC's public support for the concept of non-utility generators bidding for projects, and the expected impact of such bidding." (Verified Complaint, 23–24)

In an affidavit, NorCon's counsel noted that "The PSC in its March 12, 1991 Order instituting the LRAC proceeding … publicly stated that the "[present] LRACs may be substantially overstated". … Mr. Coram [one of the Niagara executives involved in negotiating the contract] testified that this March 1991 Order gave him reason to believe the LRACs would be substantially reduced, and heightened his concern over the risk of non-performance in the later years of these contracts." (Affidavit of Thomas J. Hall in Support of Plaintiff's Motion for Summary Judgment) He also noted that Niagara made internal calculations of the effects of differences between the contractual LRACs and possible future Niagara avoided costs.

NorCon did offer one possible explanation for the sharp reduction in the LRAC schedule: "The 1988 LRACs reflected the costs of new power plants that Niagara Mohawk would have to build over the next 20 years to meet demand. By 1992, NorCon and other cogenerators had contractually committed to build those power plants and supply that energy, so the costs of those plants were not reflected in the 1992 incremental cost study." (Plaintiff Brief, 10) That is, the capital costs of new construction would not be incorporated into the LRAC. Still, one would have thought that this possibility would have occurred to Niagara.

Given the timing, it would seem that Niagara failed to recognize an obvious problem. Anyone negotiating a deal in 1991 should have seen the LRAC decline coming. If Niagara were the only one to err, that would be a powerful argument. But Niagara was not alone. Other utilities were also stuck with contracts with 1988 LRACs. Despite the fact that such a large drop in the projected LRACs should have been anticipated by anyone paying attention, everyone seemed to have missed it.

Eugene Meehan, who was Niagara's economic expert, has suggested to me how this puzzle might be resolved. NorCon originally petitioned the PSC to order Niagara to sign a contract in December 1988. A contract based on 1988 LRACs, which were still fresh at the time of signing, was signed in April 1989. While that contract was not approved by the PSC until the 1991 amendments, the obligation from a regulatory perspective was incurred with the signing of the original contract and NorCon was entitled to the 1988 LRACs. The regulatory process, therefore, would have locked in the 1988 LRAC long before the amended agreement was executed. Hence, when the contract was finally executed in 1991, Niagara knew what it was getting into but was incapable of avoiding a terrible deal, as the original contract signed in 1989 would have locked in NorCon's entitlement to the 1988 LRACs. That would resolve the puzzle, but it suggests another one: why did the parties fail to mention this in their briefs? NorCon's omission is understandable – it wanted to emphasize Niagara's awareness of the likelihood that LRACs would be reduced. Niagara's silence is more problematic. Rather than arguing that it was aware that the LRACs were too high (and implicitly saying that it had accepted the risk) when it entered into the agreement, it might have felt more comfortable arguing that changed conditions had upset the initial deal.

B. Volatility

The volatility of LRAC projections was well understood by industry participants before Niagara and NorCon began negotiating their agreement. In a 1988 report, FERC noted the problems with any long-term, fixed-price contract: "Efficiency problems are especially likely when a long-term contract attempts to predict future fuel prices. Relative fuel prices have been especially volatile in the last few years. The potential for rapid and significant change in relative fuel prices in the presence of fixed-price contracts suggests the possibility of problems in the electric utility industry similar to the take-or-pay problems that developed in the natural gas industry." (*Administrative Determination of Full Avoided Costs, Sales of Power to Qualifying Facilities, and Inter-Connection Facilities*, 23) It continued: "To avoid problems such as those associated with take-or-pay contracts in the natural gas industry, the Commission wishes to stress the danger of including forecasted fuel costs in the fixed rate structure of long-term contracts." (26) Ironically, fuel prices were not the cause of the decline in both the measured LRAC and the actual avoided costs of Niagara and other utilities; oil prices actually were higher in mid-1992 than they were in 1988.

FERC noted that fixed-price, front-loaded contracts presented a number of problems. Even if they worked properly, there would be intergenerational equity problems. Today's ratepayers would subsidize future payers. There would be short-term inefficiency because the utility would have to take power from the QF even if its costs exceeded the current LRAC. And, of course, if the contract price turned out to be substantially higher than the current LRAC, as in fact happened, ratepayers would be hurt and the utility's viability might be threatened. "The Commission believes that designers and evaluators of fixed-price contracts need to encourage contracts that strike a balance between increased QF security and lowered transactions costs on the one hand, and increased inequity to ratepayers and economic inefficiency on the other. Such a balance can be achieved by manipulating both the pricing mechanism and other, non-price features of the contract." (*Administrative Determination*, 23) Whether parties could produce a contract structure that achieved such a balance is problematic; the NorCon–Niagara agreement didn't even try.

Niagara, and everyone else in the business, was aware of the risks of significant price changes. The second period pricing established a fixed range of prices – the projected LRACs, plus or minus ten percent. Niagara's risk if the floor were binding for a reasonable length of time was substantial.

C. Security

Niagara's concerns about the adequacy of its security pre-dated the NorCon contract. In a 1988 decision rejecting Niagara's position in an earlier dispute, the court recognized Niagara's concern about the risk of an IPP's non-performance in a front-loaded contract, but it nonetheless upheld the PSC's finding that the security was adequate:

> The PSC's authorization of front-loaded pricing contracts of the type employed here are not uncommon in the case of hydroelectric facilities. That PSC is keenly aware that front-loaded contracts subject the purchaser, ultimately ratepayers, to the peril that the facility may never be capable of producing electricity at rates less than or equal to avoided costs is apparent from the agreement PSC ordered petitioner to enter into, for it capped the extent of the advanced payment to an amount equal to the asset value of the Shawmut facility and also gave petitioner a security interest in the plant with the option of possessing and operating it until repayment was accomplished. *Petitioner's dissatisfaction with the adequacy of its repayment security, though understandable,* does not, as Supreme Court observed, warrant a court substituting its judgment for that of the agency, where, as here, it has not been shown that the manner in which PSC exercised its judgment was irrational. (*Niagara Mohawk Power Corp. v. Public Service Comm'n of State of N.Y.*, 629, emphasis added)

In 1988, prior to the NorCon–Niagara agreement, FERC explicitly recognized the problem: "One risk to ratepayers is that a QF may simply go out of business or otherwise abrogate the contract in the later years of a front-loaded contract. This would mean that the future benefits paid for in the early years would never materialize. To the extent that this is a real problem, it may be dealt with through contractual provisions, such as liens on the QF's physical assets or through other legally enforceable sanctions for non-compliance." (*Administrative Determination*, 24)

FERC also noted that substantial problems had arisen with QF contracts: "Complaints of overpayments to QFs have been well publicized. For example, Houston Lighting and Power Co. estimates it will incur over $500 million in overpayments over the next eight years; Niagara Mohawk Power Co. claims that the New York Public Service Commission estimated the company will incur $180 million in overpayments by 2000 and Pacific Gas and Electric Co. claims it will incur $857 million in overpayments *per year* by 1990." (Note 24)

In his affidavit, NorCon's lawyer cited substantial deposition testimony by Niagara executives regarding their concerns about the adequacy of the security in this contract. For example:

> Q. Now, am I correct that Niagara Mohawk foresaw the possibility that the lien on the plant might not be sufficient to satisfy the balance of the tracking account at the end of the term of this contract?
>
> A. Yes, we were convinced [of] it. [Niagara Mohawk] did sensitivity studies to determine what the exposure was in the event that there was deviations from [the] then current LRACS. (Affidavit of Thomas J. Hall, 18)

What remains unclear is whether Niagara conveyed the inevitability of disaster, given the newer information, and whether the PSC took it into account.

D. In Sum

So, by the time Niagara was negotiating the NorCon agreement, it and the rest of the industry were well aware of the need for security in the long-term QF contracts. It wanted greater security, fought for it, but was unable to convince the PSC that it should have it. When the contract turned out to be a disaster, Niagara sought the security it could not get in the initial bargain. The court gave it at least a fighting chance of succeeding. The PSC, reversing itself, now believed that the security was inadequate (true) and that the court should require the additional security (since the PSC could not legally do so). To be clear, if Niagara did actually have the right to demand assurance, NorCon could not have provided it. The result would have been the same as if the court had excused Niagara by invoking impracticability, frustration, or mutual mistake.

VI. SETTLEMENT

In 1996, while the *NorCon* case was still pending, Niagara initiated negotiations to terminate, restate, or amend a substantial portion of its above-market PPAs, including NorCon's. The negotiations culminated in a Master Restructuring Agreement (MRA); the initial version was for 16 IPPs, but NorCon and one other opted out. NorCon did, however, agree to continue negotiating in good faith. Niagara paid a substantial price in cash and stock; the agreement reduced annual IPP payments by about $500 million. Niagara summarized the essential features of the deal:

> The MRA was consummated on June 30, 1998 with 14 IPPs. The MRA allowed the Company to terminate, restate or amend 27 PPAs which represented approximately three-quarters of the Company's over-market purchase power obligations. The Company terminated 18 PPAs for 1,092 MW of electric generating capacity, restated eight PPAs representing 535 MW of capacity and amended one PPA representing 42 MW of capacity. Niagara Mohawk paid the IPP Parties an aggregate of $3.934 billion in cash, of which $3.212 billion was obtained through a public market offering of senior unsecured debt, $303.7 million from the public sale of 22.4 million shares of common stock, and the remainder from cash on hand. In addition, Niagara Mohawk issued 20.5 million shares of common stock to the IPP Parties. (Niagara Mohawk Holdings, Annual Report (Form 10-K), (March 17, 2000), Part II, item 7)

The NorCon dispute was remanded, and a bench trial was held in summer 1999. At trial Niagara's expert testified that the tracking account stood at $107 million in 1998 and he projected that it would grow to $835 million by 2007; the contract rate in year 16, he said, would be negative $90 per megawatt hour. (Transcript of Oral Argument, 620–622) That is, NorCon would have defaulted and surrendered its plant to Niagara.

Judge Sprizzo professed to being unclear as to his mandate and he urged the parties to settle:

> It is really a question of how we fit the law to this set of facts. We are in uncharted territory. The first time around, I thought the law was clearer. I dismissed the action on the theory they were not entitled as a matter of law to reasonable assurances. Now the Court of Appeals says that maybe they are entitled to assurances as a matter of fact. Then you are in the realm of what I call equitable discretion and how much I have. That has to be briefed for me at the end of the case. The Court of Appeals will be operating on an abuse-of-discretion standard.
>
> I don't practice law any more – although, in a sense, I guess I do – but it is big dice to roll on the exercise of any judge's discretion. I don't care who the judge is – I say that with all humility, having sat on the bench for almost eighteen years – we don't always get it right. And sometimes, when we get it right, we get reversed, and sometimes, when we get it wrong, we get affirmed. It is a big risk to take.
>
> I think, if you have some money out there in the family tree, so to speak, as apparently you do, then maybe settlement should get on the table here, and maybe they will take something less than 100 cents on the dollar by way of assurances with respect to the contract. (Transcript of Oral Argument, 329–30)

Before a verdict was rendered, on November 23, 1999, the parties did indeed settle. The PPA would be terminated and NorCon would receive $125 million. And so, five years after Niagara sent its demand letter, the dispute was resolved. Whether the court's answer to the certified question impacted the settlement, we cannot be certain, although the judge's comments do suggest that it did. Still, since NorCon would have had to default if Niagara's right to demand assurance was upheld, the $125 million payment is pretty good evidence that the effect on settlement was modest at best.

VII. CONCLUSION

Sometimes judges talk too much. Had they simply invoked the Restatement, there would have been no basis for criticizing the decision. But they didn't. Instead, they took what they characterized as a more nuanced approach, invoking "our customary incremental common-law developmental process, rooted in particular fact patterns and keener wisdom acquired through observations of empirical application of a proportioned, less than absolute, rule in future cases." (661) Missing from the opinion, however, are the "particular fact patterns" and "observations of empirical application." Had it practiced what it appeared to preach, the court could have disposed of this case by recognizing that the contract had been imposed on Niagara Mohawk as a matter of public policy (however misguided that turned out to be) and had gone through a regulatory process that dealt explicitly with the assurance issues. The risks of a fixed-price, front-loaded 25-year agreement were obvious. The parties knew what they were and attempted to provide for them in the contract. Assurance was not an afterthought; Niagara had been concerned about assurance questions in this type of contract for a decade. For whatever reasons, Niagara could not, at contract formation, convince the PSC to give it more security.

The New York court clearly liked the idea of recognizing a common law right to demand assurance. If it had wanted to do so while still following its incremental process, it could have stressed the conditions in which it *would not recognize* the right. It could have said that while it was sympathetic in general to the notion that an insecure party should be able to demand assurance, the facts precluded it from doing so "in this kind of controversy," since the assurance question had been thoroughly vetted. For reasons unstated, it chose not to do so. This is not to say that the court's bottom line was necessarily wrong – only that you can't get there from here.

One rationalization proffered by the court for its position was that it might encourage settlement of disputes. "The availability of the doctrine may even provide an incentive and tool for parties to resolve their own differences, perhaps without the necessity of judicial intervention. Open, serious renegotiation of dramatic developments and changes in unusual contractual expectations and qualifying circumstances would occur because of and with an eye to the doctrine's application." (662) The court did not bother to note that Niagara Mohawk had already settled a large number of similar claims without the court's recognition of the right to demand assurance. Nor did it suggest why an open-ended standard which left the trial court judge befuddled would be a superior backdrop for renegotiation than a rule that did not recognize a right to demand assurance.

By the time the demand letter was sent, it had become apparent that, barring something extraordinary (like $140 a barrel oil), NorCon would not perform in the third period. But, so what? That simply meant that the parties had thirteen years to negotiate a buyout. That the FERC/PSC policies almost bankrupted Niagara is unfortunate, but that does not justify courts tweaking contract law to bail it out.

Niagara did not formally argue that its performance should be excused because of changed conditions or mistake. But, in effect, that would have been the result had the court affirmed its right to demand assurance. NorCon and the other QFs could not have provided acceptable assurance, so Niagara could have walked away from the deals on thirty-day notice. At least one other New York judge rejected this ploy:

> Furthermore, to suggest as NYSEG does, without apparently any sense of irony, that the parties were "mutually mistaken" about the risk that PPA rates would exceed avoided costs is paradoxical in light of the extensive attention paid to the need for a "true-up" or tracking mechanism in the contracts. Indeed, this risk was identified, discussed and reconciled by every party or entity even remotely affected by PURPA, including Congress in enacting the statute, FERC in prescribing the regulatory scheme, PSC in implementing it, utilities in forecasting LRACs, and QFs in making investment and other decisions. (*New York State Elec. & Gas Corp. v. Saranac Power Partners L.P.*, 255)

If the *NorCon* decision had come from some other jurisdiction, it might be of little import. But New York is different. It is the preeminent jurisdiction for commercial cases. It is generally considered to be a "hard law" or formalist jurisdiction. The case has had some precedential affect and the results are hardly encouraging. New York state and other state courts have essentially ignored the court's "incremental" approach, extending the adequate assurances doctrine only to "this kind of controversy." Instead, the courts have interpreted the *NorCon* decision to extend the adequate assurances doctrine to all contracts that are similar to the sale of goods. In one case that did try to figure out just what the *NorCon* court meant by "this kind of controversy," the court specifically pointed out that the doctrine of adequate assurances has only been extended to long-term contracts where a change in circumstances and security provision was not negotiated ex ante. (*River Terrace Associates, LLC v. Bank of New York*, *7) That court did not, of course, know that *NorCon* would have failed to qualify.

PART IV

Offer and acceptance

14. *Brown v. Cara*, the Type II Preliminary Agreement, and the option to unbundle

Traditional Anglo-American contract law recognized a sharp distinction. Either the parties had an enforceable agreement or they didn't. Contract-like preliminary agreements – a memorandum of understanding (MOU), letter of intent, or agreement to agree – were typically not enforceable. That line has eroded in recent decades. The modern approach now relies on Judge Leval's decision in *Teachers Ins. and Annuity Ass'n of America v. Tribune Co.* (*TIAA*). He divided the world into three categories: (1) all major terms were set and the signing was a mere formality (Type I); (2) terms were left open, but the parties were obliged to negotiate in good faith (Type II); and (3) the unenforceable. The Type II agreement was Leval's innovation. But what does it mean? How can it be applied?

Leval's decision was one of three cases in which the lender, TIAA, successfully sued potential borrowers for walking away after interest rates tumbled. The others were *Teachers Ins. & Annuity Ass'n of America v. Butler* and *Teachers Ins. and Annuity Ass'n of America v. Ormesa Geothermal.* In all three, there was a "binding commitment." There was a recognized trade custom of fixing the key economic terms prior to the final agreement. In *Ormesa*, Judge Wood described the process: the parties "'circled' the transaction at a blended rate of 10.64 percent. When a financing is 'circled,' the parties orally agree that they will do the transaction on the specified terms, and the interest rate and certain other key economic terms are, by this oral agreement, fixed. It is the custom in the financial community that once the parties circle a deal, neither party tries to change the interest rate that has been agreed." (404) In all three, the commitment was contingent on the good faith negotiation of the non-economic terms, which were presumed to have de minimis value. In *Tribune*, Leval emphasized the routine nature of the documentation: "The letter stated that the agreement was 'contingent upon the preparation, execution and delivery of documents … in form and substance satisfactory to TIAA and to TIAA's special counsel …,' and that the transaction documents would contain the 'usual and customary' representations and warranties, closing conditions, other covenants, and events of default 'as we and our special counsel may deem reasonably necessary to accomplish this transaction.'" (494)

In each case, the courts treated the negotiation sticking points as contrived and not in good faith. The *Tribune* trial was on liability only; the other two dealt with the remedy issue as well, awarding expectation damages – the present value of the difference between the agreed upon interest payments and the market rates at the time of the breach. Rather than litigate the remedy issue in *Tribune*, the parties settled; it is likely that the settlement resulted in an outcome similar to the others – had Tribune acted in good faith, the deal would have gone through and therefore the damages would be based on the interest rate differential.

The combination of the binding commitment language, agreed-upon economic terms, and an easy inference of bad faith made a strong case for finding liability in these cases. It is not so clear that it transfers well to other contexts, the successful adoption of Leval's innovation notwithstanding. Schwartz and Scott (2007) summarize the case law and note that many jurisdictions have adopted the Leval test. Not all cases follow the *TIAA* pattern, however, and determining whether there is an agreement and, if so, whether there has been good faith can present more difficult problems.

How then, should the Leval framework be applied? What sort of evidence should a court look at to determine the existence of a Type II agreement? What advice might one give litigators as to how they should marshal the evidence? One way of approaching that question is to take a sample of litigated preliminary agreement cases and see how the courts have resolved them as Schwartz and Scott have done. The advantage of such an approach is that one might be able to discern patterns of enforcement. An alternative approach, which I will follow here, is to focus more intently on a specific case. What can we learn from how the lawyers argued pro and con on that question? How did the court determine that a particular agreement fell into the Type II category?

The case I chose to focus on, *Brown v. Cara*, seemed an appropriate choice. The Second Circuit, interpreting New York law, found on summary judgment that a Memorandum of Understanding (MOU) was a Type II preliminary agreement. While the Second Circuit Court of Appeals had applied the Leval framework in the past, there was no New York precedent finding a Type II agreement. Nor has the New York Court of Appeals found such an agreement subsequently. So, *Brown v. Cara* remains the leading case recognizing a Type II agreement in the nation's most prominent commercial jurisdiction. Ironically, this is despite the fact that the opinion was not rendered by the New York court. As it turns out, drilling down resulted in a dry hole. My presumption that *Brown v. Cara* would provide a good window on how to litigate a Type II claim turned out to be wrong. The plaintiff argued, almost exclusively, that the MOU was a Type I agreement. A Type II claim was thrown in pretty much as an afterthought. The court, right or wrong, reached its conclusion with very little help from the litigants. Still, the case is of interest as it illustrates how a proper framing of the problem would have highlighted the variety of contractual solutions available to the parties.

The basic problem, as framed by the court, seemed simple enough. Cara owned a piece of property in Brooklyn, the value of which could be considerably enhanced if the property could be rezoned. Brown would invest in getting approval for a more valuable land use and, if successful, it would build the project. However, the costs of drafting the various agreements (operating agreement, construction agreement, etc.) would be substantial and the nature of these agreements might depend on what had ultimately been approved. So, went the claim, rather than write an enforceable contract, they entered into a MOU that defined some aspects of their relationship but left a lot open. If the rezoning failed, those contract-drafting costs could be avoided by waiting. If it succeeded, Cara might take advantage of the absence of a formal agreement by bypassing Brown. Brown works; Cara reaps. By finding some sort of agreement, the court could constrain Cara's opportunism.

By reframing the problem, a quite different picture emerges. Transforming Cara's property into a more valuable use requires a number of discrete, perhaps overlapping, acts – rezoning, construction, leasing, management, and, perhaps, selling all or part of the enhanced property. There are, apparently, some economies from bundling these activities and an owner, like Cara, would want the opportunity to take advantage of them. However, there are some costs as well and the owner would want to maintain the option to unbundle under certain circumstances. The parties could design their relationship to reflect the appropriate balance between Cara's flexibility and Brown's reliance. These are, after all, sophisticated parties with access to counsel. If they want the benefits of legal enforcement, then they should design their relationship accordingly. If there were only one plausible contract structure, then imposing it by implication might be acceptable; but here, there were a number of plausible structures, leading to quite different outcomes. One type of contract would have given Brown a rough equivalent of the reliance damages; alternative plausible structures, however, would have allowed Brown to share in the upside. Bypassing the formal contract requirement leaves it to the courts to choose and the courts have a blunt instrument:

determining whether the parties have entered into an agreement and if so, whether it is of the Type I or Type II variety.

In its decision, the court imposed some sort of obligation on Cara and afforded Brown some protection. The court did not say what the remedy for breaching a Type II agreement would be. In the *TIAA* cases, as noted, the remedy was expectation damages. However, if Brown had won, its remedy would almost certainly have been limited to reliance damages. Cara would get the increased value of the property and would compensate Brown for the expenses it incurred producing the increased value. That is also the remedy suggested by Schwartz and Scott (2007). In their analysis, if the project were abandoned, it would be because the passage of time had produced negative information. In *Brown v. Cara*, the information was positive – the project is worth undertaking, but Cara prefers to do so without Brown. In effect, the reliance remedy would establish a default rule with the implicit assumption that the parties would find it too difficult to contract around it. However, as noted, contracting would not have been that difficult.

Section I provides the background for the decision. It includes a description of the transaction, the MOU, and the dispute. It also summarizes the key aspects of the pre-appeal litigation – the complaint, the magistrate's decision, and the district court's opinion. The appeal will be the focus of Section II. In Section III, I will turn to the question ignored by the parties and the court: how could the parties have designed an enforceable contract instead of the MOU? In particular, it will emphasize the tradeoff between the economies of bundling the different phases versus the value of the option to unbundle.

I. THE BACKGROUND

A. The Deal

Cara owned a piece of property at 100 Jay Street in Brooklyn that was being used as a parking lot. Zoning restrictions precluded residential use and limited the size of any new building on the property. Cara and Brown entered into an MOU in March 2000 with the intention of getting the property rezoned and building and managing a project. The exact scope of the project would not be determined until the parties had obtained the rezoning and concomitant approvals. The initial plan was for a mixed use building with twelve stories of residential units, office space, ground floor retail, and underground parking. The MOU alluded to some sort of joint entity (joint venture or partnership, or perhaps something else) that would be formed in the future.

To simplify slightly, Cara would have to do virtually nothing other than contribute the property. The parties differed on the extent of Cara's expected involvement. In the First Amended Complaint (5–6), Brown claimed that Cara only needed to provide the property and Brown would be involved with the development effort including the conceptual design, the rezoning process, conceptual budgeting, arranging for financing, and establishing an effective marketing plan. In his Answer to First Amended Complaint (8), Cara denied the claims as to his required obligations.

Brown (also referred to as JMB) would provide the services that would, if successful, transform the property:

> Brown provides his company and individual experience, lender relationships, architectural/engineering relationships, legal relationships and governmental relationships to lead the development effort. This will include, but not be specifically limited to, the rezoning process, conceptual design of the project, conceptual budgeting, arranging for possible financing avenues and helping to establish an effective marketing plan. (MOU, 1)

In addition, "Brown will build the project with union labor, if needed." I suspect that this meant that if Brown did build the project, he would accede to New York rules and use union labor.

Brown agreed to pay development costs (largely legal and design related) up to $175 000. Revenues from parking, retail and similar activities would be split equally. Brown would receive 60 percent of the revenues from the sale or rental of apartments. The parties recognized that "time is of the essence" and that they "intend to enter into a formal contract shortly." The MOU concluded with their agreeing "to work together in accordance with the terms and conditions outlined above." (MOU, 2)

In the next year and a half, the project was designed, the rezoning successful, and all the approvals were granted. Instead of the 12-story structure initially proposed, the approved plan called for a 23-story building. Brown's out-of-pocket expenses exceeded the $175,000 figure; subsequently, it claimed to have spent $350,000 with an additional $400,000 for the value of Brown's time. (Declaration of Jeffrey M. Brown, 8) The rezoning resulted in a substantial increase in the value of the property. According to the plaintiff, the value increased from about $3 million to $18 million. (Reply Declaration of Jeffrey M. Brown, 12) In the months following the successful rezoning, the parties engaged in negotiations on a number of matters. Two written manifestations were a set of dueling term sheets and multiple drafts of an operating agreement.

Some aspects of the term sheets are of particular interest – I will return to them below.

Negotiations broke down when Brown sent Cara a form construction contract with terms unacceptable to Cara. According to Cara, "Brown's proposed CMA [Construction Management Agreement] contained substantive terms concerning his fees that went far beyond what the Term Sheet provided, and which Cara felt were substantially in excess of market rates for the proposed transaction." (Def. Brief, 13) Brown claimed that it had inadvertently sent the wrong form. In the court's words, "Cara's displeasure and offense were so deep that he refused to continue with negotiations and ceased all communication and collaboration with JMB." (152) The parties disagree as to whether Cara's pique was genuine or an opportunistic attempt to take all the increased value for himself. An alternative explanation is that Cara might have viewed the proffered construction contract as an attempt by JMB to increase its share of the gains. The negotiations over the term sheet suggest that this is not implausible.

1. The post-rezoning documents

In September 2002, Brown sent a proposed term sheet to Cara. A revised term sheet was agreed to shortly thereafter. There were a few substantial differences between the two. And, importantly, there were two significant terms that were identical. I will get to those shortly, but first I will highlight some of the differences, which give the flavor of the terms remaining open after the MOU. Brown proposed that it would have exclusive control of all decisions except for certain major decisions like sale of all the assets, which would require joint approval. The revised Term Sheet gave Brown exclusive decision-making authority over construction; but otherwise, the parties would share equally in control. Brown proposed that both parties guarantee the construction loan, but the revised Term Sheet made Brown solely responsible. Brown proposed that its cash contribution be repaid with interest (12 percent) out of the cash flow prior to the 60/40 and 50/50 shares specified in the MOU. The revised term sheet excluded the interest and changed the sharing rate on the apartments to 55/45. Note that this entailed revising the initial terms of the agreement unlike in *TIAA v. Tribune*. There, Leval held "each was obligated to seek in good faith to conclude a final agreement *within the terms specified* in the commitment letter, supplemented by such representations, warranties and other conditions as are customary in such transactions." (*Tribune*, 500–501, emphasis added)

In the revised agreement, Cara could terminate for cause (Brown's failure to pursue its pre-construction obligations or failure to close the construction loan by a set date) by paying all costs incurred by Brown; it could also terminate for no cause if it compensated Brown for those costs and paid a "success fee of $2.5 million representing the enhanced value of the Property as a result of the rezoning process." (Def. exh. D Term Sheet, 5) Brown's initial proposal would have allowed either party to terminate if the construction loan had not been closed within 36 months. If so, Cara would have to repay the cash expended by Brown plus $2.5 million for the enhanced value. There were other differences, but this is enough to illustrate how much remained open.

The term sheets included two identical clauses: a buy/sell clause and a non-binding clause:

> Either member (the "initiating Member") may force the other Member to either purchase the Initiating Member's interest or sell its interest to the Initiating Member at a price proposed by the Initiating Member at any time if there is a deadlock on an issue as to which the consent of both Members is required or after the 3d anniversary of completion of Construction.
>
> * * *
>
> This Term Sheet represents only proposed points that may or may not eventually become part of a definitive operating agreement for the Company. Neither party shall be bound or obligated by any of the terms hereof, any prior term sheets or correspondence or any other discussions unless and until a formal written operating agreement and related agreements containing all of the material terms of the Company and construction and development of the Project have been executed and delivered by each of the parties. (Declaration of Charles Cara, Exh. E)

I will return to the buy/sell clause in Section III. The nonbinding clause indicates the importance of written documents embodying all the material terms. The absence of such a clause in the MOU is subject to different interpretations. Silence could mean that the agreement was meant to be enforceable; alternatively, one could argue that if the detailed term sheet was nonbinding, then the MOU with even less detail should be nonbinding as well. I prefer the second interpretation, but for my purposes it is sufficient to note that disclaiming enforceability of an MOU or other pre-contractual document should not have been too hard.

The parties exchanged four drafts of an operating agreement but never settled on a final version. They dispute how close they were when Cara walked away. Cara says there remained a number of significant open terms; he noted that the letter by Brown's attorneys accompanying the last draft noted five "significant open business points." (Declaration of Charles Cara, 11) Brown claimed that the parties were in the final "wordsmithing" stage. (Pl. Brief, 18) The drafts were roughly seventy pages, single-spaced, and incorporated most of the terms included in the second Term Sheet. The simple buy/sell agreement of the Term Sheet ballooned to three pages of text without really altering anything.

Finally, there were the two construction contracts. Perhaps the most interesting point about them is that despite Brown's claim that the wrong form had been sent, the "right" form never did get sent. (Nor could I find any evidence in the record of the terms of the second contract; I have only had partial access to the record, so it is possible that the terms of both contracts were produced.) It was not clear why Brown might have two different forms and why one would have been more favorable to Cara, although Brown did provide an explanation in his Declaration:

> It was in or about this time that Mr. Cara requested a draft of the construction management agreement that would be entered into between our LLC and JMB for the construction of the Project. At the time, I was in Florida. I called my office and asked them to send Mr. Cara a form of contract. Unfortunately, my office staff misunderstood which form of contract I wanted them to forward to Mr. Cara. The one that was forwarded was a form that would be appropriate for dealings between parties operating at arm's length. It was not the correct form for the contract between JMB and the LLC. (Declaration of Jeffrey M. Brown, 11)

2. The litigation, round one

In its complaint, Brown asserted six causes of action. First, it asked for a declaratory judgment that the MOU was "in full force and effect and that it creates a binding joint venture agreement between Brown and Cara." (First Amended Complaint, 7) The second cause was for breach of contract; it asked for specific performance or, in the alternative, damages of not less than six million dollars. The third, fourth, and fifth causes of action were for breach of fiduciary duty, breach of trust, and for an accounting of any future revenues or profits. The final cause of action was in quantum meruit, claiming that Cara had unjustly retained all the benefits resulting from Brown's efforts:

> Brown and JMB are entitled to judgment in an amount equal to the fair and reasonable benefit and value of the services and Project approvals obtained, provided and/or paid for by Brown and/or JMB, which corresponds to: (i) 50% of the value of the Property attributable thereto, in an amount to be proven at trial, but not less than six million dollars; (ii) 60% percent of all revenue from the sale or rental of residential units in the Project; and/or (iii) and 50% of the revenue from the parking, retail, office, signage and other revenues from the Project. (11)

The matter was referred to a magistrate judge who granted summary judgment for Cara on the first two claims but denied Cara's motion on the remaining claims. Brown conceded that if he failed on the first two claims, claims three through five would also fail. (*Brown v. Cara*, 2004, *2) The district court accordingly dismissed those claims as well. The magistrate judge held, and the district court agreed, that the MOU was an unenforceable preliminary agreement:

> [T]here were clearly open terms to be negotiated regarding the scope of the final Project … [and] the existence of these open terms strongly supports the defendant's argument that at the time the MOU was signed, neither party had agreed to all of the terms under which the parties would move forward to complete the Project … . [T]he size and complexity of the proposed construction project, the extensive negotiations over the Term Sheets and lengthy drafts of proposed agreements exchanged between the parties after rezoning was achieved clearly demonstrates that at the time the MOU was executed, there was no binding contract because there were too many open terms. (*Brown v. Cara*, 2004, *1)

The quantum meruit claim was allowed to proceed to discovery. "The evidence demonstrates that Plaintiffs provided and Defendants accepted valuable services for which Plaintiffs expected compensation. If left uncompensated, these services would constitute unjust enrichment." (*Brown v. Cara*, 2004, *2) The denial of summary judgment on this cause was not appealed.

What of the Type II claim? The Magistrate stated that Brown had not pressed the Type II argument. "The Magistrate Judge correctly concluded that 'Plaintiffs have not pressed this argument' because they mentioned this issue solely in one sentence in a footnote in 75 pages of legal memoranda." (Def. Brief, 20) As we shall see, the Court of Appeals disagreed. Brown was granted a preliminary injunction. In February 2005, the injunction was suspended. (Def. Brief, 2) Shortly thereafter, Cara entered into a joint venture with Hudson Companies to build a project known as J Condominium. The final building was quite different from the 12-story original proposal and the 23-story plan developed by Brown. It is described on its website as: "Rising 33 stories alongside the Manhattan Bridge, J Condo is Brooklyn's premiere luxury residential building with 267 studio to three-bedroom apartments, a 424-car parking garage, and a robust mix of ground floor retail tenants including Chase Bank, Bridge Apothecary, and J's Wine and Spirits. As the tallest building in Dumbo, J Condo adds an easily recognizable icon to the Brooklyn skyline with its dramatic curved, sail-like façade of floor to ceiling windows that maximizes the building's abundant natural light and offers magnificent panoramic views of Manhattan, Brooklyn, the East River, and New York Harbor." (http://streeteasy.com/nyc/building/j-condominium)

II. THE DECISION

The litigation was quite nasty. The tone is illustrated by the opening of Brown's reply brief: "Appellants submit this Reply Brief in further support of their appeal, and in opposition to Appellees' brief, which is riddled with lies by omission, quotes taken out of context, and other equally devious ploys in a calculated effort to mislead this Court." (1) Most of the plaintiff's brief argued that the MOU was a Type I agreement. The agreement, it said, was to set up a joint venture. All the details – financing, the construction contract, the operating agreement, etc. – could be deferred until a condition subsequent, the rezoning, had occurred. None of those open elements was essential to the establishment of the joint venture. I confess that I find this implausible; the Court of Appeals gave the argument short shrift and turned to the theory less argued – it was a Type II agreement.

The plaintiff did argue, barely, that the agreement was a Type II agreement. Seventeen pages of the Reply Brief were devoted to the Type I argument, while the Type II claim warranted fewer than three; most of those three were only concerned with the question of whether the Type II argument had been preserved, not with the merits of the argument itself. The court rejected the position taken by the magistrate, district judge, and defendant that the plaintiff had waived any claim of a Type II agreement. (156, note 2) It also rejected the defendant's claim that New York law did not recognize Type II agreements. (153, note 1) It then turned to considering the five factors that would determine whether a binding Type II agreement existed. These are essentially the same factors regarding the existence of a Type I agreement, although the court gives them different weight:

(1) whether the intent to be bound is revealed by the language of the agreement;
(2) the context of the negotiations;
(3) the existence of open terms;
(4) partial performance; and
(5) the necessity of putting the agreement in final form, as indicated by the customary form of such transactions. (157)

The court concluded:

> Measuring the MOU by the relevant factors in light of this limited contractual goal it is clear that it is a binding preliminary agreement to work toward the goal of developing the Jay Street Property within a defined framework, preserving for later negotiation in good faith business, design, financing, construction, and management terms necessary to achieve the ultimate goal of developing and exploiting the Jay Street Property. (157–58)

All five factors, said the court, favored finding the existence of a Type II Agreement. I will not go through the court's analysis of all five. Two factors are enough to get the flavor of the court's reasoning. With respect to the second prong, the court said:

> [T]he parties elected to negotiate a general framework within which they could proceed while preserving flexibility in the face of future uncertainty. While it was possible in the abstract to negotiate a more definitive contract, using determinative methodologies to be applied to open issues, the context of the negotiations did not require derivation of such algorithms if the parties opted instead for a more open arrangement. The MOU is evidence of such an arrangement, and, as a Type II agreement, is consistent with the context of the negotiations. (158)

The court appears to be saying that a "determinative methodology" existed that could have resulted in an enforceable agreement, but that the parties did not have to use it. Alternatively, it might have meant that the "algorithm" existed in principle, but that implementation was not feasible. I will return to this in the next section where I will show that implementation was feasible.

Turning to the third factor, where the existence of open terms creates a presumption against finding a binding contract as to the ultimate goal, these same omissions may actually support finding a binding Type II agreement. The MOU leaves open terms critical to every aspect of the Jay Street Project from design, to business structure, to ownership and management. However, these omissions do not warrant against finding the MOU enforceable as a Type II agreement. In view of indeterminate regulatory and market conditions, JMB and Cara simply elected to pursue rezoning first, leaving finalization of project design and execution for later negotiation within the framework described in the MOU. (158)

In the *TIAA* trilogy, the open terms were of minor importance, having little or no impact on the value of the deal. Contrast that with this court holding that the agreement "leaves open terms critical to every aspect." If the existence of open terms counts in favor of finding a Type II agreement, what will count against it? Perhaps the court meant only that it is not unreasonable in this situation to defer the open issues until the rezoning question is resolved. But, there is a big difference between "simply elected" and "not unreasonable," and the court provides no guidance on how it got from the one to the other.

So, the court concluded that this was a Type II agreement. That did not mean, however, that the plaintiff had won. It only meant that the plaintiff now had to prove that the Type II agreement had in fact been breached – that Cara's refusal to continue the negotiations was not in good faith. That would not be easy. Had Cara walked away right after the rezoning had been completed, that would most likely have failed a good faith test. But, that is not what happened. Cara hung on for over a year, negotiating the term sheets and four drafts of the operating agreement. I suspect that would be enough to satisfy a good faith standard, but that remains a jury question.

What if Brown were to win? What remedy would be available? New York precedent, the *TIAA* trilogy notwithstanding, is that the remedy would be reliance damages. Allowing Brown to recover expectation damages "would, in effect, be transforming an agreement to negotiate for a contract into the contract itself." (*Goodstein Const. Corp. v. City of New York*, 1361). In Farnsworth's (1998, § 3.26a) words: an "award based on [the expectation interest] would give the injured party the 'benefit of the bargain' that was not reached. But if no agreement was reached and it cannot even be known what agreement would have been reached, there is no way to measure the lost expectation." In *Goodstein*, the defendant breached an agreement that had given the plaintiff an exclusive right to negotiate. Plaintiff sued for $800 million lost profits; the court allowed recovery only for $1 million in reliance damages. "[a] party's alleged failure to bargain in good faith is not a but-for cause of [plaintiff's] lost profits, since even with the best faith on both sides the deal might not have been closed [and] attributing [plaintiff's] lost profits to [defendant's] bad faith may be speculative at best." (*Goodstein Construction Corp v. City Of New York*, 373)

However, some courts have held expectation damages to be an acceptable remedy and at least one court has shown willingness to grant specific performance. (*Stanford Hotels Corp. v. Potomac Creek Associates, L.P.*) Professor Eisenberg (2000, 1809) favors compensating the expectation interest:

> A final issue raised by the enforcement of commitments to negotiate in good faith concerns the appropriate measure of damages. Where such a commitment is part of a bargain, the injured party should be awarded expectation damages. Of course the deal might have broken down even if the other party

had negotiated in good faith. However, because that party's wrongful acts made it impossible to determine what would have happened if she had acted in good faith, she should bear the burden of proving the deal would have broken down even if she had so acted. If expectation damages are too uncertain, the court should award reliance damages measured by out-of-pocket costs or, where appropriate, by lost opportunities.

III. DISCUSSION

The project contains a number of discrete steps, running from rezoning through construction, to managing the completed project. This suggests that the parties perceived some economies from bundling them all together with a single provider. The greater the perceived economies, the more reliant the owner would be on the future performance of the provider. I need take no position on whether the economies could be real and substantial; the MOU suggests that the parties believed that there would be some. Casual observation suggests that the advantages of bundling are not great – certainly construction and management of the final project are often provided by independent entities. In fact, Brown had contacted at least two property management companies to manage the completed property. (Declaration of Jeffrey Brown, Exhibits H and I)

Assuming that there are at least some economies to bundling, the owner would have a number of concerns about committing to a particular provider for the entire project. There is the usual potential holdup problem; as the project goes forward, the provider could reshape the deal, taking advantage of the owner's vulnerability. Brown sending the "wrong" construction contract and some of the proposed language of the first term sheet might have been manifestations of this. In addition, during the process, the owner would acquire information. It would learn things about the provider's competence, character, and financial ability, and about the availability of alternative providers. (Gilson, Sabel and Scott, 2009) The option to unbundle, to replace the provider, could turn out to be quite valuable even if it meant sacrificing some of the economies associated with there being a single provider. However, giving the owner the discretion to terminate subjects the provider to the risk alluded to in the Introduction – the provider works, the owner reaps. And, of course, the costs of designing the relationship ex ante and enforcing it ex post must be taken into account as well. The structure of the transaction would reflect the answers to these questions. The parties face the same sort of reliance/flexibility tradeoff discussed in Chapter 2; they too have to price the option to abandon.

Brown's counsel proposed one solution to the problem:

> [W]hen a real estate development project requires a very substantial discretionary governmental approval or permit, without which the project would not be possible, it is typical for co-venturers who are seeking the government approval to wait until that permit is issued and the project becomes definite before incurring the expense of preparing detailed documents, such as an LLC operating agreement. Co-venturers often first execute a skeletal agreement setting forth the essential business terms of the joint venture that is sufficient to bind the parties to their joint venture and postpone creation of expensive and time consuming detailed documents until the project becomes "real" by issuance of the necessary governmental approval. (Plaintiff Brief, Special Appendix, 42)

Deferring the full documentation would indeed be a sensible policy, although the concern would not be the costs of negotiating the detailed contract documents, but the fact that the project is likely to change shape as the process proceeds. Brown failed to explain how the MOU set forth the "essential business terms." In particular, it failed to specify whether Cara would have the option to unbundle and, if so, what would happen if Cara chose to exercise that option. If the costs of designing and negotiating an enforceable agreement dealing with that were prohibitive, then perhaps the MOU would have been the best they could do. However, designing such an agreement would not have been difficult. In a sense, all that was necessary was a mechanism for pricing Cara's option to unbundle.

Suppose that there are substantial economies from bundling the phases, from rezoning through construction, marketing, and managing into a single agreement, but that the owner wants some discretion to adapt as it learns more. One solution would eschew interfirm contracts and would simply merge the two firms – pure vertical integration. While it is possible that in certain circumstances, some form of integration would be viable, that does not seem plausible in the context Brown and Cara found themselves in; I will pursue this no further. What sort of contract solutions would be available? First, the contract could simply require that Cara reimburse Brown's expenses; recall that in the Term Sheet, if Cara had terminated Brown for cause, he would have had to reimburse Brown. Second, the contract could initially be only for the rezoning effort. If the rezoning were successful, the owner would be free to hire anyone for the next phase. However, if the owner chose someone else, it would have to pay the initial provider's costs (or some fraction thereof). Easy enough to write. It would give the initial service provider a cost advantage over competitors at the subsequent phase. If the costs incurred are high, the lock-in effect could be considerable. This sort of mechanism is commonly used in other contexts. "Turnaround" fees in the movies are an example. Biotech deals employ a similar mechanism. Note that this is roughly the equivalent of the reliance damages that would have been assessed if the finder of fact were to find that a Type II agreement had been breached.

Third, the owner could have the right to terminate without cause by paying a fixed fee. The Term Sheet and the last version of the operating agreement both included such a mechanism, the "success fee." However, they did not decide on a success fee until well into the project. It might be too difficult to determine ex ante what the structure of termination fees ought to be. That could be resolved by deferring the decision to a third party, perhaps an arbitrator. As long as the mechanism were defined, the agreement would be enforceable.

Finally, a variation on the previous mechanism is a buy/sell arrangement. This is hardly esoteric. The parties, as noted, had included such a mechanism in the term sheets and draft operating agreement. Rather than have an outsider determine the value, the parties can do it themselves. If after some defined milestone (perhaps following the rezoning) either party wanted to go it alone, it could trigger a buy/sell. It would name a price at which it would be willing to either take full ownership of the property or sell out. Since the property would have been solely owned by the owner, the deal would require that the owner convey all the property if the counterparty succeeds; if the owner succeeds, the counterparty would simply give up any claim it had to the property. After the buy/sell is triggered, the counterparty would then determine whether it should take the money or pay for the property. Note that with this mechanism, as well as the previous one, if the owner buys out the service provider, the payment would be roughly equivalent to the expectancy damages – the provider's share of the gains.

The parties could have opted for a zero price on Cara's option – namely, no agreement. A finding of "no agreement" would have meant that Brown would have borne the initial costs without any protection from Cara's decision to use someone else for the next phases of the project. Brown's counsel (and the magistrate and trial judge) made this point:

> Essentially Cara would have this Court conclude that Brown acted as a mere volunteer at all times, expending hundreds of thousands of dollars to obtain the Property's rezoning for Cara's … sole benefit based solely on the hope that Cara – someday – would see fit to enter into a binding agreement with Brown. The Magistrate quite properly rejected that absurd position:
>
> Indeed, the Court finds that it is disingenuous for Cara to argue that Brown expended two years of time and effort and significant funds – over $350,000

> in costs alone – to obtain the rezoning of the Property, a result that would exclusively benefit Cara… on the pure hope that Brown could possibly participate in the development of the Property. (Plaintiff Reply Brief, 11)

Is it really that absurd? If Brown believed that Cara would incur high costs of switching to another supplier at any future phase of the project, then it might well have found the risk worth bearing. In *Trianco, LLC v. International Business Machines Corp.* the court did indeed find that a party would incur pre-agreement costs with only the hope that an agreement would come to pass. The case is unusual in that it relied on *Brown*, but the roles were reversed. The *defendant* argued that theirs was a Type II agreement while the plaintiff argued that no agreement existed. Because the plaintiff had conceded that IBM had acted in good faith, it would have lost if the court had found an agreement; so it argued instead for unjust enrichment. The court used *Brown* against the plaintiff:

> If one acknowledges the role of a preliminary agreement such as is recognized under New York law, one cannot allow a party to recover under unjust enrichment for the performance promised in order to secure the "hoped-for" contract and future negotiation. Trianco made a business decision to enter into the Teaming Agreement and help IBM secure the government contract *without the expectation of being directly compensated* for this help. Instead, Trianco believed that in exchange for their work they would be able to negotiate a satisfactory subcontract with IBM. Unfortunately this did not occur … . To compensate Trianco for the expenditures promised to obtain a return promise of future negotiations would undermine the legal concept of binding preliminary agreements. (655, emphasis added)

Ironically, if this reading were adopted in the remand of *Brown v. Cara*, if Cara were found to have acted in good faith, then Brown's quantum meruit claim, which survived summary judgment, would have failed.

My point is fourfold. First, contrary to Brown's counsel's argument, it would not have been very difficult to have written an enforceable contract initially. Second, the provider's fate, if the owner were to terminate at any stage, would depend on the structure of that contract. The structure, in effect, prices the option to unbundle. One approach would result in a payoff similar to reliance damages and another would result in a payoff similar to expectation damages. Third, all the contract solutions provide room for the parties to negotiate over the operating agreement and construction agreement. They simply define what would happen if the parties fail to agree. There would be no need to argue about whether the failure to agree stemmed from the lack of good faith by one of the parties.

IV. CONCLUDING REMARKS

The Leval framework has caught on in many jurisdictions. But what of New York? *Brown v. Cara* is one of the few decisions applying New York law to find the existence of a Type II agreement. However, as in *TIAA*, the decision was by a federal court interpreting New York law, a law that did not exist. The New York Court of Appeals has yet to endorse the notion that there exist enforceable Type II agreements. Indeed, the one opinion that even mentioned a Type II agreement was, at best, skeptical: "The parties debate whether the settlement is a Type I or Type II preliminary agreement as used in federal line of cases, such as *Brown v. Cara*, 420 F.3d 148 [2d Cir. 2005] and *Teachers Ins. & Annuity Ass'n. of Am. v. Tribune Co.,* 670 F.Supp. 491 [S.D.N.Y. 1987]. While we do not disagree with the reasoning in federal cases, we do not find the rigid classifications into 'Types' useful." (*IDT Corp. v. Tyco Group*, 915 n. 2)

As an exemplar of how to litigate a Type II agreement, *Brown v. Cara* fails. Brown did virtually nothing to make the argument. The court came to its conclusion with no help from counsel, which was fruitlessly arguing the existence of a Type I agreement. So, one goal of this project was not achieved. On the one hand, it is disappointing that the litigation history provides no guidance for future litigators. On the other hand, it is disappointing that a court could come to a conclusion (on a summary judgment motion) with so little evidence being produced.

Ironically, the Court of Appeals, in rejecting Brown's Type I claim noted that if Brown had desired, it could have entered into a fully binding contract:

> JMB argues that, given the circumstances, this level of detail was impossible to achieve when the MOU was signed. Assuming this to be true does not make the MOU a more binding contract, however. Moreover, *we are not convinced that, had they so desired, the parties could not have negotiated a fully binding contract* regardless of the unknown. Contracting parties faced with similar uncertainty routinely negotiate objective methodologies by which open terms are later to be determined. *See, e.g., Carmon*, 614 N.Y.S.2d at 556 ("It is well settled that an agreement to agree, in which material terms are left for future negotiations, is unenforceable unless a methodology for determining the material terms can be found within the four corners of the agreement or the agreement refers to an objective extrinsic event, condition, or standard by which the material terms may be determined."). JMB may claim that such an exercise would have been pointless until the rezoning process was completed. Of course, that says no more than that JMB, rather than expending the resources necessary to achieve a fully-binding agreement, decided to assume the risk that the parties would not, in the end, be able to "work together." (155)

Why the court finds it dispositive for a Type I claim, but, apparently, irrelevant for a Type II claim, I know not. The availability of a "methodology" (multiple methodologies, actually) should, I maintain, counsel against imposing an agreement, whether Type I or Type II, on the parties.

There were, I have shown, a number of plausible contractual solutions to the problem and these would have yielded different outcomes. Which is right? It would depend on how the parties reckon the gains from bundling the provider's tasks and the value of the option to unbundle. How that would work out in any given context, we can't say. And that is precisely the point. By requiring an enforceable contract, we require that the parties engage in the balancing exercise. Their needs are not well served by having a court determine after the fact which of the different contract structures should be imposed on the parties.

15. Traynor (*Drennan*) v. Hand (*Baird*): much ado about (almost) nothing

The contrasting opinions of Learned Hand (*Baird v. Gimbel*) and Roger Traynor (*Drennan v. Star Paving*) are a longstanding feature in Contracts casebooks. Over forty years ago, Professor Harry Jones noted: "[T]his is the judicial big league. Learned Hand on one side, for his court, Chief Justice Traynor for his court on the other. You can't do much better than that. I would suggest, without lack of respect, that is somewhat like comparing a Joe Dimaggio of the generation immediately past with a Willie Mays of the present generation." (Kelso, 1971, 623) We could perhaps update the baseball references, but the core sentiment of Professor Jones's remark remains intact. The central issue in the two cases was the revocability of an offer. Hand held that an offeror was free to revoke prior to acceptance, while Traynor held that the offer was irrevocable so long as the offeree had relied on it. Traynor's decision was well received, since contract scholarship at that time was pushing to expand the domain of promissory estoppel. The fact that Traynor's opinion is prominently featured in most Contracts casebooks suggests that some really important contract principle had been promulgated. Indeed, it was the basis for a whole new section of the Restatement, Section 87(2).

The specific context of the two opinions was a dispute between a general contractor and a subcontractor. When a subcontractor informed a contractor that it had submitted a mistaken bid before the contractor had accepted it, Hand held that the bid was an offer and the sub was free to revoke its offer. A quarter century later, Traynor, faced with the same problem, made an estoppel argument: so long as the contractor was relying upon the sub's bid, the offer was irrevocable. Implicit in the decision's favorable reception is the notion that the *Drennan* rule generalizes beyond its narrow context.

In fact, it doesn't. Examination of every decision citing *Drennan* or *Baird*, yields a number of significant facts. First, while *Drennan* has prevailed in most jurisdictions, application of the reliance qualification has been, at best, problematic. Second, *Drennan* doesn't travel well. Aside from the general contractor (GC) versus subcontractor context, very few opinions rely on *Drennan*. Third, its spawn, Section 87(2), has been a dud. Like *Drennan*, it is rarely cited outside the GC-sub context; but, unlike *Drennan*, it is rarely cited even in that context. Fourth, and most importantly, *Drennan*'s context has been ignored. Nearly all *Drennan*-type GC-sub cases involve a *public* construction project. The issue rarely gets litigated when the project is being done for private owners. They, apparently, have figured out how to cope with the problem; public owners, saddled with regulation of the bidding process, have been less successful.

Drennan and *Baird*, it should be emphasized, are not free-standing contract disputes, a fact that judges and contract scholars seem to ignore. They are embedded in regulation of public construction, both of the owner–GC and GC–sub relationships. The case law, by and large, ignores the regulatory context, implicitly treating all the cases as if the winner of a competitive sealed bid gives the owner an irrevocable option to use it at the bid price. Moreover, the law either ignores regulation of the GC–sub relationship or treats the regulations as unrelated to the contract issues. Thus, we have the peculiar phenomenon of a supposedly general contract doctrine that applies only in a specific context but which ignores the features of that context.

That the problem is largely confined to public competitive bidding suggests two important conclusions. First, while contract principles might make it difficult for contractors on public projects to vary the irrevocability of subcontractor bids (offers), there is no reason to rely on the common law. Governments could determine whether some or all subcontractor bids should be irrevocable as part of the overall regulatory scheme. Or, at least, they could make it easy for GCs to alter the default rule, whatever it happened to be. Of course, given that the regulations are the product of a political process, whether governments will do that intelligently is an open question. Second, analyses purporting to analyse the efficiency of the two rules are largely beside the point. Without an understanding of the nature of the public regulations, we cannot say anything about the efficiency of either rule. If we want to know the "efficient" rules, then we should look at how private owners resolve the problem. And on this, the case law is unhelpful.

The *Drennan* rule is asymmetric. That is, while the sub's bid is irrevocable, the GC is not bound. At least that is what one might think if one looked only at contract decisions. But, the picture on the ground is more complicated. The GC's freedom is constrained both by legal regulations and extra-contractual mechanisms, specifically bid depositories. For decades subs have complained bitterly about the GC's ability to renegotiate the price after the winning bid had been announced. Their complaints about the "evils" of bid shopping, chopping, and chiseling are a recurring theme in legislation, commentary, and opinions. My impression is that contracts professors have by and large bought into the notion that such behavior is inappropriate, not the sort of thing that respectable businessmen would do. However, once we recognize that these are the public bidding counterpart to the haggling that takes place in the private contracting, these lose at least some of their negative connotations. The fact that the behavior appears to be common in both the public and private construction projects has implications for the analysis that I will develop below.

The structure of the chapter is as follows. Section I summarizes *Baird* and *Drennan*. Section II provides a brief description of the public competitive bidding process for construction projects. It pays particular attention to the so-called evils of bid shopping. Section III analyses the GC versus sub cases. Section IV concerns the reverse cases in which the sub is plaintiff. It emphasizes the role of government regulation and collective action in cabining the common law solution. In Section V, we turn to the limited role of *Drennan* and Section 87(2) outside the GC-sub context.

I. THE CORE CASES

A. *Baird v. Gimbel*

The Pennsylvania Department of Highways put the contract for a new building out to bid using a sealed bid process. Gimbel, the large New York department store, submitted bids to over twenty general contractors, including Baird, to supply the linoleum. Baird submitted the low bid and was given the contract. The Gimbel estimator had erred by understating the amount of linoleum necessary for the task. When it realized its error, it promptly telegraphed all the GCs, including Baird. However, it was too late – Baird had already submitted its bid. Gimbel refused to perform and Baird, insisting that it had a valid contract, sued for breach.

Hand held that Gimbel had made an offer but had withdrawn it before Baird had accepted. Hand refused to apply the new-fangled notion of promissory estoppel, treating it as applicable primarily to donative promises. He likewise rejected the notion that Baird had received an option "if its bid was accepted, but not binding it to take and pay, if it could get a better bargain elsewhere. There is no reason to believe that the defendant meant to subject itself to such a one-sided obligation." (346)

If the parties wanted to make the offer irrevocable, Hand noted, they could have done so explicitly: "The contractors had a ready escape from their difficulty by insisting upon a contract before they used the figures; and in commercial transactions it does not in the end promote justice to seek strained interpretations in aid of those who do not protect themselves." (346) There was no need to imply that the offer was irrevocable since it could have been done explicitly. He left unstated how they could have practically contracted over this, a point to which we shall return in Section IV. Hand's bottom line was simply that an offer is revocable until the offeree accepts. The offeree's reliance would not create an enforceable obligation.

B. *Drennan v. Star Paving*

The essential facts of Drennan have been drilled into law students for decades; I will only briefly summarize them here. I will, however, add one fact which Traynor left out of the opinion.

The GC, Drennan, was bidding on the Monte Vista School Job in the Lancaster school district. The subcontractor, Star Paving, submitted its bid by telephone the day the GC's bid was due. The GC submitted its bid to the authority, naming Star as the contractor (as required by statute). Drennan's bid was the low bid and it was, therefore, chosen for the project. Before Drennan could say to the sub "I accept," the sub announced that it had made a mistake and couldn't (and wouldn't) do the job for the quoted price. Drennan found a substitute for about 50 percent more, completed the job, and sued for the difference. "Thus," said Traynor, "the question is squarely presented: Did plaintiff's reliance make defendant's offer irrevocable?" (760) Following the courts below, Traynor found that it did. His reasoning was an amalgam of Restatements 45 and 90:

> Thus section 45 of the Restatement of Contracts provides: "If an offer for a unilateral contract is made, and part of the consideration requested in the offer is given or tendered by the offeree in response thereto, the offeror is bound by a contract, the duty of immediate performance of which is conditional on the full consideration being given or tendered within the time stated in the offer, or, if no time is stated therein, within a reasonable time." In explanation, comment b states that the "main offer includes as a subsidiary promise, necessarily implied, that if part of the requested performance is given, the offeror will not revoke his offer, and that if tender is made it will be accepted. Part performance or tender may thus furnish consideration for the subsidiary promise. Moreover, merely acting in justifiable reliance on an offer may in

> some cases serve as sufficient reason for making a promise binding (see s 90)." (759–60)

He continued: "Given [that the GC] is bound by his own bid, it is only fair that [the GC] should have at least an opportunity to accept [the sub's] bid after the general contract has been awarded to him." (760) However, he added a qualification not in the lower courts' opinions: "It bears noting that a general contractor is not free to delay acceptance after he has been awarded the general contract in the hope of getting a better price. Nor can he reopen bargaining with the subcontractor and at the same time claim a continuing right to accept the original offer." (760) Such behavior would indicate a lack of reliance and would let the sub off the hook. The subsequent case law, as we shall see in Section III, shows that implementing this qualification is not so easy. Traynor concludes by asserting that it is appropriate to assign the risk of the sub's mistake to the sub: "As between the subcontractor who made the bid and the general contractor who reasonably relied on it, the loss resulting from the mistake should fall on the party who caused it." (761)

While Traynor alluded to the statutory restraints on the GC (it was bound by its bid), he did not recognize any other statutory restrictions on the public bidding process. There were significant statutory constraints on the GC–sub relationship defined by California's "naming" statute:

> No general contractor whose bid is accepted shall, *without the consent of the awarding authority*, either:
>
> (a) Substitute any person as subcontractor in place of the subcontractor designated in the original bid.
>
> (b) Permit any such subcontract to be assigned or transferred or allow it to be performed by anyone other than the original subcontractor listed in the bid.
>
> (c) Sublet or subcontract any portion of the work in excess of one-half (1/2) of one per cent (1%) of the general contractor's total bid as to which his original bid did not designate a subcontractor.
>
> (d) The awarding authority may consent to the substitution of another person as a subcontractor, when the subcontractor named in the bid after having had a reasonable opportunity to do so, fails or refuses to execute a written contract, when said written contract, based upon the general terms, conditions, plans and specifications for the project involved, or the terms of such subcontractor's written bid, is presented to him by the contractor. (*Southern California Acoustics Co. v. C. V. Holder, Inc.*, 979–80, emphasis added)

What's going on? This statute is designed to give substantial protection to subs. If the GC named a particular sub, the GC is stuck with that sub, unless the awarding authority grants permission to change. If another sub came along with a better deal, the GC and the authority could figure out a way to take advantage of the deal so the sub's protection would only be partial. The statute appears to be silent on the specific issue: the GC's freedom to walk away is somewhat limited, but the statute says nothing about the sub's freedom. Traynor's opinion provides some limits on that freedom without noting that it is part of an overall regulatory scheme. In the next case, we will see why that matters.

C. Son of *Drennan*

About a decade later, Traynor had another GC-sub dispute on his plate. (*Southern California Acoustics Co. v. C. V. Holder, Inc.*) Here he dealt with the reverse problem, a sub complaining that although he was low bidder, the GC (Holder) replaced him with another. Holder, the winning low bidder for the general contract told the school district that it had inadvertently listed this sub rather than its preferred sub and it asked permission to change; the school district consented and the disappointed sub sued for damages. The sub claimed that it had relied on the presumption that it had been selected, the reliance consisting of refraining to bid on other jobs in order to remain within its bonding limits. The trial court granted the GC's motion to dismiss. Traynor, in agreeing with the lower court on contract grounds, came up with the usual asymmetric result – the GC is not bound (to be discussed in Section IV). The GC did not make a promise; ergo, there could be no promissory estoppel.

But he's not done. In the years between *Drennan* and this case, California had amended the aforementioned naming statute. Now the GC needed not only the *authority's* consent, but also the *sub's* as well:

> The amendments made by the 1963 Subletting and Subcontracting Fair Practices Act stated the purposes of the statute in a preamble and completely revised the section dealing with substitution of subcontractors … . The purpose of the amended statute is not limited … to providing the awarding authority with an opportunity to approve substitute subcontractors. Its purpose is also to protect the public and subcontractors from the evils attendant upon the practices of bid shopping and bid peddling subsequent to the award of the prime contract for a public facility. Thus [the revised statute] clearly limits the right of the prime contractor to make substitutions and the discretion of the awarding authority to consent to substitutions … . Unless a listed subcontractor "becomes insolvent or fails or refuses to perform a written contract for the work or fails or refuses to meet the bond requirements of the

> prime contractor," the prime contractor may not substitute another subcontractor for the listed subcontractor and the awarding authority may not consent to such a substitution until the contract is presented to the listed subcontractor and he, after having had a reasonable opportunity to do so, fails or refuses to execute the written contract. (981–82)

Leaving aside the rationale for the revision, the effect is clear. The original legislation gave subs limited protection – the GC needed only the authority's approval to replace the named sub. The 1963 amendments meant that the named sub could not be replaced without its acquiescence (with some qualifications). That was enough for Traynor to overrule Holder's demurrer. "Accordingly, under the facts as pleaded in this case, Holder had no right to substitute another subcontractor in place of plaintiff." (981) The sub loses on its *breach of contract* claim, but its *breach of a statutory duty* claim survives.

It is not clear to me why Traynor puts things into two discrete boxes. When people are contracting in the shadow of the statute, there is no reason to disassociate the contract from its context. He could easily have reframed the statute in contract language: the GC in any situation covered by the statute would be making an irrevocable offer to all listed subs. By submitting a bid, the sub gives a conditional acceptance of the offer. If the sub's bid is listed (whether it is lowest or not) and if the GC is awarded the contract, then the GC is bound to use the sub. There are additional qualifications, as Traynor noted. The net effect is to turn *Drennan* on its head – the GC is bound, but the sub is not.

My concern is not with the precise reasoning of this decision. I want to draw three morals from this case. First, the GC–sub relationship for public works is typically regulated by statute. Second, the statutes typically are sub-friendly. Third, the notion that contract principles can dictate outcomes independent of the statutory regulations is incorrect.

This decision provides a hint of the irony in *Drennan* and its ilk; the point will be developed more below. The statutes tend to favor the subs; moreover, the judicial rhetoric complements the statutes, invoking the evils of bid shopping and concerns about injustice. The natural trajectory of this mix of statutes and rhetoric would, I should have thought, have yielded a string of contract decisions favoring the subs. Yet, the reality is the opposite of that. The post-*Drennan* cases generally favor the GC. One might surmise that what we observe is the result of courts compensating for the statutory imbalance favoring the subs. However, nothing in the language in the decisions even hints at that. The decisions either ignore the statutes or, like Traynor in this case, treat them as if they were from another planet.

II. CONSTRUCTION BIDDING

In the typical *Drennan*-type case, the general contractor submits a sealed bid to the owner who must choose the lowest responsible bidder. Responsible has two meanings. First, is it responsive – did it comply with the conditions imposed by the owner (including statutes)? Second, is the bidder up to the task, technically and financially? Not all competitive bidding processes award the project to the lowest bidder. In a dispute over a cable television system, the court said:

> In *American Totalisator*, the bid documents required that the "lowest responsible bidder" be awarded the contract; thus, the Court would not permit an applicant to lower its bid after examining a competitor's bid. In the instant case, however, the RFP does *not* provide that the lowest responsible bidder will be selected. Rather, because of the advanced state-of-the-art of cable television, the Ordinance and the RFP stress an examination to reveal "the most qualified applicants." Although the amount of the bid is to be considered in reviewing these proposals, it is by no means the only criterion in this particular selection process. (*McCloskey v. Independence Cablevision Corp.*, 442)

After the owner determines the lowest responsible bid, that bidder is bound, but the owner is not; it maintains the right to abandon the project. With some exceptions, the GC is strictly bound to its bid price; the claim that the GC cannot renegotiate its price with the owner often shows up in the decisions.

I will provide a little more flesh to the bidding process below. But first, we should recognize the identity of the "owner." Typically, it is a governmental entity. Most government construction projects require competitive sealed bids. The procedures are typically spelled out in statutes and these statutes vary over jurisdictions, subject matter, and time. Private owners are much less likely to use a sealed bid competition. The private owner is concerned with price, quality of performance, and duration; it will choose the procurement mechanism that is expected to best balance these factors. Seldom will that be a sealed bid process.

The public owner has to consider these factors as well but has one additional concern – corruption:

> The purpose of requiring governmental entities to open the contracts process to public bidding is to eliminate favoritism, fraud and corruption; avoid misuse of public funds; and stimulate advantageous market place competition. … Because of the potential for abuse arising from deviations from strict adherence to standards which promote these public benefits, the letting of public contracts universally receives close judicial scrutiny and contracts

> awarded without strict compliance with bidding requirements will be set aside. This preventative approach is applied even where it is certain there was in fact no corruption or adverse effect upon the bidding process, and the deviations would save the entity money. The importance of maintaining integrity in government and the ease with which policy goals underlying the requirement for open competitive bidding may be surreptitiously undercut, mandate strict compliance with bidding requirements. (*MCM Const., Inc. v. City & County of San Francisco*, 369)

The sealed bid process has the apparent virtue of reducing sweetheart deals between elected officials or bureaucrats and the construction firms. So, to police corruption, governments must rely on a procurement system that is less efficient than that which is available to the private sector. To anticipate Section III B, that is why the case law is so heavily tilted toward government projects.

The generic process of putting together the GC's bid for a government project has been described in a number of cases.

> Despite the rise of alternative project delivery systems and related changes to procurement methodologies, competitive, sealed bidding remains a mainstay in the award of construction contracts, particularly on public projects. Competitive bidding creates extraordinary time and price pressures on the bidders' side of the process. General contractors, subcontractors, and suppliers at each level are straining to get the right price in at just the right time, while still meeting the owner's bidding deadline. It is a pressure cooker environment fraught with opportunities for mistake and miscommunication. (Dendy and Sweeney (1999))

The owner puts the project out to bid and establishes a firm deadline (e.g., October 9 at 2 p.m.) for bid submission. The GC's request bids for pieces of the project from subs and each sub submits a bid (usually the same bid) to some (or all) of the GCs. The subs submit their bids as close to the deadline as possible, both to prevent the GC from shopping their bids and to incorporate the most up-to-date information. The GC uses those bids as inputs in determining how much it would bid. If its bid happens to be the lowest responsible bid, compliant with the owner's conditions, the GC wins the bid and will have a batch of offers from the subs. It will not, however, have an agreement with the owner. In effect, the GC gives the owner an irrevocable option. The GC is committed, but the owner need not go forward. If it does choose to go forward, it would be bound to use this general contractor. The sub might attempt to back out before the GC accepts its offer, as in *Drennan* and *Baird*. Or, the GC might negotiate with the sub or its competitors to get a better deal.

There are a number of variations on this generic story. In the minority of cases that mention the price for the entire project, the sub's bid typically accounted for less than 2 percent of the total. However, there were a handful of extreme outliers. In *Pavel Enterprises, Inc. v. A.S. Johnson Co., Inc.*, for instance, the sub's bid was for more than half the project. The sub's bid might be oral or written. The GC might simply request bids or it might interact with the potential subs prior to the closing date. The scope of subs' bids might not be directly comparable. The number of subs might be large, but there are some instances in which there is only one sub bidding. The sub might submit bids to only some of the GCs and it might not submit the same bids to each. The time between the bids being revealed and the owner entering into a contract with the GC could drag on for months. These factors, as well as others, will have a differential impact on the attractiveness of irrevocability. However, there is no indication in the case law that the courts pay any attention to the differences.

If the sub's bid were treated as an irrevocable offer, the GC would have a valuable option. The value increases with the length of time and the variance of the sub's costs, in particular, its opportunity costs. If the expected value of the option to the GC were greater than the expected cost to the sub of providing it, the parties would have an incentive to agree to make the option irrevocable. Both the value to the GC and the cost to the sub depend on the context. There is no reason to believe that a one size fits all rule would work. The plasticity of both "reliance" and "injustice" allows the *Drennan* rule to tailor the rule to the situation. However, since neither concept is linked to the costs and benefits of the option, any success would be fortuitous.

A. Bid Shopping and Related "Evils"

In its dealings with the subs, the GC could attempt to bargain down the price. For generations, subcontractors have complained about the GC's post-bid attempts to renegotiate the price. The GC's flexibility is characterized in unflattering terms as bid shopping, bid chopping, bid peddling, and chiseling. It is evil or immoral, so they say. California, as noted above, has legislation restricting the GC's option as do many other jurisdictions. The preamble to the California statute is instructive:

> The Legislature finds that the practices of bid shopping and bid peddling in connection with the construction, alteration, and repair of public improvements often result in poor quality of material and workmanship to the detriment of the public, deprive the public of the full benefits of fair

> competition among prime contractors and subcontractors, and lead to insolvencies, loss of wages to employees, and other evils. (CAL. GOV. CODE § 4101) (West 1943)

In 1995, the American Subcontractors Association and the American Specialty Contractors issued a joint statement: "Bid shopping or bid peddling are abhorrent business practices that threaten the integrity of the competitive bidding system that serves the construction industry and the economy so well." (White and Bolema, 2004, 37) One commentator has presented a lengthier litany of the evils associated with the GC's post-bid flexibility:

> Bid shopping and peddling have long been recognized as unethical by construction trade organizations. These "unethical," but common practices have several detrimental results. First, as bid shopping becomes common within a particular trade, the subcontractors will pad their initial bids in order to make further reductions during post-award negotiations. This artificial inflation of subcontractor's offers makes the bid process less effective. Second, subcontractors who are forced into post-award negotiations with the general often must reduce their sub-bids in order to avoid losing the award. Thus, they will be faced with a Hobson's choice between doing the job at a loss or doing a less than adequate job. Third, bid shopping and peddling tend to increase the risk of loss of the time and money used in preparing a bid. This occurs because generals and subcontractors who engage in these practices use, without expense, the bid estimates prepared by others. Fourth, it is often impossible for a general to obtain bids far enough in advance to have sufficient time to properly prepare his own bid because of the practice, common among many subcontractors, of holding sub-bids until the last possible moment in order to avoid pre-award bid shopping by the general. Fifth, many subcontractors refuse to submit bids for jobs on which they expect bid shopping. As a result, competition is reduced, and, consequently, construction prices are increased. Sixth, any price reductions gained through the use of post-award bid shopping by the general will be of no benefit to the awarding authority, to whom these price reductions would normally accrue as a result of open competition before the award of the prime contract. Free competition in an open market is therefore perverted because of the use of post-award bid shopping. (Comment, 394–96)

Most of the "evil" rhetoric, both on the pre-bid and post-bid level, is overblown, if not just wrong. Note first that the sixth point assumes that GCs would not anticipate in their bids the gains from shopping. It focuses on the ex post, ignoring the ex ante. If, however, a GC expects that he can knock 10 percent off the lowest sub bid, his bid for the project will reflect that, in which case the gains would accrue to the awarding authority. If it doesn't reflect that saving, the GC is unlikely to win that bid.

Consider the pre-bid context. A sub's concern about bid shopping is its fear that the GC would take its bid and use it as the basis for inducing some other sub to quote a lower price. In effect, the second sub would rely on the first's bid, thus avoiding the costs of bid preparation. This would be a classic free-rider problem. However, there is no evidence that courts really care or that these costs are substantial enough to matter. Of the more than sixty *Drennan*-style cases, only one even mentions bidding costs, and there is no indication that the costs had any impact on the court's analysis or disposition of the case. In one case in which a sub sued the GC, the sub argued that it would have been willing to incur bidding costs only if the GC would promise that it would use the sub, conditional on the GC getting the job. Otherwise, the case law pretty much ignores the magnitude of the sub's pre-bid costs.

If bid preparation costs are expected to be high, the possibility of free-riding might present a problem. Each sub would have an incentive to wait for others to incur the costs. If they all wait, the quality of the cost estimates is compromised. One case mentioned a bidding strategy that could arguably be construed as an attempt to thwart free-riding. "The trial produced evidence that the practice of initially submitting high bids and then submitting lower bids in the final minutes before deadline is common among subcontractors in a competitive bidding situation and is done to confuse the competition in the event the subcontractor's bid amounts become known to other bidding subcontractors." (*Montgomery Industries Intern, Inc. v. Thomas Const. Co., Inc.*, 93) However, even where the bid preparation costs might be high and bidders do not obfuscate, free-riding is not likely to be much of a problem. The free-riding second sub would be subject to the "winner's curse." That is, since the first sub would have better information, the second sub would win the contract only when the first sub believed it could not profit by further cutting its price. Over time, free-riding would be a losing proposition.

Bid chopping and shopping sounds bad (and chiseling sounds even worse). But consider a typical private sector construction project. The owner could play the GCs off against each other and the GCs, in turn, could play the subs off against each other. A sub would have to decide whether incurring the estimation costs would be worth bearing and, if so, how aggressively it should compete. If the chosen GC did not have a conditional contract with a sub, it would be free to negotiate with all the subs – that is, to shop. It's called haggling. Post-bid shopping by the GC, following its success in a sealed bid auction, would be no different from the haggling that takes place in private construction projects. The arguments against post-bid shopping should apply equally to the freely negotiated construction contracts as well. Or, to turn that around, if we think that the negotiated contract market is working tolerably well, then perhaps the evils of shopping are overstated. There is no reason to believe that quality in non-sealed bid construction would be impaired (the "Hobson's choice") by shopping.

I am not arguing that "the market" works perfectly. For half a century, the irrevocability a la *Drennan* model has been available to private parties. If it were truly superior, it is hard to imagine that the parties have been unable to figure it out. After all, the general contractors and subcontractors typically compete for both the public and private projects. There should not be any learning impediment to their adopting a more efficient mode. My point is a modest one. Outside the sealed bid, public contract world, the parties do have to deal with bid-shopping, and they somehow manage to do so.

Nor am I suggesting that all the arguments against the evils of shopping are bogus. But, it is clear that courts have been quite willing to accept the anti-shopping rhetoric without much thought. Their willingness to accept it, however, appears to be context-sensitive. Compare the following two characterizations of shopping. The first concerns a naming statute; the second concerns an antitrust claim against a "bid depository":

> Bid shopping is the use of the low bid already received by the general contractor to pressure other subcontractors into submitting even lower bids. Bid peddling, conversely, is an attempt by a subcontractor to undercut known bids already submitted to the general contractor in order to procure the job.... The statute is designed to prevent only bid shopping and peddling that takes place after the award of the prime contract. The underlying reasons are clear. Subsequent to the award of the prime contract at a set price, the prime contractor may seek to drive down his own cost, and concomitantly increase his profit, by soliciting bids lower than those used in computing his prime bid. When successful this practice places a profit squeeze on subcontractors, impairing their incentive and ability to perform to their best, and possibly precipitating bankruptcy in a weak subcontracting firm.... Bid peddling and shopping prior to the award of the prime contract foster the same evils, but at least have the effect of passing the reduced costs on to the public in the form of lower prime contract bids. (*Southern California Acoustics Co. v. C. V. Holder, Inc.*, 981)

* * *

> Plaintiffs' complaint states that the purpose of the Depository was to inhibit 'bid peddling' which refers to the disclosure, for the purpose of obtaining a more favorable bid, by a general contractor of one subcontractor's bid to a

> competing subcontractor prior to award and the practice of 'bid shopping' which refers to such disclosure for the same purpose after an award has been made to a general contractor. Plaintiffs contend that defendant engaged in 'bid peddling' by soliciting lower subbids outside the Depository for the floor covering and painting work. Instead of being a vice, however, it is readily apparent that the practice defined as 'bid peddling' is illustrative of open price competition in its purest form. To the extent that general contractors disclose the lowest subbids to competing subcontractors and thereby induce the subcontractors to make still lower subbids, the general contractors are able to offer lower prime bids to the awarding authority. The awarding authority, the taxpayers in the case of public projects and consumers in other instances, are the true beneficiaries. To obtain the lowest possible bid is the object of competitive bidding. (*Oakland-Alameda County Builders' Exchange v. F. P. Lathrop Const. Co.*, 231)

It is not uncommon for a court at one time and place to view things differently from a court at another time and place. What is unusual about the two preceding paragraphs is that they come from the same court, a mere twenty months apart. Both are en banc unanimous decisions of the California Supreme Court. Five of the six judges are the same – the only change is the replacement of Roger Traynor by Donald Wright. The difference, it appears, is not in the facts. Nor would the single change in membership produce such a change. Rather, it seems to depend on whether the judges are wearing their legislative interpretation hats (the legislature says it is bad, therefore, it is bad) or their antitrust hats (price competition is good).

III. THE CASE LAW

A. Public Contracts

Since *Drennan* was decided in 1958, it has been cited in 80 percent of the cases in which GCs are suing subs, whereas *Baird* has been cited in less than 30 percent. Courts explicitly adopted *Baird* in only two cases, both prior to 1966. Decades after *Drennan*, in *Home Electric Co. of Lenoir, Inc. v. Hall and Underdown Heating and Air Conditioning Company*, the North Carolina Court of Appeals adopted the *Baird* rule, refusing to find a contract or to apply promissory estoppel to a dispute; however, it cited neither *Baird* nor *Drennan*. It turned the "injustice" rhetoric of the pro-*Drennan* cases and commentary on its head:

> Allowing a cause of action based on promissory estoppel in construction bidding also creates the potential for injustice. It forces the subcontractor to

> be bound if the general contractor uses his bid, even though the general contractor is not obligated to award the job to that subcontractor. The general contractor is still free to shop around between the time he receives the subcontractor's bid and the time he needs the goods or services, to see if he can obtain them at a lower price.
>
> Using the doctrine in this context is also inequitable in that it allows the general contractor to sue the subcontractor if the subcontractor is unable to perform after the contractor has used his bid, but before he has formally accepted the subcontractor's offer. The subcontractor, however, is powerless and has no grounds on which to sue the contractor if the contractor refuses to use the subcontractor for the actual work. (545)

The court went on to assert, as Hand did, that if GCs don't like it, they can contract for irrevocability: "Finally, general contractors can avoid this problem entirely by securing a contract with the subcontractor at the outset, conditioned on a successful bid. Contractors should be responsible for protecting themselves without having to resort to the use of promissory estoppel for relief." (545)

Drennan and promissory estoppel have carried the day. Even so, the GC still has lost around one-quarter of the time. In a handful of cases, the court finds that the sub's bid did not amount to an offer. There was no promise; it was only a quotation or an estimate. Or, if the sub's bid "expressly stated or clearly implied that it was revocable at any time before acceptance" (*Drennan*, 759), then the GC could not claim to have relied upon its irrevocability. Both of these are exemplified in *Fletcher-Harlee v. Pote*. The court said: "Fletcher-Harlee's solicitation letter stipulated that bids must be held open for a minimum of 60 days and that subcontractors must agree to be accountable for the prices and proposals submitted. In response, Pote Concrete Contractors, Inc. submitted a written price quotation for providing the concrete for the project. Pote's 'bid,' however, did not conform to Fletcher-Harlee's terms; rather, it stipulated that its price quotation was for informational purposes only, did not constitute a 'firm offer,' and should not be relied on." (249) The court found for the sub, noting that "[t]he disclaimer language was in normal print in the last paragraph of Pote's one-page submission letter. Fletcher-Harlee does not argue that it was worded or presented in a deceptive manner." (250, n. 2) I am always suspicious when a court says that. Does it mean that the GC was aware of the language and did not complain? Or, more likely, it was unaware, but failed to make the argument? If the bidding process was as frantic as it is often portrayed, it is doubtful that someone at the GC's office bothered to read the disclaimer before submitting its bid.

The court distinguished *Lyon Metal Products, Inc. v. Hagerman Const. Corp.*, which refused to enforce a similar disclaimer: "The bid was on a Lyon's quotation form. On the bottom of the form, in small print, the following limitation is found: 'This quotation is subject to final acceptance and approval by our home office at Aurora, Illinois and the further condition contained on the reverse side hereof.' On the reverse side, in smaller print yet, eight conditions are found. One of these has relevance to this appeal: 'This quotation may be withdrawn and is subject to change without notice after 15 days from date of quotation.' The specifications for the project, which Lyon admittedly read, required that bids remain open for 120 days." (1153) In both instances, I suspect, the sub was attempting an end run around the GC's determination of a period of irrevocability and was counting on the GC not reading the fine print when putting together its bid. The courts seem to believe that the success of this ploy should hinge on the size of the print and the location of the disclaimer.

The big wild card, however, is reliance. That, coupled with the injustice proviso, gives courts tremendous discretion. If the GC did not reasonably rely on the bid, wrote Traynor, his claim would fail: "Of course, if plaintiff had reason to believe that defendant's bid was in error, he could not justifiably rely on it, and section 90 would afford no basis for enforcing it." (*Drennan*, 761) Shopping a bid would be problematic: "[a] general contractor is not free to delay acceptance after he has been awarded the general contract in the hope of getting a better price. Nor can he reopen bargaining with the subcontractor and at the same time claim a continuing right to accept the original offer." (*Drennan*, 760) If in the post-bid period the GC were to attempt to get better terms (or if GCs typically do so), then a court might well conclude that it did not reasonably rely on the sub's bid. There are three major problem areas: (1) the GC should have known the bid was in error; (2) the GC proposed new terms; (3) GCs in general, or this specific GC, are known to shop the bid, and/or the GC shopped the bid in this instance. Any of these might be enough to defeat reliance. I'll consider these in turn.

1. Known error

In *Drennan*, Traynor concluded that the GC should not have inferred an error "since there was usually a variance of 160 per cent between the highest and lowest bids for paving in the desert around Lancaster." (*Drennan*, 761) What the GC should have known is a fact question and in a few instances courts have found against the GC. A court found a 125 percent difference acceptable on the basis of testimony by the GC that it is "not uncommon" to have differences between the low and high bids submitted by subcontractors that are "more than double." (*Powers Const. Co., Inc. v. Salem Carpets, Inc.*, 33) Bid differences on which courts found reliance unreasonable ranged from between 35, 40, 50, and up to 290 percent.

2. Counteroffer

"It is undisputed that the customary practice in the construction industry is for the general contractor who is awarded a contract to enter into a written contract with the subcontractor, which written contract embraces far more than the price which the subcontractor has bid by telephone. The additional matters would include such things, as whether the subcontractor would furnish a bond, who would provide for insurance, how payments would be made and many other matters." (*Saliba-Kringlen Corp. v. Allen Engineering Co.*, 109) If a court were to deem these terms a material alteration of the sub's offer, it could treat the proffered written contract as a counteroffer. If the sub then were to reject the counteroffer, the GC would not be able to resurrect the original offer and the sub would be off the hook.

Of the fifteen cases in which the sub proffered the counteroffer defense, the court accepted it in six, rejected it in seven and remanded in two. The courts in some instances listed the non-conforming clauses and labeled them as either material or non-material, although in most instances it is hard to tell how the court came to that conclusion. For example, in one of the cases holding for the sub, the court recognized two clauses (among the seven) that made the GC's written contract a counteroffer: "The sub-contract prohibited the sub-contractor from continuing to employ any person deemed by the owner, architect or contractor to be a nuisance or a detriment to the job … [and] the sub-contract authorized the architect to discharge any workman committing a nuisance upon certain parts of the premises." (*Hedden v. Lupinsky*, 610–11) It is hard to imagine that these would be deal-breakers. There are instances of proof by adjective, labeling the new terms as onerous. In rejecting a GC's claim, a trial judge concluded that the non-price terms were too important: "I've read this subcontract in its entirety and it contains so many agreements which in my opinion are absolutely essential to the performance of this job; that it would be, in my opinion, extremely unlikely that either Nielsen or National intended themselves to be contractually bound to each other until this particular written subcontract form had been completed and signed by both parties. There are many matters that go far beyond the bid price." (*S. N. Nielsen Co. v. National Heat & Power Co., Inc.*, 947)

One tactic for rejecting the counteroffer defense is simply to say that the non-conforming clauses are not material. A second is to recognize that the sub regrets its original offer and is raising the issue opportunistically. For example, in *N. Litterio & Co. v. Glassman Const. Co.* the sub's president admitted that his refusal to go forward was based on price and had nothing to do with the additional terms:

> When the prime contract was awarded to it Glassman sent Litterio a written proposed subcontract for the brick and masonry work to be done for the amount of Litterio's bid. The proposal contained various terms which, so far as the record shows, had not theretofore been the basis of any communication between the parties, including a provision that it was not valid unless signed and returned within ten days. ... Having become convinced that its bid was too low, Litterio let the ten days elapse without executing and returning the proposed subcontract. In the proceedings in the District Court the President of Litterio deposed, and the District Court found, that Litterio would have accepted the contract except for the error in estimating the cost of the work. The refusal to go ahead, in other words, was based on the price, not on other provisions in the proposed contract. (739)

Nonetheless, since promissory estoppel is ordinarily a question of fact, the court remanded so that the case might go to trial.

3. Bid shopping

Adding new, more onerous, terms can be characterized as a form of chiseling – chopping the bid. In most of the cases, however, it appears that the additional terms were simply language included in a GC's form contract and there was no attempt to rebargain, but that is not always clear from the court's presentation of the facts. When the rebargaining is explicitly about price, the chiseling issue is more squarely framed.

There are two interrelated questions regarding GC's attempt to renegotiate the price. First, is it meaningful to say that a GC relied on a sub's bid if renegotiation in this market or by this GC is common? And, second, should a GC that has attempted to renegotiate this particular contract be allowed to claim that it had reasonably relied? If chiseling were endemic, one would expect reliance on a bid to be unreasonable. Only a handful of opinions raised the question. They do suggest that post-bid renegotiation is common, but that might just be a reflection on a small, nonrepresentative sample. In two instances, the court recognized that shopping was common, but that there was no evidence of it in the specific case. In a Minnesota case, the court noted that the sub contended "that 'bid shopping' and 'bid chopping' are so common to the Twin

Cities area construction industry that prime contractors and subcontractors do not expect to be bound by prices submitted by the subcontractors to the prime contractors and that defendant was therefore not bound on its bid on the ventilation work because further and final negotiations would take place at a later time." (*Constructors Supply Co. v. Bostrom Sheet Metal Works, Inc.*, 76) However, since there was no evidence that the GC had shopped this bid, the court found for the GC, holding that its reliance was reasonable.

For a most peculiar twist on the reliance argument consider this:

> The facts of this case demonstrate precisely in what way the general contractor relied upon the bids of prospective subcontractors. As already indicated, the general contractor entered into several subcontracts at less than the original bid price, sometimes with the original bidder and sometimes not. In at least one case, the general contractor entered into a subcontract with someone who did not make the low bid, but at the exact price of the low bid. But in no case did the general contractor ever enter into a contract with a subcontractor or supplier at a price higher than the low bid. It is thus quite clear from the record that unless the general contractor negotiated a contract with another subcontractor or supplier at or below the low bid, the contract was made with the low bidder. Therefore it is obvious that the general contractor relied upon the low bids in the sense that those bids provided a protective ceiling on the cost of work to be contracted out to subcontractors and of supplies to be obtained from materialmen. (*Saliba-Kringlen*, 102)

That is, the GC could shop the bid at will, so long as it ended up with a price at or below the sub's bid. If it failed to do better, it could still hold the sub to its bid. That hardly seems consistent with Traynor's reasoning in *Drennan* – a GC could not "reopen bargaining with the subcontractor and at the same time claim a continuing right to accept the original offer." (*Drennan*, 60) But, it does exemplify the plasticity of the reasonable reliance concept.

More in line with *Drennan*, two opinions found that bid shopping precluded a finding of reliance:

> In accordance with industry practice of shopping for the lowest possible price after the bid selection, I & R determined to contact other dealers in an effort to secure the lowest possible price for the boilers.
>
> * * *
>
> In concluding that there was no reliance, the trial judge found that I & R expressly reserved the right to shop among suppliers after the subcontract was awarded, and found that I & R admitted that it was actively seeking a better price, that reserving the right to shop the suppliers after a subcontractor is

> awarded a bid is standard practice in the industry, and that I & R did not intend to be bound by Hazelton's facsimile quote. (*I & R Mechanical, Inc. v. Hazelton Mfg. Co.*, 801, 805)

In a second opinion finding no reliance, the court said: "In fact, it is Complete General's customary practice to contact other subcontractors to determine whether they are willing to reduce their bids before Complete General awards a subcontract, a tactic commonly referred to as bid-shopping." (*Complete Gen. Constr. Co. v. Kard Welding, Inc.*, 967)

Pavel Enterprises, Inc. v. A.S. Johnson Co., Inc., perhaps the oddest of the bid shopping cases, came to the right result, but the reasoning was bizarre. The subcontract itself was for about 60 percent of the entire project. Commentary on GC–sub disputes usually notes a power imbalance between large GCs and small subs. Here, at least, the situation was reversed. Ironically, the initial low bidder was disqualified because it did not qualify as a small business while Pavel did. The sub, Johnson, made an error in calculating its bid; it did not inform Pavel (aka PEI) because PEI was not the low bidder. However, after the low bidder was disqualified, PEI received the contract. It did not enter into the contract with the government for another month, a fact the court found significant. After it was named the winning bidder, but before it entered into a contract with the government, it sent the following fax to Johnson and its competitors:

> We herewith respectfully request that you review your bid on the above referenced project that was bid on 8/05/93. PEI has been notified that we will be awarded the project as J.J. Kirlin, Inc. [the original low bidder] has been found to be nonresponsive on the solicitation. We anticipate award on or around the first of September and therefor request that you supply the following information.
>
> 1. Please break out your cost for the "POWERS" supplied control work as we will be subcontracting directly to "POWERS".
> 2. Please resubmit your quote deleting the above referenced item.
>
> We ask this in an effort *to allow all prospective bidders to compete on an even playing field.* (524, emphasis added)

A few days later, PEI informed Johnson that it had accepted Johnson's bid. Johnson responded by saying that it had discovered a mistake in that bid but had not informed PEI because it had assumed that PEI had not won the contract. Johnson declined to perform. One month later, PEI was formally awarded the contract; it brought in a second sub at a higher price and sued Johnson for the difference.

This should have been an easy case under *Drennan*. The first point involved a change of scope and the second (an even playing field) made clear that there would be a new round of bidding. A holding for PEI would mean that in the new bid for a differently configured project, Johnson would be bound by its previous bid. Somehow, the court, while holding for Johnson, found the reliance question to be "indisputably a close call." (533) The court then added a second reason for denying PEI. Even if it found that PEI had accepted Johnson's offer, that offer was subject to a condition precedent that PEI be awarded the contract. "Prior to the occurrence of the condition precedent, Johnson was free to withdraw." (533) On this reading, Johnson was free to revoke any time prior to the government formally awarding the contract to PEI and since the formal award came nearly one month after Johnson revoked, Johnson wins. Given that there is often a temporal gap between the determination of the winning bidder and that bidder entering into a formal contract with the owner, this line of argument would undercut the reliance rationale. The GC would remain bound to the owner but in the interim period between the closing of the bid and the awarding of the primary contract, the sub would be free to walk.

What to make of all this? The *Drennan* standard has all the warts that Robert Scott and his various co-authors have cataloged for years. The GC's reliance is a fact question, but there is not much theory to frame those facts. That does not necessarily make it wrong. *Drennan* is only a default rule and if it were completely out of touch, then we should expect parties to contract away from it. There does not seem to be much evidence of that for *public* projects. There was a hint in the preceding discussion that contracting away from *Drennan* might not be a simple matter. Even if the bid document were to say that a sub's bid would be irrevocable for sixty days, a sub might in its bid negate that by including language limiting the period of irrevocability to a matter of days or hours. In Section IV, I will return to the question of ex ante contracting.

B. Non-Government Construction Contracts

Three facts about the cases involving non-governmental owners stand out. First, there are so few of them. The paucity of cases involving private projects suggests that in that context the parties have succeeded in dealing with the problem. They needed neither *Baird* nor *Drennan*. Second, the fairness justification – GCs are legally bound to their bid with the public owner and so, therefore, should the subs be bound – doesn't carry over to the private context. Third, with but one exception, the courts were entirely indifferent to the identity of the owner. Nongovernmental owners showed up in about 10 percent of the cases. Some were large retailers engaged in major construction projects – Macy's, Walmart, and Home Depot. In none does the court describe how the owner chose the GC; the implication is that it was a sealed bid process, but there is no reason to believe that to be true. Nor is there any reason to believe that the GC had given the owner an irrevocable option. The judicial indifference is illustrated by the fact that in a few of the decisions, the identity of the owner remained entirely unknown. In only one case did the court appear to consider the difference between a public and private owner and in that case, it is fair to say, the discussion was muddled:

> We recognize that in public bidding cases the bidding process is governed by statute and that the legislative objectives of obtaining the lowest prices and establishing an honest and open procedure for competition for public contracts ... are furthered by allowing the award of reasonable bid preparation costs for "the failure to give fair consideration to a bidder in accordance with the statutory procedure." To the extent that the decisions are based on an implied contract or on promissory estoppel, however, those bases for recovery may be equally applicable to private solicitations for bids. There is surely no policy which would be served by allowing solicitors of bids in the private sector to ignore the conditions they themselves set and ask others to rely upon. (*New England Insulation Co. v. General Dynamics Corp.*, 1000)

There are two problems with that statement. First, there is no reason to believe that the bases for recovery would be "equally applicable." The court does not consider what, if anything, might distinguish the public and private cases. Second, it is not clear from the remainder of the discussion that the owner was in fact a private entity. This might have been mere dicta. The statement is followed by a footnote: "See, in another bidding context in the private sector, *Drennan v. Star Paving Co.*, 51 Cal.2d 409, 333 P.2d 757 (1958)." Since the owner in *Drennan* was, of course, a local school district, one cannot be confident that the owner in this case was in fact private. So, the only case suggesting that there might be some difference between the public and private owner manages to put *Drennan* in the wrong box.

Private owners do not have a direct interest in the GC–sub relationship. Unless they have reasons for using a particular sub, they will be content with the GC's evaluation of the subs and its means of choosing them. Major construction projects nowadays are run by construction managers (a fancy name for general contractor) and the contracts typically have a guaranteed maximum price (GMP). That is, they are partially cost-based with the GMP establishing a ceiling. The contracts allow for adaptation by including a mechanism for making and pricing change orders. Their concern would be the price, the quality, and the speed with which the project can be completed. To the extent that a private owner is able, it will convey to the GC its tradeoffs between these. Because they are so rarely litigated, the case law provides no insights into the process, and since one size does not fit all, one cannot generalize from the anecdotal material available. Still, it appears that the typical pattern is that owners negotiate with GCs who simultaneously negotiate with subs and the GCs do not receive firm commitments from the subs until the final agreement is reached. That is, the GC engages in haggling with both the owner and the subs with the subs either providing estimates or irrevocable options with a short fuse.

IV. THE CASE LAW: SUB V. GC

If a sub submits the lowest bid, would the GC be estopped from selecting another contractor? Where there are no other constraints on the GC's discretion than contract law, the subs have invariably lost. Traynor's *Southern California Acoustics* decision (discussed above in Section I. C.) is an accurate statement of the default rule. General contractors rely on subs, but subs, it is said, do not rely on general contractors. The default rule is not, however, where the action is. In some instances, subs have argued that they had successfully contracted for the contingent right to perform. More significant are the extra-contractual constraints on the bidding process. In particular, many jurisdictions have adopted statutory restrictions on the GC–sub relationship and in some instances, subs have set up private mechanisms – bid registries or depositories – to regulate the relationship. The driving force behind these extra-contractual constraints is the sub's concern with the so-called evils of bid shopping.

A. The Default Rule

The case for the asymmetric treatment of subs was made in *Holman Erection Co. v. Orville E. Madsen & Sons, Inc.* The sub, it wrote, does not rely on the general contractor:

> A subcontractor submits bids to all or most of the general contractors that it knows are bidding on a project. The subcontractor receives invitations to bid from some generals and submits bids to others without invitation. The time and expense involved in preparing the bid is not segregated to any particular general. The total cost is part of the overhead of doing business. The same bid

> is submitted to each general. Thus, whether or not any particular general wins the contract is of little or no concern to the subcontractor. (698)

The court noted further that, because of the way bids are typically prepared, the sub and GC are under very different pressures: "The subcontractors have the luxury of preparing their bids on their own timetable, subject only to the deadline for submitting their bids to the general contractors. The same bid goes to all the general contractors and covers the same work. The generals, on the other hand, are dealing with all the various construction aspects of the project and with numerous potential subcontractors." The GC, as noted above, gives the owner an irrevocable option.

Moreover, binding the GC would limit its flexibility. Specifically, since the GC "was forced to juggle the subcontracts in order to comply with the MBE [Minority Business Enterprise] regulations," (699) the GC had to replace at least one named sub with a minority-owned firm. Although the court does not spell this out, the flexibility gives the GC a second round to meet statutory constraints. Rather than trying to put together the appropriate mix of minority and small business concerns (and any other mandated types) in their initial bid, the winning GC can, in effect, hold a separate post-bid competition between them. MBE firms from different categories would compete against each other – minority electrical subcontractors would compete with tile subcontractors, cement subcontractors, and others. Regardless of whether one finds any or all of these arguments compelling, *Holman* is an accurate statement of the law. More precisely, of contract law, for, as we shall see, much of the action is outside the scope of contract law.

In a few decisions, the courts refused to find a contract, invoking arguments that would have led to denial of a GC claim against the sub. Without raising any reliance issues, two courts invoked the mirror image rule when declining to find a contract:

> In the absence of agreement to essential terms, such as bonding, penalty provisions, manner of payment, and work progress completion dates, it can readily be seen that the plaintiff and the defendant must have intended to set out those particulars (and others) in the written contract which was to be executed at a later date. (*Plumbing Shop, Inc. v. Pitts*, p. 385)

> The depositions here also show that even if plaintiff's dollar amount had been acceptable to defendant, other material provisions of a written contract, including conditions and bonding terms, would have had to be agreed upon. The bid submitted by plaintiff in this case was not capable of being acted upon without reference to these matters so could not be considered complete in any event. (*O. C. Kinney, Inc. v. Paul Hardeman, Inc.*, 631)

It is not clear that these courts would have found a lack of an agreement had the suit been brought by the GC. A court might have concluded, as in III. A 2, that there was no contract but that a GC could recover under promissory estoppel. Neither court considered an estoppel theory.

Suppose that prior to the bid the GC had agreed that if it were the low bidder and it had used the sub's bid in preparing its own, then it would use the sub for the project. In *Electrical Const. & Maintenance Co., Inc. v. Maeda Pacific Corp.*, the sub alleged an oral agreement claiming that it was "unwilling to bid unless [the GC] agreed to award [it] the subcontract if it were the lowest bidder on the subcontract and [the GC] were the successful bidder on the prime contract." (620) In reversing the dismissal of the sub's claim, the court held that there was consideration for the GC's promise, namely the sub's submission of a bid. Whether there actually was such an oral agreement was a fact question to be determined on remand.

One sub alleged that it had agreed to give the GC "protection," that is, submit inflated bids to all the GC's competitors, and in return, the GC promised to give it the deal if the GC were the low bidder. (*Premier Elec. Const. Co. v. Miller-Davis Co.*) The trial court held that there was no contract and even if a contract had been formed, it would have been illegal. On appeal, the court did not have to deal with the latter question, holding that no contract had been formed. In *New England Insulation Co. v. General Dynamics Corp.*, the GC promised that bids would be retained in a locked file and only opened after the bid closing date. However, in a kickback scheme, some of its officers revealed the content of one sub's bid to another, which then won the bid. Overturning a dismissal, the court held that "an invitation to bid upon certain conditions followed by the submission of a bid on those conditions creates an implied contract obligating the bid solicitor to those conditions." (31)

Notwithstanding these exceptions, the asymmetric treatment of the sub's claims remains the dominant contract law outcome. Subs have attempted to overcome this asymmetry by group action, either through legislation or through private organizations like bid depositories.

B. Statutes

In *Southern California Acoustic*, Traynor presented two generations of California "naming" statutes. The earlier statute simply required the GC to list all subs with more than 0.5 percent of the total cost. To replace the named sub, the GC would have to get permission from the owner. If a GC were to offer the owner a better price-quality deal, nothing in the statute would prevent the owner from approving the substitution. So, while the statute gave the sub some assurance, it did not protect it from post-bid shopping. The revised statute, as noted above, made replacement of the named sub more difficult.

The extent of protection varies between jurisdictions and even within jurisdictions as the rules can differ for different agencies or different types of projects. A Kentucky decision illustrates a weak naming statute:

> The requirement for listing is set out in the "Instruction to Bidders" and "General Conditions" issued to all prospective general contractors, which documents state that the name of each proposed subcontractor shall be submitted with the proposal and that no subcontractor may be employed or substituted without the approval of the Department of Finance, Division of Contracting & Administration. The sole evidence herein relating to this procedure is that the requirement has the purpose of assisting the Division in its evaluation of bids, and other portions of the above documents specifically provide that no contractual relationship shall arise between the Division and the subcontractor by submission of its name by the general contractor. (*Finney Co., Inc. v. Monarch Const. Co., Inc.*, 858)

Despite a dissent decrying bid shopping, the court held that the statute did not give rise to a contractual relationship:

> The basic question confronting this court is whether the incorporation of the name and amount of bid of a subcontractor by a general or prime contractor in its bid to the owner constitutes an acceptance which would create a contractual relationship between the general contractor and the subcontractor should the general contractor become the successful bidder. Our answer is that in the absence of a contrary statute, it does not. We are unable to find a single case to the contrary. (859)

Other jurisdictions give the sub a lot more protection. The second generation California statute discussed above is one example. *Hoel-Steffen Const. Co. v. U. S.*, a case concerning a federal naming clause, provides a nice illustration of the type of clause and the difficulty one might have in avoiding the obligation to use the named sub, even when both parties would like to. The naming clause permitted a change of subcontractors only if the contracting officer (CO) approved. It stated that the contractor must list its subcontractors and may make a change only with the CO's consent in accordance with paragraph 17.10 of the subcontractor's listing clause, which states:

> No substitutions for the individuals or firms named will be permitted except in *unusual situations* and then only upon the submission in writing to the Contracting Officer of a complete justification therefor and receipt of the Contracting Officer's written approval. The Contractor shall not be entitled to

> any increase in the contract price if substitution is authorized. However, the contract price shall be reduced if the Contractor's cost of performing the work is decreased as a result of approval of the subcontractor's substitution. In the event the Contracting Officer finds that substitution is not justified, the Contractor's failure or refusal to proceed with the work by or through the named subcontractor shall be grounds for termination of the contract under the provisions of Clause 5 of the General Provisions. (845, emphasis added)

The Procurement Regulations provided a non-exhaustive list of nine factors (including bankruptcy, loss of license, failure to furnish a performance bond) that would define an unusual situation. In putting together its bid, the low bidder made an error. It requested that it be replaced by another bidder and stated that it would pay the difference. Its costs would have exceeded its bid price by around $200,000 and the alternative sub would have performed the job for only $46,000 more. However, the contracting officer declined to find the circumstances unusual and refused; the sub then performed the job and sued the government claiming, successfully, that the contracting officer's decision was arbitrary and capricious. The court recognized that a principal purpose of the regulation was to prevent bid shopping and since there was no shopping here, the contracting officer should have permitted the substitution. (849)

In the course of interpreting a Nevada listing statute, a federal court relied on the legislature's purpose and similar statutes in other states. (*Clark Pacific v. Krump Const., Inc.*) The statute required that general contractors bidding on public works projects list the major subcontractors and circumscribed the grounds upon which the subs could be removed. "The drive to enact state statutes requiring listing of subcontractors on public works project, and limiting the grounds for post-award substitution of listed subcontractors, came about at least in part because of pressure from subcontractors' trade associations,... The Nevada State Senate approved S.B. 474 by a vote of 20-1-0; the Nevada State Assembly approved the bill by a vote of 42-0-0." (1338, 1340) The sub could be replaced if the awarding authority objected to the sub. "Absent an objection by the awarding authority, a listed subcontractor may be replaced only with the approval of the awarding authority, which approval may be granted only on [certain] grounds." (1340) The one contested ground was the refusal of the sub to execute a written contract "*with the same terms that all other subcontractors on the project were offered.*" (1340, emphasis added by court) A literal reading of that language, said the court, would lead to an absurdity – electrical subcontractors would have to agree to the same terms as cement subcontractors and so forth. The court interpreted this to mean that the contract terms had to be in "reasonable conformity." (1342) It also looked to what other states had done to deal with the "evils of bid-shopping": "But the court need not construe in a vacuum: At the time the Nevada Legislature enacted S.B. 474, numerous other states had adopted subcontractor listing statutes; indeed it seems from the considerable similarity of language among these statutes to be likely that Nevada copied its listing statute from that of another state." (1341)

The court noted similar statutes in Delaware, Alaska, Connecticut, California, and New Mexico. It granted the sub a preliminary injunction, rejecting the GC's attempt to replace it with the one other bidder. It noted, with disapproval, the testimony of the state's contracting officer that the state had no obligation to investigate the grounds for removal asserted by the GC. (1351–52) The defendant took an even more extreme position: "Krump Construction's president, Mr. Ron Krump, testified that he believed the statute imposed absolutely no limits on post-award negotiations between a winning general contractor and its listed subcontractors. In Krump's view, the terms of the subcontract bid, and the fact that a general contractor makes use of the sub-bid in its own prime bid, have no relevance to, and do not in any way restrict the scope of, post-award negotiations." (1344) In determining that the sub's behavior in the post-bid negotiations was reasonable, the court cited the testimony of the sub: "listed subs should be prepared to negotiate subcontract terms which depart from the terms of a sub's bid by as much as five per cent of the total sub-bid price." (1345) Thus, even in a state with tight restrictions on bid shopping, the sub testified that it was the norm, within a certain range. Because the GC was insisting on terms outside that range, the court held for the sub.

In the Nevada case, the court granted a preliminary injunction, delaying the beginning of construction. A similar defense by the GC was rejected in a case under the Massachusetts listing statute. (*Roblin Hope Industries, Inc. v. J. A. Sullivan Corp.*) The GC argued that the statute allowed it to reject a sub without giving any reason. It replaced the sub and the job was performed by a competitor. The first sub sued and the trial court awarded it the costs of bid preparation. On appeal, the court deemed this inadequate for deterrence and awarded anticipated profits.

While some courts have interpreted the statutes to apply to any post-bid attempts to negotiate, others have held that negotiating with the chosen sub was okay:

> Under New York Public Bid Law, which is essentially the same as Louisiana's, the courts have distinguished between post-bid negotiations with the original low bidder and negotiations with others, which could lead to the

> hiring of a contractor other than the original low bidder. … These courts have reasoned that post-bid negotiations with the announced lowest bidder are not inconsistent with the policy of avoiding favoritism; negotiating with any other bidder, on the other hand, directly contravenes the policy. (*Percy J. Matherne Contractor, Inc. v. Grinnell Fire Protection Systems Co.*, 822)

It is not clear whether this distinction matters very much. After all, if the GC has no outside alternative and is bound to the owner, it's bargaining leverage is limited at best.

Two California decisions illustrate variations on the listing statutes. The former ups the ante, the latter suggests one way of gaming the law. In *MCM Const., Inc. v. City & County of San Francisco*, the plaintiff GC was disqualified as non-responsive because it failed to list all subcontractors and the dollar amounts for each accounting for more than one-half of one percent of the total, and to indicate which of the firms, if any, were Minority Business Enterprise (MBE) and Woman-owned Business Enterprise (WBE). The disappointed GC argued to no avail that the city could not impose conditions over and above those embodied in the state listing statute. Although the court did not put it this way, it held that San Francisco could if it so chose, pay more for construction to satisfy other social goals.

In *Thompson Pacific Const., Inc. v. Los Angeles Unified School Dist.* the GC, Thompson, took advantage of an exception in the statute. The GC could reject the sub if, after a reasonable time, the sub refuses to enter into a written contract at the price specified in the sub's bid. The school district claimed, almost certainly correctly, that Thompson:

> had violated the Act by listing with its prime contractor bid "placeholder" subcontractors (that is, subcontractors who had not submitted a bid for the work for which they were listed) or "captive" subcontractors (owned and controlled by Thompson). After Thompson was awarded the prime contract, the District argued, Thompson sought to find the lowest price it could from other subcontractors, and then requested permission to substitute the newly-found subcontractor with the placeholder or captive subcontractor on the grounds that the listed subcontractor had failed or refused to sign a subcontract. (2)

If all the subs refuse to sign the contract, then Thompson would be free to negotiate each subcontract unconstrained by the statute – that is, to shop, just as if this were a non-government project. Thompson argued that these were not placeholders and it just happened that each of the subs was offered the work but declined. The key to making this ploy work is the willingness of the District to accept the substitution. It could have refused the replacement and if Thompson failed to put together a team, from the listed subs, it could have replaced Thompson. Or, it could have fined him for violating the Act. "When Thompson requested substitutions of six of its listed subcontractors, the District clearly had the authority to investigate the reasons for the substitutions, to determine whether Thompson had violated the Act, and to cancel the contract or impose penalties if it found such a violation. The District declined to exercise this authority, for the perfectly sound reason that no listed subcontractor objected to the proposed substitutions." (5) So, the strategy is not without risks. (An additional risk is that the opinion is unpublished and, under California's rules, cannot be cited, so it has no precedential value.) Notice, however, that by "accepting" bogus bids Thompson was, in effect, incorporating into its bid its own judgment as to the costs of the six subcontracts. In at least this instance, a GC had more confidence in its judgment (and ex post bargaining ability) than in the price discovery of the sealed bid process.

C. Bid Depositories

The GC–sub relationship is further constrained by the use of bid depositories. Subcontractor trade associations have established depositories throughout the country. These have often run afoul of the antitrust laws, but they continue to exist in one form or another. The basic structure has been characterized in this way by William Orrick (1968) (who was counsel for the defendant subcontractor in *Oakland-Alameda County Builders' Exchange v. F. P. Lathrop Constr. Co.* in which the court held the depository rules to be a per se violation of the Sherman Act):

> A "locked box" procedure is the most common method of depository operation. Subcontractors wishing to bid to one or more general contractors on a certain job submit bids in sealed envelopes to the depository. An envelope containing a bid addressed to each general contractor to whom the subcontractor wishes to bid is placed in the "locked box," and another envelope containing a copy of that bid is addressed to the depository itself and similarly deposited in the box or another secure receptacle. There will be a cut-off point, typically 4 hours or so before the prime bid opening time (i.e., the time by which all bids must be submitted to the owner or awarding authority), and after that cut-off point (or depository closing time) is reached, no more bids may be received, and none received may be amended or withdrawn.
>
> Promptly at the depository closing time, the locked box is opened, and the envelopes contained therein are dispensed to the general contractors to whom addressed. Each general contractor then prepares his own bid to the owner or

> awarding authority based upon the subbids received and his estimates of his own work costs. (520)

If all the subs in a trade are required to place their bids through the depository, and if the rules preclude any sub's revising its bid, then there would be no room for post-bid chiseling. The process identifies the low bidder and all the others are estopped from altering their bids. From the point of view of the subs, this would kill two birds with one stone. The locked box maintains confidentiality for the bid so that there could be no pre-bid free-riding and the restriction on amending or withdrawing bids means that there could be no post-bid shopping.

However, a depository that bound all subs in a trade to use it and be bound by its rules would violate the antitrust laws. So, subcontractors have tried to accomplish almost the same thing with rules that are less stringent. Some succeed, many don't. Schueller (1959–60) produced a compilation of federal antitrust prosecutions from the late 1930s to the late 1950s. Despite a significant California Supreme Court ruling in 1971 that a bid depository's rules were illegal per se, depositories continue to survive in modified forms. If GCs could only use subs that submitted bids to the depository, that would be a clear violation. Various means of enforcing the use of the depository short of formal requirements have been deployed and some have weathered the antitrust challenge.

My concern here is not with the subtleties of antitrust compliance. Rather, it is to underscore the point that the sub's bid takes place within a specific context. Under a depository system, the sub's bid would almost always be irrevocable; promissory estoppel would be irrelevant. If the depository rules were relaxed enough to grant subs some freedom to withdraw, a *Drennan*-type rule would impose an additional restriction on that freedom. Ironically, by invoking injustice, the court could enhance the anti-competitive effects of the depository, contrary to the purpose of relaxing the depository's rules.

D. Summing Up

So, while the contract doctrine holds that the sub's bid is irrevocable (subject to reliance/injustice), but the GC is not bound, the doctrine is often trumped by pro-subcontractor statutes or by extra-contractual mechanisms, like bid depositories. Subs complain about the evils and immorality of shopping but absent such restrictions, it seems clear that post-bid negotiation would be common. Indeed, even with many of those restrictions in place, post-bid negotiation appears to be common. I am quite confident that the negotiation would be so common that it would not adversely affect the reputations of GCs or subs that engaged in it. After all, the subs and GCs also work on projects for private owners in which the subcontracts are negotiated. Since haggling is the norm in that context, it is unlikely that the same behavior would be anathema in the public competitive bidding context.

Suppose that neither regulations nor depositories constrained post-bid negotiations. That is the implicit assumption of most of the post-*Drennan* cases and commentary. A second implicit assumption is that the parties are incapable of figuring it out for themselves. While Learned Hand had suggested that the parties could deal with this by pre-bid contracting, much of the case law treats this as impractical because it would require multiple contingent contracts with subs. Recall that in two cases discussed earlier, the GC's solicitation stated that the bids be irrevocable for a period of time, but that the sub's form stated that the bid could not be relied on; and in one of the cases, the ploy worked. I would think that this problem could be resolved either by tweaking contract doctrine or by designing the sealed bid regulations so that GCs could establish in the bid requests the extent to which the sub's bid would be irrevocable. If in its solicitation of bids the GC could state that a condition for having a bid considered was that the sub accept its terms and that submission of a bid constituted acceptance of the GC's terms, the multiple contract problem would be resolved – if the courts would honor the clause. The GC would be offering a unilateral contract that the sub would accept by submitting a bid. That might be sufficient to avoid the mirror image problem in which the sub submits a bid conditional on a different set of terms.

Assuming that the courts could avoid this ploy, the GC could determine unilaterally whether the sub's bid would be irrevocable and whether it would have the freedom to shop post-bid. If it so desired, it could give itself a pure option – the sub offer is irrevocable, GC is free to shop. As noted above, the option is valuable for the GC, and costly for the sub to provide. The GC must recognize that ultimately it must pay for the option – the more one-sided the arrangement, the more it must pay. If the terms favor the GC too much, subs might refuse to bid or they might submit bids that convey little information. I suspect that in many (most?) contexts, GCs would find that an irrevocable option, even one modified by the *Drennan* rule, would give them more protection than they needed and they would opt for less. That is, if parties were free to bargain over the issue (no statutory constraints, no worry about enforceability), the majority would most likely arrive at the *Baird* solution. That appears to be what happens in non-government projects.

V. BEYOND CONSTRUCTION

A. *Drennan*

Once we get beyond the GC v. sub and sub v. GC cases (or when one of them is suing a supplier), there's not much left of *Drennan*. It shows up in the well-known case of *Hoffman v. Red Owl Stores, Inc.* as part of a list of cases supporting the proposition that relief has been granted for promissory estoppel. In another case, the court distinguished *Drennan* in finding that a conditional commitment letter from a lender did not give rise to a claim of promissory estoppel. (*Laks v. Coast Fed. Sav. & Loan Ass'n.*) In *Steiner v. Thexton*, *Drennan* played a tangential role. When the seller of property refused to convey, the court found there was no contract (the agreement was illusory) and also rejected a promissory estoppel claim. The court distinguished *Drennan* by noting that in this case only one party, the buyer, had a right to revocation. Only three cases outside the construction context did much to extend *Drennan*'s reach. In *Aronowicz v. Nalley's, Inc.*, Nalley's, a food distributor, encouraged plaintiffs to develop a sliced meat business (Major), describing in some detail the future relationship between the parties. Nalley's would be the exclusive distributor in Los Angeles and Orange County. Major spent over $100,000 getting the business up and running:

> On June 16, 1965, Gardiner [the local Nalley's manager] wrote to an executive in Nalley's home offices in the state of Washington. … He described the product and its packaging in favorable terms. He stated that Nalley's would increase the sales of its own products in its Los Angeles District by $100,000 a year by adding the Major line, converting now unprofitable retail accounts to profitable ones. He went into detail about the financial benefits to defendant and stated that he personally and the sales organization were enthusiastic.
>
> Apparently Washington thought otherwise. Whatever the reason, on June 22, 1965 Gardiner telephoned Duncan and stated that defendant was not going to distribute Major's products. He gave no reason. …
>
> Disaster resulted to Major. Immediate efforts were made to secure other distribution, handicapped by the fact that in light of the Nalley's distributorship Major had not developed a sales organization as such, and owned no trucks in which to distribute by itself. … Although some sales were made through a food broker, and a few other sources, the business faltered. In little more than six months it was through. … With no market for its products Major defaulted on its various commitments to equipment suppliers and others. Machinery was foreclosed and repossessed. The individual plaintiffs

> and others were sued by a bank on guarantees which they had executed, eventually settling the claims. (429–30)

The court upheld the damages verdict although there was at least some reason to question how the jury got there. "This juror told counsel that the million dollar verdict was based upon the assumption that there were about 100 shareholders of Major and one million dollars seemed about right for that number of shareholders; the juror further said that if the jury had known there were fewer shareholders the verdict would have been less. Aside from the fact that counsel's declaration is the rankest kind of hearsay, the matter recited does not at all show that a verdict was reached by chance." (At 432) In fact, there were only two shareholders.

The court held for the plaintiff, blurring the theories of liability. It did not find it necessary to decide whether liability arose under contract or under promissory estoppel. Perhaps, it said, an exchange of letters established a bilateral agreement. Or maybe Nalley's letter might have been an offer to enter into a unilateral contract which was accepted when Major built its plant. Or, citing Restatement Section 45 and *Drennan*, it could have found a subsidiary promise not to revoke its offer. The court did not explain why it is a good idea to encourage investment of substantial funds in a business when the survival of that business hinges on a not-yet consummated distribution arrangement. Nor did it explain how all these losses could have been incurred in the one week between Gardiner's positive letter and negative telephone call.

Strata Production Co. v. Mercury Exploration Co. concerned the enforceability of a "farmout" agreement for oil. "A farmout agreement is an assignment of a lease and drilling rights by a lease-owner not interested in drilling to another operator interested in drilling. The primary characteristic of a farmout agreement is that the assignee is obligated to drill one or more wells on the assigned acreage as a prerequisite to the completion of the assignment." (825) Strata entered into farmout agreements on three adjacent properties. One of the agreements was with Mercury which would convey 100 percent of the "working interest" to Strata. "The working interest is the right to exploit the oil and gas in the leased land. Working interest owners are entitled to a proportionate share of profits from the oil extraction but are responsible for paying the costs of that extraction. A grant of 100 percent of the working interest gives the lessee the exclusive right to exploit the minerals in the land." (825) The agreement gave Strata the option, but not the obligation, to drill a test well within 120 days. If it failed to do so, the agreement would terminate. Strata paid nothing for the option. Mercury warranted that it owned the entire working interest, when, in fact, it did not. Strata went ahead with the drilling and sued Mercury for its damages – the revenues it had lost because it did not have the entire working interest.

Mercury argued that this was only a unilateral contract and could be accepted only by performance. Prior to performance, it was revocable. Because Strata learned of the error before it began drilling on this tract, Mercury argued, Mercury was free to revoke. Under Restatement Second § 45, partial performance by Strata would have made the unilateral agreement enforceable, but Strata's drilling on this tract would have been too late. The court distinguished the partial performance theory from promissory estoppel, in which the action or forbearance rendering the offer irrevocable need not be the initiation of performance under the contract. The court cited *Drennan*, as well as Restatement Sections 90 and 87(2), in arguing that the elements of promissory estoppel made Mercury's offer irrevocable. Strata's action in reliance upon the offer, the court held, was to commence drilling on one of the *adjacent tracts*. The rationale for this was that the tracts were from the same geologic formation and evidence from one test drilling would indicate the likely productivity of the Mercury tract; drilling a wildcat well was risky and expensive (over $600,000) and it might not have been undertaken but for the Mercury farmout. Hence, "Strata's reliance served as a consideration substitute for the option contract, which in turn made the underlying unilateral contract irrevocable and unmodifiable for the time allotted by the option." (829) This is the clearest extension of the *Drennan* rule outside the construction context.

Roel Const. Co., Inc. v. Fladeboe Automotive Group, Inc. involved a construction contract, but it presented a very different problem and *Drennan* played a very different role. The owner was a private firm and the procurement mechanism was far from a competitive sealed bid. The contract was for the construction of an automobile showroom and the dispute was between the dealership and the general contractor (Roel):

> The parties entered into a form contract requiring the contractor to perform the work for its cost plus a contractor's fee. The contract specified a guaranteed maximum price. But it also contained a specially inserted provision allowing the contractor to "re-bid" the project after the plans were complete. … The new paragraph was entitled, "GUARANTEED MAXIMUM PRICE TO BE DETERMINED." It provided, "Owner and Contractor agree that the plans for the project are incomplete and will be re-bid at completion of the permit set. The GMP shall be adjusted accordingly by change order for any deletions or additions to the scope of the work. (1–2)

The dealership became dissatisfied with Roel's performance. It stopped paying and found a replacement GC. In the meantime, Roel submitted a rebid of $1.2 million. Roel sued for, among other things, the lost profits from being deprived of the opportunity to rebid. It won on the issue of breach but lost on this element of damages:

> The rebid provision suggests the contractor had the duty to begin work based on the preliminary plans; the dealership had the duty to pay for that work and allow the contractor to submit a rebid based on the completed plans. At that point, the contract would simply be discharged by performance, subject to the formation of a new contract at a new price if the dealership accepted the rebid. The rebid provision does not suggest the dealership was bound to accept any reasonable rebid, regardless of price, as the contractor claims. Nor does it suggest the contractor could earn its entire contractor's fee by merely submitting the rebid. (9)

Drennan's role was to provide support for the notion that the contractual right to rebid did not support the GC's claim to lost profits. "No reasonable probability exists the contractor would have earned its contractor's fee. The contract did not require the dealership to accept the contractor's rebid. The term "rebid," like the term "bid," implies an offer. (See *Drennan v. Star Paving Co.* (1958) 51 Cal.2d 409, 413, 333 P.2d 757 [bid is an "offer" or "promise to perform"] … . Thus, while the contractor had the right to begin work on the project and *submit* a rebid upon completion of the plans, the dealership retained the right to *reject* the rebid." (8, emphasis in original) Thus, rather than creating an obligation as Traynor had, here *Drennan*'s role is to negate the obligation. A rebid is only an offer and, according to this court, there is no duty to accept it.

B. Section 87(2)

Drennan begat Restatement Second § 87(2). "An offer which the offeror should reasonably expect to induce action or forbearance of a substantial character on the part of the offeree before acceptance and which does induce such action or forbearance is binding as an option contract to the extent necessary to avoid injustice." The construction bid cases get along just fine without it. Only five of these cases even mentioned that section. Of the five, three found an agreement, and two did not. On the other hand, § 90 was mentioned in about 2/3 of the cases. Whether or not one agrees with *Drennan*, it is clear that the courts have found § 90 adequate to deal with the problem. (Four of the five cited § 90 as well.) The innovation has been a dud, even on its home turf.

It hasn't fared any better elsewhere. Only a few cases outside the construction bidding context even consider § 87(2), and in even fewer is it successful. Of the 13 cases, the plaintiff succeeded in only four. The aforementioned *Strata* case is one. The others are *Dankrag, Ltd. v. International Terminal Operating Co.*, *Guckenberger v. Boston University*, and *In re Donovan's Third Case*. In the first of these, the cost of shipping goods turned out to be much greater than the carrier had anticipated. It tried to get out of the contract by arguing mutual mistake. The court rejected this defense and found that there was an enforceable contract, a perfectly routine result with no need to call upon § 87(2). The court tacked on a footnote invoking it: "The doctrine of promissory estoppel also provides authority for the Court's conclusion that ITO was bound to perform at the offered rate of $15.75 per long ton, since the CARIB EVE had proceeded up river to Albany in reliance, at least in part, on ITO's offer." (364)

In *Guckenberger*, students at Boston University with learning disabilities sued under the Americans with Disabilities Act, claiming that the school had reneged on certain promises to them. The court cited the precursor to § 87(2) finding that the school had promised to accommodate students with learning disabilities and had failed to adequately do so. One such disability was a "history of difficulty with foreign language learning." (119) The students' reasonable reliance on the school's promises had created a contract, the court held, and the university's failure to honor the agreement entitled the student to damages.

Finally, *Donovan* concerned a lump sum settlement of a disability claim with an insurer (Liberty). Donovan withdrew his appeal of a denial of a finding of total disability and on the same day an agreement to pay him a lump sum of $50,000 was memorialized in a letter. The lump sum payment had to be approved by a state agency, the Department of Industrial Accidents (DIA). Before it gave its approval, Donovan was hospitalized (on unrelated grounds) and died. All the paperwork had been done for the lump sum payment, save a signature by the insurer's counsel. He refused to sign and Liberty refused to pay. The DIA and the court concluded that Donovan's withdrawal of his appeal was induced by the promise to pay the lump sum. "This interrelationship of Liberty's offer and the withdrawal of the appeal is well supported in the record by the July 16, 1997, letter of Donovan's counsel to Liberty, which confirmed the receipt of the offer and at the same time indicated "[t]he employee [ac]cepts that offer subject to approval of the [DIA], and … will withdraw the appeal and request lump sum proceedings." (390) Since Donovan's withdrawal was made in reliance on Liberty's promise, the court invoked § 89B(2) and found the contract valid. Why the court in 2003 chose to cite the tentative draft of 1973 is beyond me.

These few positive citations don't amount to much – one win every nine years. And, even then, the court could probably have gotten to the same result without relying on § 87(2) at all. The more numerous cases rejecting § 87(2) generally conclude that there was not substantial reliance or that denying the existence of a contract would not result in an injustice. To give the flavor of these opinions I will summarize two. In *2949 Inc. v. McCorkle*, the dispute centered on the interpretation of a pre-printed form contract with an irrevocability clause that the plaintiff, a sign company, had presented to a client. The court held that there was no consideration for the irrevocability clause and, therefore, the only way that the clause would be enforceable would be to find that the plaintiff had relied to its detriment. The court distinguished § 87(2) from § 90, noting that the former included the modifier "substantial," while the latter did not. The plaintiff's asserted reliance was performance of a credit check and a reference check, and an examination of the order. This the court found to be insubstantial and it therefore granted the defendant buyer's motion for summary judgment.

The facts in the second case, *First Nat. Bankshares of Beloit, Inc. v. Geisel*, are more complicated so I will simplify them somewhat. In essence, in 1989 the five top managers of a bank held 39 percent of the bank's shares and were granted an option to buy the remaining 61 percent within one year of the death of the majority shareholder. This turned out to be a valuable option; when the dispute arose the option price was about $1.9 million and its value was about $4.5 million. The agreement was for "One Dollar ($1.00) and other valuable consideration," but no monetary consideration had actually been paid. Years later, after the majority shareholder's death, the trustee for the majority shareholder repudiated the option agreement, saying that there had been no consideration. At that point the managers attempted to pay the $1, but the proffer was rejected and the court held that it was too late. (1351) Apparently, had the dollar been paid initially, this court would have found adequate consideration. The court then turned to the estoppel arguments. There was some evidence that the managers had been promised that they would have the option if they continued to work at the bank during the majority owner's lifetime. Even if this were so, the court held, the plaintiffs would still lose:

> [d]efendants argue that the plaintiffs cannot establish that they relied on the alleged promises to their detriment. They contend that the plaintiffs *were adequately compensated for their services as employees* of the bank, and

> therefore evidence is lacking that any of the individual plaintiffs detrimentally relied on the promises allegedly made....
>
> The court agrees that the evidence advanced by the plaintiffs does not demonstrate detrimental reliance on the part of the plaintiffs "of a substantial character." *See Restatement (Second) of Contracts* § 87(2). Hence the refusal of the court to enforce the alleged promise would not result in injustice. The plaintiffs *do not dispute that they were very adequately compensated for the years they remained employees of the bank.* Some of the plaintiffs testified by deposition that they had declined to pursue other opportunities based upon their understanding that they would someday have the opportunity to control the bank. However, this is insufficient evidence as a matter of law to support an inference that the plaintiffs substantially relied on the alleged promises and as a result suffered detriment. *See Restatement (Second) of Contracts* § 87(2) cmt. e. (1356, emphasis added)

The court did not indicate how it determined (on a summary judgment motion) that the managers had received adequate compensation already and that either the $2.6 million that the managers would have split was not substantial, or that depriving them of those shares would not be an injustice. I would have thought that a bonus averaging half a million dollars per person should have crossed the substantiality hurdle. But that is not my point. The decision is an indication of the futility of relying on § 87(2) as a substitute for consideration.

VI. CONCLUSIONS

Contracts casebooks and treatises treat *Drennan* as if it were a Really Big Deal. Traynor invented something new, an irrevocable option, albeit one tempered by concerns about reliance and injustice, that dramatically altered the offer-acceptance framework. It didn't happen. Rather than revolutionizing contract doctrine writ large, it has been confined to its facts – disputes between general contractors and subs. In practice, its domain has been even narrower, GC–sub disputes in which the owner is a public entity.

Given its practical irrelevance, the question is: why *Drennan*'s favored place in the contract doctrine universe? Part of the answer most likely stems from the drama of one giant (Traynor) taking on another (Hand). Part, no doubt, is the result of history – at that time, contracts scholars were looking for vehicles to advance the promissory estoppel alternative to consideration. And part of the answer is that, whatever its warts, *Drennan* is fun to teach.

I think there is a deeper problem. The authors of casebooks and treatises try to distill abstract principles from the case law. Their focus is on decided cases. The context, particularly any regulatory constraints on the parties, is given little attention. Traynor's treatment of contract law and the naming statute in *Holder* as being from two unrelated bodies of law is a striking example of the disconnect. And there is even less attention to what parties actually do. To be sure, a number of casebooks include a brief discussion of Shultz's (1952) study of the GC–sub relationship in the middle of the last century. But none emphasizes the limited scope of that project – public projects only. I do not mean to suggest that litigators should be given free rein to introduce context arguments into every dispute. But, there is no reason for scholars to so restrict their inquiry. If we are going to restate contract law, we might as well restate the law that parties actually use rather than attempting to generalize from context-specific decisions in which the context has been excised.

16. Concluding remarks

The unifying concept of this book is that an economic understanding of contract design will illuminate both contract doctrine and contract interpretation. With regard to remedies, I have followed Scott and Triantis (2004) in calling into question the primacy of the expectation damages remedy, especially when it is presented as making the victim of a breach indifferent as to whether or not the promisor had performed. I observed the explicit termination clauses, in effect options to abandon, in a number of areas and the methods parties used for pricing these options. In order to adapt to changed circumstances, one party was given the discretion to adapt, but it would be confronted with a price reflecting the counterparty's reliance. From the behavior of parties with explicit termination clauses, I drew some inferences about the pricing of an implicit termination clause – that is, the remedy for breach. This led to the conclusion that the default remedy of making the "victim" whole was not, in general, what parties would prefer. I recognize that the compensation principle is so well entrenched that a full frontal assault will be futile. But, we can at least nibble away at the corners of the doctrine.

I suggested that one of the areas that would benefit from rethinking is the lost-volume-seller remedy. Unfortunately, there is a statute (§ 2-708 (2)) and an Official Comment which put some constraints on courts. I believe the statute gives some leeway for creative interpretation. The Comment says:

> The provision of this section permitting recovery of expected profit including reasonable overhead where the standard measure of damages is inadequate, … [is] designed to eliminate the unfair and economically wasteful results arising under the older law when fixed price articles were involved. This section permits the recovery of lost profits in all appropriate cases, which would include all standard priced goods. The normal measure there would be list price less cost to the dealer or list price less manufacturing cost to the manufacturer. It is not necessary to a recovery of "profit" to show a history of earnings, especially if a new venture is involved.

However, since the older law was neither unfair nor economically wasteful, the rationale for compensation disappears. Since the section is supposed to apply only to "appropriate cases," at least some of the harm from the statute can be avoided by narrowly defining "appropriate." The Comment refers to "fixed price articles" and "standard priced goods." A pretty good argument can be made that most consumer durables no longer fall into that category; an even stronger argument can be made that in the B2B world, there are no "fixed price articles." The domain of the statute can be narrowed by some aggressive interpretation.

The last sentence of the Comment suggests another area, which I only touched upon, the "new business" doctrine. As I noted in Chapter 8, most jurisdictions have abandoned the doctrine. In *Fera v. Village Plaza, Inc.*, which many casebooks use to introduce the near-demise of the new business rule, the court gave the rationale for the doctrine and also for rejecting it: "These cases … should not be read as stating a rule of law which prevents every new business from recovering anticipated lost profits for breach of contract. The rule is *merely an application* of the doctrine that '(i)n order to be entitled to a verdict, or a judgment, for damages for breach of contract, the plaintiff must lay a basis for a reasonable estimate of the extent of his harm, measured in money'. 5 Corbin on Contracts, s 1020, p. 124. The issue becomes one of sufficiency of proof." (643, emphasis added). So, since it is only an application of a general rule, it should not bar recovery if damages would not be too speculative and that, the court argued, is a fact question.

The new business restriction is too broad, but not on the grounds stated – damages would be "too speculative." The bright line rule of non-recovery should be limited to rejecting claims that, but for the breach, the plaintiff would have made an investment and that investment would have earned it a lot of money. The question is not whether the investment would make *any* money, but rather whether the expected return on this investment should exceed the next best use of the funds. And the answer has to be No. The *expected return* on an investment in a new business should be, at best, the opportunity cost – the cost of capital.

For the *Fera* court, the possibility of recovery would be a fact question. Indeed, the court used the fact that both parties spent a considerable amount of effort on proving damages as evidence that the damage measure would not be speculative:

> This issue (damages for lost profits) was the most completely tried issue in the whole case. Both sides put in testimony that took up days and encompassed experts on both sides. This fact was adequately taken from the category of speculation and conjecture by the testimony and placed in the position of those cases that hold that even though loss of profits is hard to prove, if proven they should be awarded by the jury. In this case, the jury had ample testimony to make this decision from both sides. (647)

These jurors only had to sit through days of nonsense as opposed to the poor jurors in *Kenford* who had to endure months. Still, the only purpose of the "factual" inquiry was to mislead the jury. The estimates were not speculative; they were silly. Fera's claim was that he had taken a ten-year lease on a space in a shopping center for a "book and bottle" shop and because the shopping center leased the space to someone else, he had lost profits for the ten-year period. After the breach, he still had the concept, his cash, and other potential spaces to lease. Awarding any lost profit damages assumes that this shop in this location was better than any alternative he might have, which makes no sense. So, rather than having a per se rule against recovery of a new business's profits, the rule should recognize that for a new business, the opportunity cost of capital would reduce many claims to zero. It would not bar claims based on something other than the claim that a particular investment would have earned more than the normal rate of return on capital.

Termination is, of course, an extreme form of adjustment to changed circumstances. The reliance/flexibility tradeoff also shows up in a less extreme form – deferring the quantity decision. In my previous book (2006), I examined the problem in greater detail; I concluded there that parties were quite capable of pricing the discretion and that the courts were not particularly good at applying the blunt tool afforded them by the UCC – good faith. In this book, I only considered one instance of quantity discretion, the minimum quantity clause in the *Lake River* contract. Published opinions sometimes hide crucial facts and this was one such case. Sections of the contract not mentioned in the opinions clarified the role of the minimum quantity clause in providing an implicit price for the counterparty's discretion. Once the additional terms were recognized, the structure of the deal became apparent. The case provided one more bit of data questioning the economic logic of the penalty clause doctrine. (For another, see my analysis of *Wasserman v. Township of Middleton* (Goldberg (2006, ch. 17))

Lake River provides one example of the value of "legal archeology" in reassessing decisions. In some instances, digging into the facts shows that the opinion was flawed but because the holding has become so well entrenched, there is little to be done. Cardozo's opinion in *Wood v. Lucy, Lady Duff Gordon*, which I discussed in my previous book (Chapter 2), is an example. To find consideration for Wood's promise, Cardozo found a duty to use reasonable efforts. He, apparently, was unaware that when the contract was executed, Wood was being sued on a similar contract, one that did have an explicit best efforts clause. It would have been easy enough for Wood to include a best efforts clause to make this contract enforceable; there was no need to imply a reasonable (or best) efforts obligation for this purpose. The effect of Cardozo's Band-Aid for finding consideration has been the creation of an ill-defined implied obligation to use reasonable or best efforts. Nonetheless, there is no way that the *Wood* precedent will be overturned.

The *Norcon v. Niagara Mohawk* precedent is more vulnerable. The fact that Niagara Mohawk had been fighting over the security issue for a decade prior to entering into the contract undermines the court's implication that the parties were not capable of contracting over the security issue. The court's extension of the right to demand assurance in "this kind of controversy" ignored the fact that this controversy was not the kind of controversy the court claimed it was describing. Since the opinion was tailored to the alleged facts, the disconnect between the court's characterization and the actual situation should give future courts room to rethink the doctrine. Perhaps a default rule recognizing a right to demand assurance would be appropriate in some contexts – just not this one. Future courts could follow the Court of Appeals' incrementalist approach; but they should not end up in the same place.

By mischaracterizing the facts, courts can lead commentators astray. Professor Eisenberg, for example, was misled by the opinions in both *Freund* and *Kenford*. In *Freund*, he made the plausible argument that there should have been at least some sales, so there should have been some loss of royalty payments. However, the record uncovered two facts not available to him. First, no court was ever asked for royalty payments as part of the damage remedy; it was a nonissue. Second, the royalties would have been offset against the $2,000 advance; it would have been much more difficult to argue that the sales would have been large enough to recoup the advance. In *Kenford*, he accepted the court's glowing picture of the quality of the plaintiff experts' testimony. A closer look at that testimony revealed the low quality of the experts' evidence. The experts used the same flawed methodology. As an indication of how flawed the methodology was, one of the experts concluded that the value of the right to buy the New York Yankees at the fair market value was ten times the fair market value.

I noted in the Introduction the significant role that protection of reliance would play in the book. I have tried to indicate how parties price reliance in various contexts and the richness of their solutions. In the discussion of the reliance/flexibility tradeoff, I found that in some instances the price of reliance was effectively zero; the counterparty was free to terminate (or to vary quantity) without having to pay any compensation. In other instances, the party with discretion would have to pay a significant price. In my discussion of pre-contract reliance in *Brown v. Cara*, I noted that it would have been fairly easy for the parties to maintain the ability to defer decisions on the structure of their future relationship and still have an enforceable agreement. I suggested a number of different mechanisms that would have priced the reliance on the continuation of the arrangement, again with a wide range of plausible prices, including zero. My point is that parties have an incentive to price the reliance and, perhaps more controversial, they are likely to be better at it ex ante than judges or juries ex post, especially when the doctrines they employ fail to frame the issue properly.

Reliance showed up in other places as well. If a party has made expenditures in reliance on a contract and performance is excused, should the party be able to recover its reliance expenditures? The default rule in both the U.S. and England is: Maybe for reliance and Yes for restitution of payments. I have argued for a simpler default rule that would leave the parties where they were at the time of the excuse. Parties should be free to contract out of this. Although, it appears that in England if a contract is deemed frustrated, the court looks to the statute, not the contract, to determine what happens next. The revocability of an offer (bid) hinged on reliance in Traynor's *Drennan* decision. I showed that courts have difficulty in determining whether the reliance is adequate. More significantly, the reliance inquiry deflects attention from the relevant question: Can the GC include in the bid solicitation a condition that would define the extent to which the bid would be irrevocable? At that time, the GC can weigh the costs and benefits of establishing a period in which the bid would be irrevocable.

In putting so much emphasis on the contract design decisions of sophisticated parties, I am making the implicit assumption that they are pretty good at it. Or, at least I am assuming that their self-interest would produce better results than doctrinal arguments not based on the underlying economics. I must emphasize "pretty good." They can make mistakes and some can survive for long periods. I think the treatment in the publisher's standard forms of the publisher's option to publish is one example of the persistence of language that is unnecessarily ambiguous. (Chapters 5 and 6) The treatment of redelivery in time charters (Chapter 10) is another example. The Kenford–Erie contract was an embarrassment. (Chapter 9) The Alcoa–Essex contract analysed in my previous book (Chapter 20) was extensively negotiated by sophisticated parties and yet managed to get almost everything wrong. Transactional lawyers are far from perfect. If they were, contract litigators wouldn't have much to do.

Bibliography

Ayres, Ian and Richard E. Speidel. 2008. *Studies in Contract Law* (7th edn.) West Academic Publishing.

Ben-Shahar, Omri and James J. White. 2005–2006. "Boilerplate and Economic Power in Auto Manufacturing Contracts," 104 *Michigan Law Review* 953.

Bolema, Theodore R. and Nancy J. White. 2004. "Federal Antitrust Law Implications of Bid Shopping," 24 *The Construction Lawyer* 37.

Coase, Ronald. 1960. "The Problem of Social Cost," 3 *Journal of Law and Economics* 1.

Coghlin, Terence et al. 2008. *Time Charters*. Routledge.

Cohen, George. 1994. "The Fault Lines in Contract Damages," 80 *Virginia Law Review* 1225.

Corbin, Arthur L. 1951. *Corbin on Contracts*. Matthew Bender & Company, Inc.

Craswell, Richard. 1988. "Contract Remedies, Renegotiation, and the Theory of Efficient Breach," 61 *Southern California Law Review* 629.

Cunningham, Lawrence A. 2012. *Contracts in the Real World*. Cambridge University Press.

Dagan, Hanoch. 2000. "Restitutionary Damages for Breach of Contract: An Exercise in Private Law Theory," 1 *Theoretical Inquiries in Law* 115.

Dawson, John P. 1983. "Judicial Revision of Frustrated Contracts: Germany," 63(5) *Boston University Law Review* 1039.

— 1984. "Judicial Revision of Frustrated Contracts: The United States," 64 *Boston University Law Review* 1.

— et al. 2013. *Cases on Contracts and Contract Remedies* (10th edn.) Foundation Press.

Dendy, Geoffrey and Neal J. Sweeney. 1999. "Holding Subcontractors to their Bids, Edition II," *Construction Briefings*.

Dunn, Robert L. 2005. *Recovery of Damages for Lost Profits* (6th edn.) Lawpress Corporation.

Eder, Bernard et al. 2011. *Scrutton on Charterparties and Bills of Lading*. Sweet & Maxwell.

Eisenberg, Melvin A. 1998. "Probability and Chance in Contract Law," 45 *UCLA Law Review* 1005.

— 2000. "The Emergence of Dynamic Contract Law," 88(6) *California Law Review* 1743.

— 2005. "Actual and Virtual Specific Performance, the Theory of Efficient Breach, and the Indifference Principle in Contract Law," 93 *California Law Review* 975.

— 2009. "Impossibility, Impracticability, and Frustration," 1 *Journal of Legal Analysis* 207.

— 2010. "Impossibility, Impracticability, and Frustration – Professor Goldberg Constructs an Imaginary Article, Attributes It to Me, and Then Critiques It," 2(7) *Journal of Legal Analysis* 383.

Epstein, Richard A. 1989. "Beyond Foreseeability: Consequential Damages in the Law of Contract," 18 *Journal of Legal Studies* 105.

Farnsworth, Allan E. 2001. *Farnsworth on Contracts, Second Edition*. Aspen Publishers.

— 2008. *Farnsworth on Contracts, Third Edition*. Aspen Publishers.

— et al. 1998. *Contracts: Cases and Materials, Seventh Edition*. Foundation Press.

Foxton, David. 2008. "Damages for Late or Early Redelivery under Time Charterparties," *Lloyd's Maritime and Commercial Law Quarterly* 461.

Friedmann, Daniel. 1989. "The Efficient Breach Fallacy," 18 *Journal of Legal Studies* 1.

Fuller, L.L. and William R. Perdue, Jr. 1936. "The Reliance Interest in Contract Damages: 1," 46 *Yale Law Journal* 52.

Garvin, Larry T. 2012. "*Globe Refining Co. v. Landa Cotton Oil Co.* and the Dark Side of Reputation," 12 *Nevada Law Journal* 659.

George, Tracey E. and Russell Korobkin. 2012. *K: A Common Law Approach to Contracts*. Wolters Kluwer Law & Business.

Gergen, Mark P. 2009. "A Theory of Self-Help Remedies in Contract," 89 *Boston University Law Review* 1397.

Gibson, Michael T. 1997. "Reliance Damages in the Law of Sales under Article 2 of the Uniform Commercial Code," 29 *Arizona State Law Journal* 909.

Gilson, Ronald, Charles Sabel, and Robert Scott. 2009. "Contracting for Innovation: Vertical Disintegration and Interfirm Collaboration," 109(3) *Columbia Law Review* 431.

— & Alan Schwartz. 2005. "Understanding MACs: Moral Hazard in Acquisitions," 21 *Journal of Law, Economics, and Organization* 330.

Goldberg, Victor P. 1984. "An Economic Analysis of the Lost-Volume Retail Seller," 57 *Southern California Law Review* 283.

— 1998. "Bloomer Girl Revisited or How to Frame an Unmade Picture," *Wisconsin Law Review* 1051.

— 2006. *Framing Contract Law: An Economic Perspective*. Harvard University Press.

— 2008a. "Cleaning Up *Lake River*," 3.2 *Virginia Law & Business Review* 427–45.

— 2008b. "Lawyers Asleep at the Wheel? The GM-Fisher Body Contract," 17 *Industrial and Corporate Change* 1071.

— 2010. "Excuse Doctrine: The Eisenberg Uncertainty Principle," 2(1) *Journal of Legal Analysis* 359–72.

— 2011a. "Traynor (*Drennan*) versus Hand (*Baird*): Much Ado about (Almost) Nothing," 3 *Journal of Legal Analysis* 1–47.

— 2011b. "After Frustration: Three Cheers for *Chandler v. Webster*," 68 *Washington & Lee Law Review* 1133.

— 2013a. "A Precedent Built on Sand: *Norcon v. Niagara Mohawk*," 2013 *Columbia Business Law Review* 38–78.

— 2013b. "*The Achilleas*: Forsaking Foreseeability," 66 *Current Legal Problems* 107–30.
— 2014. "Protecting Reliance," 114 *Columbia Law Review* 1033–81.
— & John Erickson. 1987. "Quantity and Price Adjustment in Long-Term Contracts: A Case Study of Petroleum Coke," 30 *Journal of Law & Economics* 369.
Goodhart, Charles A.E. 1995. "Restitutionary Damages for Breach of Contract," 3 *Restitution Law Review* 1.
Hillman, Robert A. 2014. "The Importance of Fault in Contract Law," *Duquesne Law Review* 278.
Hoffmann, Lord Leonard. 2010. "*The Achilleas*: Custom and Practice or Foreseeability?" 14 *Edinburgh Law Review* 47.
Holmes, Oliver Wendell. 1897. "The Path of the Law," 10 *Harvard Law Review* 462.
Janes, Hurford and H.J. Sayers. 1963. *The Story of Czarnikow*. Harley Publishing Company.
Kaleta, Paul J. 1996. "Reassessment of PURPA Power Purchase Agreements, and PURPA Itself, Is Imperative with the Advent of Competitive Electric Markets," 2(1) *Journal of Project Finance* 6.
Kelso, Charles D. 1971. "Teaching Teachers: A Reminiscence of the 1971 AALS Law Teachers Clinic and a Tribute to Harry Jones," 24 *Journal of Legal Education* 606.
Kessler, Friedrich. 1957. "Automobile Dealer Franchises: Vertical Integration by Contract," 66 *Yale Law Journal* 1135.
Kull, Andrew. 1991. "Mistake, Frustration and the Windfall Principle of Contract Remedies," 43 *Hastings Law Journal* 1.
Lord, Richard A. 1990. *Williston on Contracts*. Thomson West.
Lowe, John S. 1987. "Analyzing Oil and Gas Farmout Agreements," 41 *Southwestern Law Journal* 759.
Macaulay, S. 1966. *Law and the Balance of Power; the Automobile Manufacturers and Their Dealers*. Russell Sage Foundation.
— et al. 2010. *Contracts: Law in Action*. LexisNexis.
McElroy, R.G. and Glanville Williams. 1941a. "The Coronation Case – I," 4(4) *The Modern Law Review* 241.
— 1941b. "The Coronation Case – II," 5(1) *The Modern Law Review* 1.
Orrick, William H. Jr. 1968. "Trade Associations are Boycott-Prone—Bid Depositories as a Case Study," 19 *Hastings Law Journal* 505.
Posner, Richard A. 1990. *The Problems of Jurisprudence*. Harvard University Press.
Ray, Edgar. 1979. *Grand Huckster: Judge Roy Hofheinz*. Memphis State University Press.
Schueller, George H. 1960. "Bid Depositories," 58 *Michigan Law Review* 497.
Schultz, Franklin M. 1952. "The Firm Offer Puzzle: A Study of Business Practice in the Construction Industry," 19(7) *University of Chicago Law Review* 237.
Schwartz, Alan and Robert E. Scott. 2007. "Precontractual Liability and Preliminary Agreements," 120 *Harvard Law Review* 661.

Scott, Robert E. and George G. Triantis. 2004. "Embedded Options and the Case Against Compensation in Contract Law," 104 *Columbia Law Review* 1428.

— & George G. Triantis. 2006. "Anticipating Litigation in Contract Design," 115(4) *Yale Law Journal* 814.

Selz, Thomas D. et al. 1997. *Entertainment Law – Second Edition*. Shepards/ McGraw-Hill.

Thel, Steve and Peter Siegelman. 2009. "Willfulness Versus Expectation: A Promisor-Based Defense of Willful Breach Doctrine," 107 *Michigan Law Review* 1517.

Treitel, G.H. 2004. *Frustration and Force Majeure*. Thomas/Sweet & Maxwell.

Trimarchi, Pietro. 1991. "Commercial Impracticability in Contract Law: An Economic Analysis," 11(1) *International Review of Law and Economics* 63.

Virgo, Graham. 2006. *The Principles of the Law of Restitution*. Oxford University Press.

MISCELLANY

'The Crowning of Our King and Queen,' *The Graphic*, Aug. 13, 1902. No. 1706A.

16 U.S.C.A. § 824a-3 (West).

Administrative Determination of Full Avoided Costs, Sales of Power to Qualifying Facilities, and Interconnection Facilities, 53 FR 9331-01, 55 FR 31882.

BPTime3 Time Charterparty, *Onecle*, http://contracts.onecle.com/scorpio-tankers/ bp-charter-2007-07-20.shtml.

Building: J Condominium. *Zillow Inc. Sites*, http://streeteasy.com/building/j-condominium.

Cal. Gov. Code § 4101 (West 1943) (repealed 1986).

ContractsProf Blog. Law Professor Blogs, LLC, http://lawprofessors.typepad.com/contractsprof_blog/2004/11/paula_abduls_ve.html.

Gryta, Matt. 'Hofheinz Widow Starts Suit against Cottrell,' *Buffalo News*, Nov. 11, 1989.

Hoffmann, Jan. 'In Nail-Biting Last Chapter, Our Heroine Gets Her Million,' *New York Times*, Feb. 14, 1996.

Law Reform (Frustrated Contracts) Act, 1943, 6 & 7 Geo. 6, c. 40.

New York Times, June 22, 1902, 'The Coronation Gamble.'

New York Times, June 25, 1902, 'Coronation Insurance Risks.'

New York Times, June 26, 1902, 'Immense Business Losses.'

Restatement (Second) Contracts.

Sample Business Contracts from SEC Filings, *Onecle*, http://contracts.onecle.com/hp/hurd.emp.2005.03.29.shtml.

U.C.C. Section 2.

Index